Tuskegee Airmen

Tuskegee Airmen

Barry M. Stentiford

Landmarks of the American Mosaic

 GREENWOOD

AN IMPRINT OF ABC-CLIO, LLC
Santa Barbara, California • Denver, Colorado • Oxford, England

Library of Congress Cataloging-in-Publication Data

Stentiford, Barry M.
   Tuskegee airmen / Barry M. Stentiford.
      p. cm. — (Landmarks of the American mosaic)
   Includes bibliographical references and index.
   ISBN 978-0-313-38684-8 (hardcopy : alk. paper) — ISBN 978-0-313-38685-5 (ebook)
   1. United States. Army Air Forces. Fighter Group, 332nd. 2. United States.
Army Air Forces. Composite Group, 477th. 3. World War, 1939–1945—Aerial
operations, American. 4. United States. Army Air Forces—African American
troops. 5. World War, 1939–1945—Regimental histories—United States.
6. World War, 1939–1945—Participation, African American. 7. World War,
1939–1945—Campaigns—Europe. 8. African American fighter pilots—History.
I. Title.
   D790.252332nd .S74   2012
   940.54'4973—dc22   2011013524

ISBN: 978-0-313-38684-8
EISBN: 978-0-313-38685-5

16   15   14   13   12   1   2   3   4   5

This book is also available on the World Wide Web as an eBook.
Visit www.abc-clio.com for details.

ABC-CLIO, LLC
130 Cremona Drive, P.O. Box 1911
Santa Barbara, California 93116-1911

This book is printed on acid-free paper ∞

Manufactured in the United States of America

Contents

Series Foreword

THE LANDMARKS OF THE AMERICAN MOSAIC series comprises individual volumes devoted to exploring an event or development central to this country's multicultural heritage. The topics illuminate the struggles and triumphs of American Indians, African Americans, Latinos, and Asian Americans, from European contact through the turbulent last half of the twentieth century. The series covers landmark court cases, laws, government programs, civil rights infringements, riots, battles, movements, and more. Written by historians especially for high school students on up and general readers, these content-rich references satisfy more thorough research needs and provide a deeper understanding of material that students might only otherwise be exposed to in a short section in a textbook or superficial explanation online.

Each book on a particular topic is a one-stop reference source. The series format includes

- Introduction
- Chronology
- Narrative chapters that trace the evolution of the event or topic chronologically
- Biographical profiles of key figures
- Selection of crucial primary documents
- Glossary
- Bibliography
- Index

This landmark series promotes respect for cultural diversity and supports the social studies curriculum by helping students understand multicultural American history.

Preface

THIS VOLUME IN ABC-CLIO'S LANDMARKS of the American Mosaic series places the Tuskegee Airmen at the junction of two historical trends: the growth of airpower and its concurrent development as a critical factor in the American way of war and the early stirring of the civil rights movement. Blacks were beginning to become a political force outside the South. These two trends intersected during a dangerous period in history when the United States and its allies found themselves fighting a powerful alliance of foes that represented a very different way of life. Blacks and their liberal white allies were able to use the crisis of World War II to push the administration of President Franklin D. Roosevelt to fulfill the desire of blacks to see black pilots in the Army Air Corps. The Air Corps pilot represented the pinnacle of military elites, and blacks wanted to see some of their number join that elite.

Tuskegee Airmen is intended for high school students and general readers rather than the specialist in military aviation or civil rights, but readers with a firmer understanding of either World War II or the early civil rights movement will profit from this volume. The work is organized chronologically, but in the later chapters it becomes more organized by subject as the roles of the pilots who trained at Tuskegee became more varied. This work builds on the works of others, forming a synthesis from earlier studies that approached the topic from either a "black struggles" or a military history perspective. Colonel Robert W. Tomlinson (U.S. Air Force, Retired) read early drafts and provided important criticism and served as a sounding board. Dr. Daniel L. Haulman, the chief of the Organizational Histories Branch at the Air Force Historical Research Agency, generously shared his work with me and provided me with copies of many important primary documents. My wife Vitida and son Geoffrey gave me constant support. All shortcomings in facts and interpretations are mine.

Introduction

THE "TUSKEGEE AIRMEN" were the African American men who served in the 99th Fighter Squadron, the 332nd Fighter Group, and the 477th Bombardment Group during World War II. The 332nd Fighter Group contained the 100th, 301st, and 302nd Fighter Squadrons, and the 99th was later added to it. The 332nd fought in the European Theater of Operations and earned fame for its escort of bombers on long-range strategic bombing missions. The 477th Bombardment Group contained the 616th, 617th, 618th, and 619th Bombardment Squadrons. The war ended before the 477th deployed to combat. While the name "Tuskegee Airmen" more properly belongs to the approximately 994 pilots, navigators, and bombardiers who received their initial flight training at Tuskegee Army Airfield, Alabama, the name is often extended to all black members of those organizations—including the 15,000 aircrew members and ground personnel. These mostly enlisted men served in the 318th Base Squadron, the 96th Maintenance Group, the 1000th Signal Company, the 1051st Quartermaster Service Group Aviation Company, the 1765th Ordnance Supply and Maintenance Company, Aviation, the 1902nd Quartermaster Truck Company (Aviation), the 387th Service Group, and other units that supported the flyers. The Tuskegee Airmen struggled against enormous obstacles in order serve their country in the deadly field of aerial combat. They persevered while understanding that many of their own countrymen hoped and expected them to fail in training or in combat.

While the legend that the 332nd never lost a bomber it escorted was not true, the 99th Fighter Squadron and later the 332nd Fighter Group nevertheless established impressive combat records (Haulman, 2009). They participated in more than 15,000 combat sorties, with more than 6,000 performed by the 99th alone. Members were credited with shooting down at least 94 enemy aircraft in aerial combat and destroying another 150 enemy aircraft on the ground. The 332nd received credit for destroying 950 railcars, trucks, and other vehicles. Members were awarded 96

Distinguished Flying Crosses, 14 Bronze Stars, and eight Purple Hearts. The 99th, 100th, and 301st Squadrons earned the Distinguished Unit Citation for service on March 24, 1945, when Group Commander Colonel Benjamin O. Davis Jr. led the 332nd on a mission escorting bombers to knock out the Daimler-Benz tank factory near Berlin. The 1,600-mile round-trip was one of the longest missions flown by the 15th Air Force during the war (Francis, 1997). The victories did not come without a price though, as 66 members lost their lives during the war, and another 32 were shot down and captured.

Despite the desire of some Americans to see black military pilots, powerful forces worked against the idea. The high tide of racism in the United States ran from the 1880s through World War II. Black participation in American wars had largely been purged from public memory or their service denigrated. The American soldier as represented in art, books, plays, or movies about any war was a white man. One popular book from 1926 claimed that blacks played no part in the Civil War and that African Americans were the only people in history who "became free without any effort of their own." The author claimed that during the war they "twanged banjos around railroad stations, sang melodious spirituals, and believed that some Yankee would soon come along and give each of them forty acres of land and a mule" (Woodward, 1957, p. 217). This image is at odds with the reality of the multitudes of blacks who risked their lives to escape to Union lines during the war and the tens of thousands who served in the Union army, constituting about 10 percent of its strength by the end of the war. That service had been intentionally forgotten and replaced with a stereotype that better suited white desires to keep blacks in a subservient position. The stereotype held that blacks were natural cowards, unintelligent, and incapable of showing initiative. As a result, most black soldiers during the World War I were assigned to perform manual labor, especially as stevedores. The military routinely excluded all but a token few from the officer corps. The desire of African Americans during World War II to see black combat aviation units had to fight hard against these racist caricatures of black manhood. The struggle to get blacks into the infantry, armor, or artillery was difficult enough, and the goal of seeing blacks represented among officers in numbers that reflected their percentage of the general population seemed almost insurmountable. The Army Air Corps had been all white, but the Air Corps pilot represented the most glamorous and the most public of military elites, and blacks sought to achieve that exalted position.

The eventual success of the Tuskegee Airmen underscores the high quality of the men who served. Because of the rigorous screening, the men selected for flight training and ground crew training were uniformly highly intelligent and often well educated. Many had previous civilian experience as pilots or mechanics. They were aware that they were under heavy scrutiny and that any shortcomings on their part would be used to justify ending all military aviation training for African Americans. Not only their skills at combat flying would be questioned and scrutinized, but their very status as officers would be as well. While the idea of a black man in a U.S. uniform was offensive to many whites, the idea of a black officer was beyond belief. The failure of the well-known Tuskegee Airmen would have been used as an argument against the idea of the military having any black officers.

To be sure, not every white man inside the military and out was against the Tuskegee Airmen, or else the program never would have gotten started. Some white men supported the "experiment" and helped it succeed for a variety of reasons, from politics to altruism to simply taking at face value the idea that "all men were created equal." Others might not have liked the idea of black officers or pilots, but their professionalism allowed them to overcome their personal feelings and treat the Tuskegee Airmen properly. However, the Tuskegee Airmen would also have to deal with bigoted superiors; with smirks and disrespect from white enlisted men; and with whispers, rumors, lies, and uncertainty over the attitude of men in planes from other units, men on whom they depended and who in turn depended on the Tuskegee Airmen. The Tuskegee Airmen and their supporters had to overcome fierce and determined resistance to the idea of black men fighting for the United States in the skies over Europe. Some black Americans adopted the "Double V" as their motto during the war—victory over the enemies of the United States abroad and victory over racism at home. For the Tuskegee Airmen, the war became one of triple Vs, with victory over entrenched and official racism in the armed forces added to their burden. Their valor and sacrifice not only helped defeat Nazi Germany but also helped break down racial barriers and became a powerful argument for ending racial segregation in the armed forces after the war. But the Tuskegee Airmen were not the first African Americans to serve in the U.S. military—they came from a long tradition of black participation in American wars. To borrow an old but apt cliché, if they saw farther, it was because they stood on the shoulders of giants.

The question arises, then and now, why these men fought so hard to serve in a racist system in order to risk their lives fighting for a racist society in war. The answers are complex, as myriad motives existed in the men individually and as a group. But several reasons—from self-interest to larger issues—drove these men. Primarily was the glamour of the Air Corps and of flying. Since the early days of military aviation, the military pilot had been a heroic figure, high above, both literally and figuratively, the infantryman slogging through the mud. Black Americans were as excited by flying as white Americans. Black leaders also understood that loyal participation in war was a key argument in demanding that most important of all civil rights—the right to vote. But black leaders wanted to see black men doing more in military than performing menial tasks such as grounds keeping and laundry or back-breaking labor with a pick and shovel. Black leaders wanted to see black men in combat units—in the infantry, artillery, and tanks and well as in the elite Air Corps and Marine Corps. They wanted to see blacks in the highly trained technical roles such as mechanics. And above all, they wanted to see black officers. Too often, black men were led by white men. An officer was a leader, and in a society that routinely relegated blacks to menial tasks under the supervision of whites, the sight of black officers leading men in combat would send a powerful message of the potential of black men—to both blacks and whites. The military pilot combined all these desired attributes; he was highly trained, skilled at using the latest technology, an officer, and a fighter. Above all, the Air Corps pilot was dashing and heroic, involved in high-stakes combat where coming in second meant death. Pilots in the Air Corps were as far from the Jim Crow stereotype of black manhood as possible, and African Americans wanted to see black pilots in the Army Air Corps. For many of the same reasons, racists did not want to see black men in combat units or as officers and especially not as pilots. Such tangible symbols of black abilities as leaders and as American warriors would undercut the whole Jim Crow system and white supremacy in general.

Ideally, black leaders and their white liberal supporters would have liked the military to simply end racial segregation and open all ranks and positions to men based on ability and not skin color. While that ideal was not likely to be realized during the war, the creation of all-black aviation units was an attainable compromise but was met with opposition from both ends of the spectrum. White supremacists saw it as either a waste of resources to train black men for roles they would be unable to fulfill or, worse, the start of a change in society when blacks would start calling for their civil rights. Liberal organizations such as the National Association for the Advancement of Colored People, which included white as well as black members, feared that the creation of new black units would further entrench segregation in the military. For the administration of President Franklin D. Roosevelt, anxious to do something overt that would maintain the support of blacks where they were able to vote and, perhaps more important politically, maintain the support of liberal whites, the creation of a separate black air combat unit—an experiment—was palatable. For black men to succeed in that previously whites-only world of Army Air Corps pilots would attack the racist caricatures that had long been used to hold blacks in submission

The plan was at once so small, so tepid, but at the same time so bold, with large implications. The very best—the smartest, healthiest, most educated, most skilled—young black men from throughout the nation would be recruited. They would be trained separately from whites. The desire to avoid any chance that a white enlisted soldier might come into contact with black aviation cadets or officers was so strong that the army decided to build a whole new air base for training them. There the cadets would be put through the normal highly intense program the Air Crops conducted to train pilots and weed out those deemed unable to meet the incredibly high standards required for military pilots. Because of the desire to avoid situations with white enlisted men around black officers, black enlisted men would also have to be selected and trained to fill all the roles required to keep an air base running and the planes flying. Once trained and assembled, the new black flying unit, at first limited to a single squadron, would function almost as a separate black air force. If the first squadron proved itself in combat, more units would be created, expanding this little separate black air force. This was the bold experiment that so horrified white supremacists.

When word got out in January 1941 that the Air Corps was seeking young black men for pilot training, black men across the nation began to decide whether they believed themselves up to the task. Many decided to accept the challenge, become Air Corps pilots, and perhaps fight the war in the skies over Europe or the Pacific. But before they succeeded in the Air Corps, they would first have to struggle to get in.

References

Francis, Charles E. *The Tuskegee Airmen: The Men Who Changed a Nation*. 4th ed. Boston: Branden, 1997.

Haulman, Daniel L. "Tuskegee Airmen-Escorted Bombers Lost to Enemy Aircraft." Maxwell Air Force Base, AL: U.S. Air Force Historical Research Agency, 2009.

Woodward, W. E. *Meet General Grant*. New York: Fawcett, 1957.

Tuskegee Airmen Time Line

1861   American Civil War begins.

1862   September 22: President Abraham Lincoln issues the Emancipation Proclamation, effectively making the abolition of slavery a Union war aim during the American Civil War.

1863   First black state-raised Volunteer regiments accepted into the Union army. All the officers in these regiments were white, while all enlisted men were black.

1865   American Civil War ends in Union victory.

1866   Formation of four black regiments in Regular Army: the 9th and 10th Cavalries and the 24th and 25th Infantries. All the officers in these regiments are white, while all enlisted men are black. Later, some of the officers were black.

1877   First black man, Henry O. Flipper, completes West Point and becomes the first black officer in the Regular Army.

1881   What later became Tuskegee Institute opens as a normal school for the training of teachers.

1898   April 23–December 10: Spanish-American War.

1903   December 14: Orville and Wilbur Wright make first powered, controlled airplane flight at Kitty Hawk, North Carolina.

1907   August 1: Aeronautical Division of the U.S. Army Signal Corps established to handle "all matters pertaining to military ballooning, air machines, and all kindred subjects."

1908   September 3: Aeronautical Division, U.S. Army Signal Corps, gets its first airplane, a Wright Flyer.

1914   July 18: Congress authorizes the Aeronautical Division, U.S. Army Signal Corps, to become the Aviation Section of the U.S. Army Signal Corps.

1914   July 28: World War I begins in Europe.

1917   April 6: United States enters World War I.

1918   May 24: The Aviation Section of the U.S. Army Signal Corps becomes the U.S. Army Air Service.

November 11: World War I ends.

1926   July 2: U.S. Army Air Service becomes the U.S. Army Air Corps.

1934   May: John C. Robinson lands in a field at Tuskegee Institute.

1935   July 28: First flight of a prototype Boeing B-17 Flying Fortress heavy bomber.

October 3: Italy invades Ethiopia.

1936   June 12: Benjamin O. Davis Jr. becomes the fourth African American to graduate from West Point and accept a commission in the Regular Army.

1937   July 7: Marco-Polo Bridge Incident begins Japan's attempt to conquer China proper; the start of World War II in Asia.

1939   September 1: Germany invades Poland; the start of World War II in Europe.

September 8: President Franklin D. Roosevelt declares a limited national emergency.

June 27: Congress passes the Civilian Pilot Training Act.

December 28: First flight of a prototype Consolidated B-24 Liberator heavy bomber.

1940   August 31: President Roosevelt orders the mobilization of the National Guard and the Organized Reserves. Men brought to active military service under the emergency are not to serve outside of the Western Hemisphere or U.S. possessions in the Pacific.

September 16: Congress passes Selective Service Act, creating the nation's first peacetime conscription. It included provisions that prohibit racial discrimination in the conscription of American men for military service.

October 25: Benjamin O. Davis Sr. is promoted to brigadier general (temporary); becomes the first black general in U.S. history. His rank becomes permanent on August 1, 1941.

October 26: First flight of a prototype North American P-51 Mustang.

December 20: War Department issues Army Regulation 210-10 requiring post commanders to ensure that membership in officers' clubs, messes, and social organizations be open to all officers.

1941 January 16: War Department announces plans to create a "Negro pursuit squadron" that would be trained at Tuskegee.

March 10: The 99th Pursuit Squadron constituted.

March 19: "Air Base Detachment" created, which would later become the 318th Air Base Squadron.

March 22: The 99th Pursuit Squadron activated at Chanute Field, Illinois.

March 29: First Lady Eleanor Roosevelt visits Tuskegee Institute and accepts a ride in an airplane piloted by Charles "Chief" Anderson.

May 1: The Air Base Detachment activated at Chanute Field, Illinois, to serve as the ground support for the proposed 99th Fighter Squadron.

June 7: War Department approves the establishment of a flying school at Tuskegee Institute.

June 20: Congresses establishes the U.S. Army Air Forces, which the Air Corps falls under.

July 19: First class of black cadets (42-C) with Captain Benjamin O. Davis Jr. and 12 cadets begin preflight training at Tuskegee Institute.

July 12: Construction begins at what would become Tuskegee Army Airfield.

July 23: Tuskegee Army Airfield established. The Advanced Flying School activated.

August 21: Class 42-C begins first phase of military flight training at Kennedy Field near Tuskegee.

September 2: Captain Davis becomes first black American military pilot to fly solo.

November 5: The 99th Pursuit Squadron moves from Chanute Field to Maxwell Field, Alabama.

November 8: The seven remaining members of Class 42-C enter the second phase of military flight training, now under military instructors.

November 10: The 99th Pursuit Squadron moves from Maxwell Field to Tuskegee Army Airfield. Lieutenant Clyde H. Bynum, who was white, assumes command. The Air Base Detachment moved from Chanute Field to Maxwell Field.

December 6: Captain Alonzo S. Ward, who was white, assumes command of the 99th Pursuit Squadron.

December 7: United States enters World War II following Japanese attack on Pearl Harbor, Hawaii.

December 27: The 100th Pursuit Squadron constituted

1942　February 19: The 100th Pursuit Squadron activated.

February 28: In a major reorganization of the U.S. Army, the army is divided into three parts—the Army Air Forces, the Army Ground Forces, and the Army Service Forces. The Air Corps as a headquarters is abolished, although pilots are still branched Air Corps.

March 7: First class of four cadets and Captain Davis graduate and are awarded their pilot wings. The four cadets are commissioned as second lieutenants.

March 13: The Air Base Detachment redesignated as the 318th Air Base Squadron.

March 21: The 96th Maintenance Group (Reduced) (Colored) activated at Tuskegee Army Airfield. The 366th and 367th Material Squadrons activated under the 96th Maintenance Group.

May 15: The 99th Pursuit Squadron redesignated as the 99th Fighter Squadron. The 100th Pursuit Squadron redesignated as the 100th Fighter Squadron.

April 29: Second class of pilots graduates from Tuskegee.

May 20: Third class of pilots graduates from Tuskegee.

June 1: First Lieutenant George Roberts becomes the fourth commander of the 99th and the first black man to command a U.S. Army Air Corps squadron.

July 4: 332nd Fighter Group established. The 301st and 302nd Fighter Squadrons also established.

August 19: The 99th Fighter Squadron attached to Third Fighter Command.

August 22: Lieutenant Colonel Benjamin O. Davis Jr. assumes command of the 99th Fighter Squadron.

September 12: Second Lieutenant Faythe A. McGinnis dies in a crash during a training flight, becoming the first casualty of the Tuskegee Airmen.

September 15: The 1000th Signal Company, the 1051st Quartermaster Service Group Aviation Company, the 1765th Ordnance Supply and

Maintenance Company (Aviation), and the 1902nd Quartermaster Truck Company (Aviation) activated at Tuskegee Army Airfield. These black units would provide necessary ground and base functions for the 332nd Fighter Group.

October 13: The 332nd Fighter Group activated.

November 8: The Allies invade North Africa.

December 26: Lieutenant Colonel Noel F. Parrish becomes commander of Tuskegee Army Airfield.

1943 March 27: The 332nd Fighter Group transferred from Tuskegee Army Airfield to Selfridge Field, Michigan.

April 2: The 99th Fighter Squadron leaves Tuskegee Army Airfield to begin deployment to the European Theater of Operations.

April 24: The 99th Fighter Squadron lands in North Africa at Casablanca in French Morocco.

May 13: The 477th Bombardment Group (Medium) established, with white pilots.

May 31: The 99th Fighter Squadron arrives at Casablanca in French Morocco.

May 31: The 99th Fighter Squadron arrives at Farjouna in Tunisia to begin operations as part of the 33rd Fighter Group.

June 1: The 477th Bombardment Group (Medium) activated.

June 2: First combat mission for the 99th Fighter Squadron.

June 9: First aerial combat for the 99th Fighter Squadron.

June 11: Italian island of Pantelleria surrenders to the Allies.

July 2: Lieutenant Charles Hall becomes the first of the Tuskegee Airmen to shoot down an enemy airplane in combat.

July 10: The Allies invade Sicily. Lieutenant Richard Bolling becomes the first of the Tuskegee Airmen to bail out of his aircraft as a result of aerial combat. He landed in the Mediterranean Sea and was rescued.

June–July: The 99th fighter Squadron awarded the Distinguished Unit Citation for service in the conquest of Sicily.

August 25: The 477th Bombardment Group (Medium) inactivated.

September 3: Secret armistice signed between Italy and the Allies. First Allied troops land on Italian mainland.

October 7: Lieutenant Colonel Davis assumes command of the 332nd Fighter Group.

November 19: The 99th Fighter Squadron moves to Modena, Italy, and is attached to the 79th Fighter Group.

December 24: The 332nd Fighter Group leaves Selfridge Field to begin deployment to European Theater of Operations.

1944 January 3: The 332nd Fighter Group boards transports for deployment.

January 15: The 477th Bombardment Group (Medium) reactivated.

February 5: First combat mission for the 100th Fighter Squadron.

February 15: First contact with the enemy for the 302nd Fighter Squadron.

May 1: The 99th Fighter Squadron becomes part of the 332nd Fighter Group.

May12–14: The 99th Fighter Squadron earns the Distinguished Unit Citation for combat over Cassino, Italy.

June 6: Operation Overlord, the Allied invasion of Normandy, France, begins.

July 6: The 99th Fighter Squadron joins the other squadrons of the 332nd Fighter Group at Ramitelli, Italy.

July 12: Captain Joseph Elsberry is credited with three confirmed kills during a single mission.

July 15: The 332nd flies it first mission with all four squadrons participating.

July 18: Lieutenant Clarence Lester is credited with three confirmed kills during a single mission. The 332nd was credited with a total of 11 kills on that mission.

July 25: The 387th Service Group activated at Daniel Field, Georgia. The 387th was a support unit for the 477th Bombardment Group and would later include the 590th Air Material Squadron and the 602nd Air Engineering Squadron.

August 14: Fourteen black officers enter a part of the post restaurant at Tuskegee Army Airfield that was reserved for whites. The officers ask for service and show a copy of the 1940 War Department directive banning segregation in post facilities. The restaurant manager directs that the black officers be served. As a result, the post commander ends segregation at the post restaurant.

September 6: The 67th Army Air Forces Base Unit organized at Tuskegee Army Airfield.

September 10: Brigadier General Benjamin O. Davis Sr., on a visit to the base at Ramitelli, pins the Distinguished Flying Cross on Colonel Davis and three others for their service during an escort mission on June 9, 1944.

October 21: The 332nd flies its 100th mission for the 15th Air Force, an escort mission for B-24s of the 304th Bombardment Wing in an attack on Gyor, Hungary.

November 2: 302nd Fighter Squadron receives approval for its emblem. The emblem consists of a winged running devil with a machine gun.

November 3: Major George S. Roberts assumes temporary command of the 332nd Fighter Group.

November 3: The last non-American graduates from pilot training at Tuskegee Army Airfield, Eugene G. Theodore, from Trinidad.

November 25: The 100th Fighter Squadron receives approval for its emblem. The emblem consists of a winged panther on a globe.

December 9: On an escort mission to Brux, Germany, the 332nd first encounters Me-262 jet fighters.

December 24: Colonel Davis reassumes command of the 332nd Fighter Group.

1945 January 1: Seven men from the 332nd Fighter Group are awarded the Distinguished Flying Cross.

January 11: The 387th Air Service Group moves from Daniel Field, Georgia, to Godman Field, Kentucky.

January 22: Eleven pilots from the 332nd awarded the Distinguished Flying Cross.

March 5: The 477th Bombardment Group moves from Godman Field, Kentucky, to Freeman Field, Indiana.

March 7: The 387th Air Service Group moves to Freeman Field.

March 9: Truman K. Gibson, a civilian aide to the secretary of war, along with Major General James M. Bevans, deputy commander of the Mediterranean Allied Air Forces, visit Ramitelli.

March 10: An article by Roi Ottley, "Dark Angels of Doom," in *Liberty* magazine makes first claim of the Tuskegee Airmen never having lost a bomber.

March 24: 332nd participates in the longest raid performed by the 15th Air Force during World War II, an attack on Berlin. During the mission, the 332nd shoots down three Me-262 jet fighters. The 99th, 100th, and 301st Fighter Squadrons are awarded the Distinguished Unit Citation.

April 5: Freeman Field "Mutiny" begins when officers from the 477th Bombardment Group attempt to enter the de facto whites-only officers' club at Freeman Field, Indiana. The 115th Army Air Forces Base Unit moves from Godman Field to Freeman Field.

April 10: The 115th Army Air Forces Base unit discontinued, and the 387th assumes its functions in support of the 477th.

April 10–11: Around 100 officers from the 477th refuse to sign a copy of the new base regulations on Freeman Field and are arrested.

April 13: Last confirmed kills for the Tuskegee Airmen in World War II, when four enemy aircraft are shot down on a mission.

April 26–27: The 477th moves back to Godman Field.

April 28: The 387th moves to back to Godman Field.

April 30: The 332nd Fighter Group performs its 311th and last recorded mission, escorting a reconnaissance aircraft over Bolzano, Italy.

May 4: The 99th Fighter Squadron moves to Cattolica, Italy.

May 7: World War II in Europe ends. The 332nd flies over Brenner Pass between Italy and Austria to test the armistice.

May 8: Celebrations held to mark VE (Victory in Europe) Day.

May 29: Major William A. Campbell becomes first African American to be awarded a second Distinguished Flying Cross.

June 1: The 67th Army Air Forces Base Unit (Tuskegee Weather Detachment) discontinued.

June 8: Colonel Davis awarded the Silver Star. He left Italy that day to assume his new duties with the 477th.

June 9: Major Roberts reassumes command of the 332nd.

June 21: Colonel Benjamin O. Davis Jr. assumes command of the 477th Composite Group at Godman Field, Kentucky.

June 22: The 99th Fighter Squadron moves to Godman Field and is reassigned from the 332nd Fighter Group to the 477th. The 477th Bombardment Group (Medium) is redesignated as the 477th Composite Group.

June 29: The 301st Fighter Squadron receives approval for its emblem. The emblem consists of a cat on a flying machine gun.

July 18: The 332nd moves from Cattolica to Lucera, Italy.

August 6: United States drops the first atomic bomb used in war on Hiroshima, Japan.

August 8: Soviet Union declares war on Japan and opens an offensive against Japanese forces in Manchuria.

August 9: United States drops second atomic bomb, on Nagasaki, Japan.

August 14: Japan agrees to the demands of the Allies, and combat largely ends in the Pacific.

September 2: World War II officially ends with the formal surrender of Japan.

September 3: The 99th, 100th, and 301st Fighter Squadrons begin their trip to the United States.

October 4: The 332nd arrives at Camp Kilmer, New Jersey.

October 19: The 332nd Fighter Group inactivated.

1946 March 13: Colonel Davis assumes command of Lockbourne Air Force Base, Ohio.

June 28: Last class (46-C) graduated from Tuskegee Army Airfield. The base was closed shortly afterward.

1947 July 1: The 477th Composite Group is inactivated.

July 1: The 332nd Fighter Group is reactivated.

September 18: The U.S. Air Force established as a separate branch of the U.S. military.

1948 July 26: President Truman issues Executive Order 9981, ordering the end of military segregation.

1949 July 1: The 99th Pursuit Fighter Squadron is inactivated.

July 1: The 332nd Fighter Group is inactivated.

1954 October 27: Benjamin O. Davis Jr. is promoted to brigadier general, becoming the first African American general officer in the U.S. Air Force.

1959   May 22: Benjamin O. Davis Jr. becomes the first African American promoted to major general.

1965   April 30: Benjamin O. Davis Jr. becomes the first African American promoted to lieutenant general.

1975   September 1: Daniel "Chappie" James Jr. becomes first African American to wear four stars when he is promoted to general in the U.S. Air Force.

1985   August 8: The Tuskegee Airmen monument is unveiled at the U.S. Air Force museum on Wright-Patterson Air Force Base, Ohio.

1995   August 12: After a review by the air force, all Letters of Reprimand were removed from the officers involved in the "Freeman Field Mutiny," and the court-martial conviction of Lieutenant Roger C. Terry was set aside.

2007   March 29: Congressional Gold Medal awarded to the Tuskegee Airmen.

ONE

A Legacy to Build On

THE PARTICIPATION OF BLACK MEN in the American military began in the early colonial period. While English colonists were hesitant to arm men who were not free—a group that included not only slaves but also indentured servants and apprentices—military necessity sometimes broke down such inhibitions. Free black men in some colonies had similar militia obligations as whites, especially free blacks living in areas with little or no slavery. Around 5,000 black men fought in the Revolutionary War, both in the Continental Line and in state-raised regiments, with various state militias, and in the Continental Navy. One Rhode Island regiment was around three-quarters black (Donaldson, 1991). However, as the slavery issue became more politically charged after the Revolution and with northern states increasingly abolishing the institution, political pressure against arming free blacks grew, and the militia of most states specifically excluded blacks of any status. State laws increasingly mentioned skin color in the laws governing who had the obligation or right to bear arms for the state. Blacks were forbidden to serve in the U.S. Army, although ships in the fledgling U.S. Navy often included blacks as part of their crews.

Still, some blacks did serve in the War of 1812, serving in militia or other military forces raised by the states for the war and in scattered small wars against Indians. Only in the Mexican-American War (1846–1848) were blacks excluded. That war occurred near the height of southern slave-based culture, was of short duration, and the troops who fought it had to be transported far from their homes—all of which mitigated against black men participating in combat. At the opposite extreme was the Civil War, which dragged on for more than four years of bloody struggle, in the heart of the nation, and with the existence of slavery the central issue that tore the nation apart. All these factors worked to bring black men into uniform and into combat. In March 1863, following President Abraham Lincoln's issuance of the Emancipation Proclamation, Massachusetts raised a new Volunteer regiment, the 54th, in which all enlisted soldiers would be black, while all officers would be white. While Massachusetts was the center of abolitionist activity and Boston had a sizable free black population that had been petitioning the governor to be allowed to serve, other factors were also behind the decision of Governor John A. Andrew of Massachusetts to raise the regiment.

All states remaining loyal to the Union had been assigned a quota of troops that had to be raised and mustered into federal service. After the Union government passed draft laws, any state that failed to raise its quota would be subject to the draft. The men of the 54th would count toward Massachusetts's quota. Still, abolitionists and black leaders alike understood the powerful message that black men wearing U.S. Army uniforms fighting to restore to the Union would send. The federal government and U.S. Army had debated long enough over the potentially divisive issue of allowing black men to serve. By raising the 54th Massachusetts Volunteer Regiment and offering it to the federal government, Massachusetts forced the federal government, which was increasingly short of soldiers, to decide whether preservation of the Union was worth allowing black men to fight in U.S. Army uniforms. For the administration of President Abraham Lincoln, the answer was a hesitant "yes." Once that barrier had been breached, more and more Union states began raising similar forces, and in 1864, the federal government itself began raising regiments of black volunteers, the U.S. Colored Troops (Weigley, 1967). By the end of the war, black men made up about 10 percent of the Union army, a percentage about equal to their portion of the general population but a much higher percentage than their proportion of the population of the Union states.

Still, federal law prevented the commissioning of black men—they could serve as privates or sergeants but not as officers. As radical a step as seeing black men wearing U.S. Army uniforms and carrying weapons was for many people in 1863, the next step—seeing black officers—was too radical. A military officer had a commission, which gave him specific authority and an obligation from the federal government to command other men. In a society that still saw blacks, whether free or slave, as subordinates, the idea of black officers was seen as preposterous. Still, that black men were allowed to serve at all and even be appointed to noncommissioned officer status—up to an including regimental sergeant major—was a radical step and showed how far the crisis of the Civil War went to alter relations between blacks and whites.

If the sight of black men in U.S. Army uniforms brought pride to black communities and forced some northern whites to see blacks as something other than menial workers, the very idea of armed black men in uniform was a nightmare to southern whites, especially in areas with large slave populations. Southern whites saw the use of black soldiers by the Union government as tangible evidence of the depravity of the Union. Armed black men were long the greatest fear of the white South, and the idea that that black men were being armed by the federal government enraged them. The Confederate government reacted to the creation of black Union regiments by passing laws that held that any black found in a Union uniform would be sold as a slave, regardless of the man's previous status or place of birth, and that any white man found leading black soldiers would be executed for leading a "servile insurrection." In practice, black soldiers were sometimes killed rather than captured.

After the Civil War, Radical Republicans in Congress pushed through legislation allowing regiments of black soldiers in the Regular Army for the first time, based largely on the proven record of black men in Volunteer regiments during the war. Some congressmen were more pragmatic, reasoning that if blacks were now to be citizens of the United States, with all the rights and privileges, then they should also bear their portion of the burden of defending the country. In 1866, four regiments of black soldiers were formed, the 24th and 25th Infantry Regiments and the 9th and 10th Cavalry Regiments. These four regiments represented about 10 percent of the total strength of the Regular Army. Almost all the officers were white, but the privates and noncommissioned officers were all black. These black Regulars would later be known as the "Buffalo Soldiers" (Dobak & Phillips, 2001). In modern popular culture, the Buffalo Soldiers—a term apparently never used by the black Regulars themselves except as an insult—have entered the imagination as either elite Indian fighters on the frontier or, conversely, a much-abused group of soldiers of a despised race in a racist army.

For the black enlisted soldiers, the army did offer job security. As a general rule, the black soldiers received low pay, miserable housing, bland food, and worn-out equipment, but the same was true for all American soldiers of the period. Black newspapers increasingly ignored the black Regulars, and white newspapers did likewise for white soldiers. In general, whatever their color, soldiers of the Regular Army had little status in the United States during peacetime. The African American soldiers were not systematically materially neglected, nor were they "elite" units of the army. As with white units, some black units performed poorly in combat against

Indians, had high incidents of violence within units, and were occasionally posted away from critical areas from lack of faith in their abilities. The black regiments were maintained and performed on a level similar to white regiments. Minor differences with white regiments did exist, though. Far fewer black soldiers could read, which made finding suitable company clerks or noncommissioned officers difficult. Black regiments had a chaplain who was expected to serve as schoolteacher to the men in their off-duty hours (Dobak & Phillips, 2001). White officers often sought to avoid service in a black regiment, although some, such as later General of the Armies John J. Pershing, who had served as a captain in the 10th Cavalry Regiment, later recounted that the black Regulars he led were solid soldiers and professionals (Trask, 1981). Black soldiers were far less likely to desert than whites and more prone to reenlist. This had been expected based on the experience of the U.S. Colored Troops in the Civil War and was one of the primary arguments for creating the regiments in the first place. Neither abused victims nor elite units, they shared much of the same military experiences of their white counterparts. Whatever the shortcomings in race relations in the military and American society as a whole during the Gilded Age, the peacetime U.S. Army was simply too small and isolated to support a two-tier structure (Dobak & Phillips, 2001). Although black soldiers often received discrimination, they were paid and equipped the same as white soldiers. Racism was a fact of life, however, and often racist white officers saw black soldiers of great bravery, intelligence, or leadership as exceptions, while any lazy, unintelligent, or cowardly black soldier was seen as the norm. The black regiments, like most of the army, served mainly in the West. While white communities in the West were sometimes unenthusiastic about having a black army unit posted nearby, the black Regulars often earned the respect of local whites by their courage against Indians and outlaws. Black Regulars who spent time in the East or the South soon learned that their status as American soldiers did not shield them from racial discrimination and could actually invite more violence against them by whites who resented seeing a black man in a military uniform.

The army commissioned its first black man, Henry O. Flipper of Georgia, in 1877, after he completed the U.S. Military Academy at West Point. Second Lieutenant Flipper was assigned to the 10th Cavalry Regiment. But his pioneering effort had little effect. Flipper was dismissed from the army in 1882 after a racially charged court-martial where he was found guilty of lying. Black officers remained extremely rare, and most of the officers for the four black regiments remained white. John H. Alexander became the second black man to graduate from West Point in 1877 and Charles Young

Henry O. Flipper was the first African American to graduate from the U.S. Military Academy at West Point, graduating in 1877. His military career was cut short because of racist allegations and he was dismissed in 1882. (Hulton Archive/ Getty Images)

the third in 1889. No other African American man would graduate from West Point until 1936, when Benjamin O. Davis Jr. became the fourth black man to graduate. A few black enlisted men earned commissions through examination and served in the Regular Army, but none had the prestige that a West Point background gave an officer of the period, and most of the black officers who did exist were chaplains assigned to the black regiments. Black men also continued to earn reserve commissions through the Reserve Officers Training Corps, but most would either remain in the Organized Reserve or serve in black National Guard units. Still, the existence of the four black Regular Army regiments was looked at with some pride by the black community and was seen as a sign that blacks were participating in American society, although they were largely ignored by the black press.

Army life for the few black officers who did exist was exceedingly difficult, although the pay tended to be better than what most blacks earned in civilian life. As officers, lieutenants and captains were not allowed to socialize with enlisted men. However, racial custom prevented white officers from interacting socially with black officers. Since most black officers were the only black officer on a post, they were completely socially isolated unless middle-class black families happened to live in nearby communities, which was rare. Segregation seriously limited not only the commissioning of black officers but more so the ability of the few black officers who did exist to rise in rank beyond the company grades—lieutenants and captain.

Custom and sometimes regulations tried to prevent any situation where a black officer would be in charge of a white officer, and under no circumstances was a black officer to command white enlisted soldiers. A black captain could command a black company only if all the lieutenants in that company were black. While that was possible although difficult in the Regular Army, the next levels of command were nearly impossible and contrary to army policy. A black battalion commander, usually a major or lieutenant colonel, would have to have all captains and lieutenants in the battalion be black, and at the regimental level, commanded by a colonel, the problem was three times worse. In practice, such hypothetical all-black battalions and larger units did not exist in the Regular Army, and the single black battalion commander in the Regular Army in the years before the Great War, Charles Young, did have white officers under him, which was a constant source of friction. The army told itself that black enlisted men assigned to segregated units preferred white officers, and so black battalions in the Regular Army usually had all white officers, effectively preventing black officers from ever rising above the rank of captain.

In the National Guard, however, segregation in most states was stricter, but black officers had as a result more potential to rise above the rank of captain. Black National Guard units, in the states that had them, were all black—enlisted men and officers. However, most states with black National Guard units had no black units larger than a battalion, meaning that lieutenant colonel was as high as a black officer could rise in the National Guard. In all cases, the root problem was that the idea of a black officer holding command or authority over a lower-ranking white officer, let alone a white enlisted man, was simply unthinkable. In much of the nation, especially in the South, tradition dictated that white people had authority over black people and that white people were always the social superiors of black people. White people addressed black men in formal situations by their first names or by terms such as *uncle* or even as *boy*. Newspapers and even national magazines, if they were being polite, normally referred to a black man with the term *negro* in front of their last name, reserving *Mr.* for white men only. They were not above using a slew of less polite terms for blacks. For a white enlisted man to have to refer to a black officer as, for example, *Captain Jones* or, even more unthinkable, as *sir*, was one of those potential social situations that later military leaders saw as insurmountable. When on September 7, 1904, the *New York Times* reported on an incident at a sham battle held at Manassas, Georgia, involving black and white veterans of the Spanish-American War in which an enlisted soldier from Georgia refused to salute a black officer, the current and a former governor of Georgia saw fit to write letters to the editor of the *New York Times* praising the Georgia soldier, with the former governor writing that "any Yankee who thinks a Georgia soldier will salute a negro is a damned fool."

While racism was a powerful force in most of the nation, in the South it had legal standing under a system called *Jim Crow*. Jim Crow was a complex array of legal and social relationships that sought to keep blacks in a subordinate position. While racism outside the South could be and often was a virulent as in the states of the former Confederacy, Jim Crow laws existed mainly in the South. The key to maintaining Jim Crow was the denial of the right to vote to black men. Blacks had been kept away from the voting booth using largely extralegal violence-based methods as Reconstruction drew to a close in the 1870s. With blacks initially prevented from voting through violence, state governments were free to pass a series of laws that perpetuated the denial of black voting rights. Once Jim Crow laws were in place, the system became a legal, self-perpetuating system to keep black people from exercising basic civil rights. Sheriffs and courts, simply by enforcing the laws, effectively kept blacks repressed. Since blacks were not voters in most areas of the South, politicians had few incentives to do anything for blacks, and with blacks rendered ineligible for jury service by their lack of registration as voters, blacks who confronted the law found themselves arrested by white policemen, persecuted by white district attorneys, tried by all-white juries, and sentenced by white judges. When the law was too slow or, more commonly, when the alleged transgression involved social or sexual interaction between a black man and a white woman, the white response could be savage. Whether consensual or not, sexual relations—or even the hint of social contact—between a black man and a white woman was considered rape, and the black man who was caught by a white mob bent on revenge would normally be beaten, burned, hanged, and eventually dismembered, sometimes with pieces of the victim cut off as souvenirs. Had the actual black man involved been able to avoid the mob, one or more other black men might suffer the grim fate in his stead to "send a message" to all black men.

While Jim Crow and overall racial prejudice was detrimental to all blacks, it had a particular sting to the small black middle class. Essentially, Jim Crow was an incipient caste system where status was inherited and no amount of education, wealth, or manners could move a black person above it. When someone such as the leading black intellectual W.E.B. Du Bois, who held a doctorate from Harvard University, ventured into the South and even parts of the North, he would have to ride in the separate, dirty train cars reserved for blacks, would have to stay at the hotels that allowed only black patrons, and would be forbidden to eat in most restaurants. Had he become involved in a dispute with a white man, no matter how low the education or class of the white man, Du Bois, as a black man, would almost certainly have been the loser. There were dirty hotels, bad diners, and miserable public transportation for whites too, but the acquisition of education, manners, and especially wealth allowed a white person access to a higher standard, while no amount of wealth could buy a black person a ticket out of the Jim Crow train car.

Outside the South, few true Jim Crow laws existed, allowing blacks to form voting blocs. As long as the numbers of blacks outside the South remained small, northern politicians had only a limited interest in appealing to black voters. However, beginning during World War I, blacks began moving from the rural South, eventually settling in the urban North in what would later be characterized as the Great Migration (Dodson & Dioue, 2004). Many northern politicians who represented urban districts increasingly found their elections and reelections dependent on maintaining good relations with the black voters in their districts.

The key to civil rights has long rested on the right to vote, and the right to vote had been long tied to military service. Athenian democracy during the classical age of Greece included landless peasant men because these same men provided the masses needed for the citizen armies. The early American republic included elements of this principle in that women were not originally allowed to vote in part because they were not expected or allowed to serve in the military. Likewise, most free white adult American men had a militia obligation, and eventually the right to vote was extended to most adult free men. This linkage between voting and military service was well understood by blacks such as Frederick Douglas and Du Bois, who had a classical republican conception of citizenship. Opponents of allowing blacks to vote understood this linkage at some level and remained committed to keeping black men out of the military or by allowing them to serve only in support-type roles if they had to serve, in part to keep them out of the voting booth. The very idea of black men armed, trained to fight, and wearing U.S. uniforms struck at the heart of Jim Crow and white supremacy, and a sizable black military contribution to an American victory would provide a powerful argument against the continued denial of black civil rights.

When the United States went to war against Spain in 1898, blacks again responded to the call for troops. The four black Regular Army regiments became involved almost immediately. The black regiments had been stationed in the West but had to move into the South for deployment to Cuba. In the South, the black soldiers experienced firsthand the danger and degradation of Jim Crow. Many black soldiers came from the North, and while they had been subjected to official and unofficial racism, many were taken aback by the overt hatred they faced as the troop trains moved into the South. The federal government hesitated when accepting state Volunteer regiments composed of blacks, in part because the number of white regiments the army was forced to accept completely swamped the ability of the army to adequately house, equip, and train. Later, the army did accept four black Volunteer regiments for service in Cuba as "immunes" on the theory that blacks were somehow less susceptible to tropical diseases. To fill the officer ranks in the new black Volunteer regiments that were raised for occupation duties in Cuba, 30 experienced black Regular noncommissioned officers of proven ability were commissioned. However, as was common throughout the army of the period, when the Volunteer regiments were disbanded, these men had to return to their original regiments as privates (Coffman, 2004).

Despite the difficulties of military service, blacks stayed in the U.S. Army, and occasionally middle-class black men were able to earn a commission, usually through examination. In 1912, six black U.S. Army officers were sent to the West African nation of Liberia to train and command the Liberian Frontier Force, a constabulary composed of tribal Liberians. Black Americans commanded the force until 1924, helping to crush the Kru revolt of 1915. But as with most of the peacetime U.S. Regular Army, the black Regulars—officers and enlisted alike—served beyond the notice of most Americans. If the white Regular was often forgotten during peacetime, the black Regular was doubly so. The black soldier had been largely written out of the history books. Public acknowledgment of the black participation in war had followed a pattern—briefly celebrated and then quickly forgotten and most signs of it erased. Most Americans in 1910 would have been shocked to discover that black men had fought in the Revolutionary War or had played such a prominent role in the Union armies in the last years of the Civil War. Blacks had served and were still serving, but until their service was acknowledged, most white Americans could still tell themselves that only white men defended the country, and thus only white men had earned the right to vote and serve on juries.

World War I

While the Regular Army expanded slightly in the 1800s and much more so after the Spanish-American War and the resulting new responsibilities placed on the army, the number of black regiments remained fixed at four, so black men formed a decreasing percentage of the total strength. When the United States entered World War I, the Regular Army contained the same two infantry and two cavalry regiments of African Americans, for a total of almost 10,000 black men, including an influx of 4,000 recruits during 1916. Three of these regiments remained in the United States throughout the war, while one served in the Philippines. The National Guard contained another 10,000 black men. Thirty-four percent of black Selective Service registrants were later drafted, compared to 24 percent for whites, mainly because whites had the option of volunteering for several months after the United States entered the war, while blacks were not allowed to. A total of 13 percent of draftees were black, although blacks constituted only around 10 percent of the total population. Draftees, black or white, did not have any influence on where or how they served. Under Selective Service, the government would put a drafted man into the position the government felt he could best serve. The U.S. Marine Corps admitted no blacks, while the navy took in about 1 percent. Of 400,000 blacks who served in the war, most served in the army. Some 42,000 served in combat, a ratio slightly lower than for whites because forces both inside the army and without sought to keep black men in menial positions, performing heavy labor building roads or moving supplies or in the laundry (Edgerton, 2001, pp. 70–72). World War I occurred during the high tide of racism in the United States. Racial violence in Houston, Texas, between black soldiers and white civilians was used to justify keeping black soldiers in labor battalions and not being issued weapons (Edgerton, 2001, p. 77). As labor units, the African Americans performed superbly. One regiment, working as stevedores, was expected to unload 6,000 tons a month. In September 1918 alone, they unloaded 800,000 tons. But many blacks resented serving only as laborers and clamored for black combat units. Black leaders understood that black men in combat would give a powerful argument for respecting the civil rights—especially the right to vote—after the war. The time the United States spent fighting World War I was relatively short, about a year and a half, with American involvement in major combat lasting only about six months. But during that time, the number of black men in combat units constantly shrunk, and more and more black men were moved into support roles. By the armistice on November 11, 1918, most of the American black men still in frontline combat units were fighting in regiments attached to the French Army.

In the new National Army raised for the war, black National Guard units were consolidated and combined with new units of drafted men to form the 92nd and 93rd Divisions. In these divisions, all enlisted men were black, while officers were predominantly white. The 93rd Division was "loaned" to the French army, mainly to satisfy French demands for American troops

A group of African American soldiers, who were awarded the Croix de Guerre by the French government for gallantry in action, pose for a photo in 1919, following the end of World War I. (National Archives)

and to allow white American units to remain under American command. The French separated the regiments of the 93rd and attached them to French divisions. With French equipment, proper training, and capable leadership, the African American regiments performed well, earning 550 French decorations, including 180 of the Croix de Guerre, while suffering 35 percent casualties. They held their front for 191 days without losing territory while capturing many Germans (Edgerton, 2001, p. 85).

The experience of the 92nd Division, which remained part of the American Expeditionary Force, was far less glorious. Racism within the army created the self-fulfilling prophecy of failure of black soldiers in battle. The 92nd Division suffered from inadequate training, shortages of basic equipment, no artillery, and uneven officer quality. Many of the white officers assigned to the 92nd were self-declared racists in the belief that they "knew how to handle blacks." Thrown into battle two days after arrival in the Argonne, two battalions from the division's 368th Regiment failed in combat, while others performed well. The failure of some elements was projected to the entire division and then to all black soldiers. The failure of the 92nd was cited as "proof" that blacks were naturally unfit for combat (Edgerton, 2001, pp. 91–99). As a result, most black combat units were converted to labor units. The stereotype of blacks as cowardly, unaggressive, and unintelligent was also used to justify the exclusion of all but a token few from the officer corps. This stigma would last through World War II.

The experience of blacks in the World War I had been deeply discouraging to them and their liberal white allies. Black leaders such as Du Bois had encouraged black men to serve, believing that faithful black service would lead white Americans to see blacks as fellow citizens, whereas black refusal to fight would be used as an excuse to remove what few rights blacks retained. However, the experience of blacks during the war had instead been used to bolster racism after the war. The years immediately after the war, 1919–1921, saw some of the worst racial violence since the end of Reconstruction as whites sought to put blacks "back in their place" and crush any hopes that participation in the war would lead to greater freedoms at home. Official military racism and segregation was increasingly cloaked in pseudoscience. In 1925, the Army War College conducted a study, "The Use of Negro Manpower in War," which was theoretically an examination of how black men were employed during World War I and made recommendations on their use in future wars. The study was based on racist attitudes and assumptions. It erroneously said, for example, that whites and blacks were different subspecies of humanity and that blacks had a brain weighing, on average, only 35 ounces as opposed to 45 ounces for the brain of a white man. The study claimed that black men, in addition to possessing too little brainpower for mastering technical tasks or to be resourceful, were also natural cowards. Therefore, blacks could best serve in the military (and, by extension, in civil society) by performing menial jobs, jobs that took little skill, such as cleaning, carrying goods, and the like. And, of course, black soldiers should serve under white officers, whose innate bravery and intelligence made them natural leaders. The War College revisited the topic in 1937, and although the official position remained that while blacks lacked the innate requirements for highly skilled positions or leadership, the 1937 study argued that more of them should be allowed to serve in the military, albeit still in menial roles. However, the world was becoming increasingly dangerous, and preventing qualified men from doing their part in national defense on the basis of skin color would be increasingly difficult to maintain.

Tensions had been building in Europe since 1933, when the National Socialist Workers' Party, or *Nazis*, came to power in Germany. The election of the leader of the Nazi Party, Adolf Hitler, to German chancellor in 1933 signaled the ascension not only of a revived German militarism but also of an open and particularly vicious form of racism. Hitler's book *Mein Kampf*, first published in 1925, was a rambling hate-filled autobiography mixed with his views on various ethnic groups and his plans for a future enlarged Germany. While Hitler's strongest hatred was toward the Jews, he also described Slavic peoples as subhumans and referred to blacks as "half-apes" and disparaged them as not being fully human. Italy's Fascist Party, part of the inspiration for Hitler's Nazis, had been in power since 1922. While not originally racist in orientation, the Fascist war against Ethiopia signaled a new aggressiveness and expansionism on the part of Italy and brought deep resentment against Italy by people of African descent worldwide. On the other side of the world, Japan's fragile democracy had largely been replaced by military-based governments that sought to use military force to ensure that Japan would always have access to the raw materials and captive markets its industries believed they needed for sustained growth. Open warfare began between Japan and China in 1937, and while the United States remained officially neutral, Americans sympathized with the Chinese.

As the world drifted toward World War II, blacks in the United States could look back on centuries of black participation in American wars, although the fruits of that loyal service were hardly encouraging. Social and political forces worked to keep blacks who did serve in the military during wartime in the less glamorous roles, such as transportation and labor, while keeping blacks from technical, combat, or leadership positions. Most understood that if the military simply dropped color or race as a factor in assigning soldiers and allowed soldiers to be assigned on the basis of individual skills, intelligence, and performance, myriad injustices would go away. Black newspapers and magazines, as well as civil rights organizations such as the National Association for the Advancement of Colored People (NAACP), had long called for an end of racial discrimination and, more fundamentally, for an end to racial segregation. While the black press tended to have an ambivalent attitude toward the military in general, most understood that black men serving in integrated military units would be a powerful step forward in ending segregation in the nation.

As first the Far East and then Europe became embroiled in war, the United States began to rearm. While some dissenters raised their voices, in general most American favored keeping out of the war but believed that the nation must build up its military from its peacetime doldrums in order to prevent German or Japanese attempts to establish bases in the Americas and to be able to defeat them if deterrence failed. The U.S. military in 1939 was in desperate need of men, equipment, and training. The Regular Army consisted of about 175,000 men organized into six infantry divisions and one cavalry division, all of which were under strength and with obsolete equipment. While most military and civilian leaders understood the nation needed to build up the army and the navy, many, including President Franklin D. Roosevelt, believed that airpower would play a major role in defending America.

The emergency dreaded by national leaders came sooner than most had hoped it would. Germany's invasion of Poland on September 1, 1939, led France and Great Britain to declare war on Germany, which in turn declared war on them. Most American leaders understood that the world was entering a new and dangerous phase. The United States did not mobilize for war after Germany invaded Poland, but the nation did begin taking steps unprecedented in American history toward preparedness. On September 8, 1939, as a response to the outbreak of war in Europe, President Roosevelt declared a limited national emergency. The German invasion of France the following spring and France's unexpected collapse and surrender gave new urgency to the U.S. government. In short order, Germany had taken control not only of France but also of half of Poland and all of Denmark, Norway, Luxembourg, the Netherlands, and Belgium. Austria had earlier become part of Germany, which in early 1939 had also absorbed half of Czechoslovakia. Italy was allied to Germany, and Spain was sympathetic. Germany, Italy, and Japan joined in the Axis alliance, under which they pledged mutual support in the event of war. American leaders were acutely aware of the vulnerability of American possessions in the Pacific, specifically the Philippines, Guam, and Hawaii, to the Japanese and knew that the Japanese coveted these islands. While most Americans desperately wanted to stay out of the war, most also understood that the United States would have to become strong enough to prevent Japan from seeking to conquer U.S. possessions and to deter Germany from making any claims to territories in the New World. Denmark ruled Greenland, and France and the Netherlands had possessions in the Caribbean, off the coast of Canada, and on the South American mainland. Should Germany press for the use of these possessions of the nations it had conquered, the United States needed to be able to prevent German forces from landing at any of these New World possessions. The need for skilled pilots was only going to increase.

On July 31, 1940, President Roosevelt called on Congress for the authority to order the National Guard and Organized Reserves to active service for the year of training. Concurrent with the mobilization of the National Guard and the Organized Reserves was the institution of the country's first peacetime draft. The men mobilized for the emergency could serve outside the United States, although they were not to leave the Western Hemisphere except to deploy to U.S. possessions in the Pacific. Despite some National Guard units deploying to the Philippines, the bulk of the men called to service before the attack on Pearl Harbor spent their time training for war in camps scattered across the nation. The1937 mobilization plans called for blacks to serve in the same proportion as in the general population and that they serve in combat units; however, the Air Corps was specifically excluded from the requirement to accept blacks. The detailed plans of 1940 included provisions for an army that was only 5.8 percent black. Black leaders hoped that the building crisis would lead to allowing blacks to serve not only at the same percentage as in the general population but also in integrated units. President Roosevelt, running for his third term, accepted that blacks should serve at the same proportion but would not agree to desegregation (Coffman, 2004).

For most black Americans, the military was an alien world. Many older black men still had bitter memories of their experience in World War I. By 1940, only 4,179 black men served in the army, while the officer corps contained only five black men. Of the five, three were chaplains. The other two were Colonel Benjamin O. Davis and his son, Lieutenant Benjamin O. Davis Jr. Colonel Davis was about to retire but was instead promoted to brigadier general in 1940, the first black general officer in the United States, and would serve in that rank for the next eight years without any further promotion. In the Organized Reserves, forerunner to the Army Reserve, there were an additional 353 black officers, which was less than 5 percent of all officers in the Reserve.

Black leaders in 1939 and their liberal white allies understood the linkage between military service and the right to vote. While stung by the World War I experience and its aftermath, they understood that the answer was not to shirk from having black men bear their share of the military burden but rather to prevent racists from denigrating that service. Opponents of the subordination of blacks would have to strive to see black men serving in the military in numbers comparable to their percentage of the general population and serving in all branches, positions, and ranks. To see that result, they would have to overcome bigotry, custom, and inertia in society, government, and the military. In the 1940 mobilization plans, the Army Air Corps was still exempted from accepting any allotment of black soldiers. Major General Henry "Hap" H. Arnold, Chief of the Air Corps, argued that having black pilots was impossible because pilots were officers and "since this would result in having Negro officers serving over white enlisted men. This would create an impossible social problem" (MacGregor, 1989).

Despite the opposition of the Chief of the Air Corps to allowing black pilots, many black Americans saw airpower as the future and wanted to be part of it. Since the waning days of World War I, airpower enthusiasts had been nourishing grandiose dreams of what airpower could accomplish, and the fledgling Army Air Service, as the Army Air Corps had been designated before 1926, formed a cabal of true believers in the supremacy of airpower. Throughout the 1920s, the Air Corps Tactical School at Maxwell Army Airfield in Montgomery, Alabama, taught a doctrine that held that strategic bombing would be key to victory in the next war. This faith developed to the point that airpower enthusiasts argued that ground and naval forces were almost obsolete and that by scientifically analyzing the economy of an enemy nation and selectively bombing key factories, rail junctions, and infrastructure, an enemy nation would be brought to economic, social, and military collapse, and the army would simply have to occupy the defeated nation. Wedded to this faith in the power of strategic bombing was the Air Corps' faith in the bomber. Believing that multiengine bomber aircraft would always fly higher, faster, and farther than fighter aircraft, the Air Corps sought to spend almost all its budget on developing bombers, arguing that any money or effort spent on fighters or ground attack missions would only prolong the next war. A fleet of properly armed bombers would be able to break through any conceivable air defense efforts by an enemy and lay waste to the ability of an enemy to wage war. All effort should go toward the bomber fleets. When the prototype B-17 Flying Fortress—a large, four-engine bomber with defensive machine guns all around—first flew in 1935, the Air Corps believed that it had the tool to carry out its ambitious doctrine.

Not all military leaders shared the view of future war developed by the Army Air Corps. More traditional officers in the army, as well as their navy and marine counterparts, saw the main value of airpower in close air support—using aircraft to deliver bombs and machine gun fire on targets near the battlefield, giving ground troops an additional source of support. The Army Air Corps only grudgingly developed aircraft and units for the close air support mission and would remain committed through the war and beyond to strategic bombing as the best use of airpower.

While most military leaders were not so convinced in the primacy of airpower, most army and navy leaders in the United States understood that airplanes would play a major role in the next war. However, the United States—the nation that gave birth to heavier-than-air flight—lagged behind most European powers in the number of pilots. At the start of 1939, the army had a total of only about 4,502 pilots, of whom 2,007 were in the Regular Army, 308 were in the National Guard, and another 2,187 were in the Organized Reserve, while the Army Air Corps had plans for fleets of tens or even hundreds of thousands of aircraft if war came (National Museum, 2010). During the late 1930s, the Air Corps trained about 200 pilots a year, but given the increasingly dangerous situation in Europe and Asia, the Air Corps planned to expand to 24 air groups by June 30, 1941. To build and sustain that size of a force, the Air Corps would need to produce around 1,200 pilots a year (Pisano, 2001). The nation needed to increase its supply of pilots and do so quickly.

The Civil Aeronautics Act of 1938 included an appropriation of $100,000 to create the Civilian Pilot Training Program (CPTP) through the National Youth Administration, one of the myriad federal programs that the Roosevelt administration created in an effort to revive the economy during the Great Depression. On December 27, 1938, President Roosevelt announced the program to the public. Under the CPTP, the federal government planned to train 20,000 civilian pilots each year. While the program was ostensibly to create more civilian pilots and increase the demand for civilian aircraft, the administration understood that its real purpose was to create a pool of civilian pilots that the military could draw on if the need for rapid expansion occurred. The administration also hoped that the program would spur interest in flying in the general population. Neither the army nor the navy greeted the new program enthusiastically. Despite the military implications of the program, it was still very much a civilian training program, and graduates incurred no particular military obligation. Even women, who were specifically banned from military flying, were allowed to participate in limited numbers. Most European nations could boast of similar civilian flight training programs, flying clubs, and glider clubs, but in Europe such programs were overtly military in nature, and their purpose of training military pilots was undisguised.

The U.S. military believed that any similar program to expand the number of pilots in the United States should be run by the military and thus that anyone accepted into such a program should be eligible to serve as a military pilot. Such criteria would automatically exclude women and blacks and many white men from participating. The army went so far as to propose ending all private flying in the United States for the duration of the emergency (Pisano, 2001). In response to the army's plan, some 83 private companies involved in civilian flying organized the National Aviation Training Association in part to lobby Congress against the army's plan, which they feared would destroy the nation's growing aircraft industry. Congress remained wary of attempts by the military to extend its control any more than was absolutely necessary for the emergency and blocked the attempt by the army to assume direct control of all flight training.

Still, passage of the act authorizing the CPTP was fraught with confusion in Congress. The army required aviation cadets to have at least two years of college, but some in Congress wanted the CPTP open to all regardless of education. Eventually, an amendment to the act inserted by James E. Van Zandt (R-PA) allowed 10 percent of people selected for the CPTP to not have any college education (Pisano, 2001). The next debate in Congress over the passage of the act came with an amendment proposed by Everett M. Dirksen (R-IL), who inserted a clause that "none of the benefits of training or programs shall be denied on account or race, creed, or color." Dirksen justified the inclusion of blacks in the program specifically on the record of black men who served in American wars back to the Revolution and from his association with black civilian fliers in the Chicago area. Dirksen, as well as the National Airmen's Association of America, an organization of blacks interested in aviation, which saw the inclusion of blacks in the CPTP as a first step toward integrating the Army Air Corps. Opposition to the Dirksen amendment came from Clarence Lea (D-CA), who argued that the law, as written, had no provisions for discrimination anyway but also that few if any "colored institutions in this country may be able to qualify as training centers under this bill" (Pisano, 2001, p. 56). In other words, since he saw few if any black colleges with the facilities for such a program, including in the bill a provision for training blacks as aviators would be moot. After long debates in both houses of Congress and in committees, the bill for the CPTP finally passed Congress on August 12, 1939, as Public Law 18. Congress authorized a budget of $4 million, which would create about 10,000 pilots. The final version of the bill contained Representative Dirksen's antidiscriminatory language. With a government program to train pilots, one that in part was to create a pool of pilots the military could draw on in an emergency, the continued exclusion of blacks from serving as pilots in the Air Corps was coming under increasing pressure. The president signed the bill soon after Congress passed it. Still, with the Army Air Corps remaining steadfast in its opposition to black pilots, the national defense implications of the CPTP remained theoretical in regard to blacks who completed the CPTP and earned their civilian pilot's license.

The CPTP would be based at civilian colleges, and women and blacks would be allowed to participate. Northern schools that wanted to admit blacks into their program were allowed to do so, but programs would also be established at black schools. Trainees accepted into the program had to pass a physical examination based on the military's standards for pilots. They had to pay a lab fee of between $35 and $50 and for life insurance. The program of instruction called for 10 hours of instruction in civil air regulations followed by 35 hours each on navigation and meteorology. Students then took 35 to 50 hours of flight instruction, which consisted of eight hours of dual flying instruction, nine hours of dual check flying time, and 18 hours of solo flying. Colleges without an airfield would have to contract with a local airport for use of its facilities for the flight portion of the course (Pisano, 2001). The standards were intentionally high for the ground portion of the course to eliminate those whose shortcomings might lead to death once the flying portion of the course began. Those who completed the course would be certified as a civilian pilot.

The CPTP was initially established at 13 colleges. The first program at what were then called *Negro colleges* was established at Tuskegee Institute in Alabama. The program expanded until programs existed at 1,132 colleges and 1,460 flight schools. In addition to the program at Tuskegee Institute, the CPTP was the established at five other Negro colleges: West Virginia State College for Negroes, Howard University, Hampton Institute, Delaware State College for Colored Students, and North Carolina Agricultural and Technical College, and more would follow (Pisano, 2001). Tuskegee Institute was one of the best known of the Negro colleges, and its CPTP soon became synonymous in the public mind with the training of black pilots. Despite the increased opportunity for flight training that the

Tuskegee students talk about flying their Stearman biplanes, an airplane used as a trainer. At far left is Captain Benjamin O. Davis Jr. (U.S. Air Force)

CPTP gave blacks, the potential for blacks who completed the training to use their skills in defending the nation remained in doubt.

The Army Air Corps had always excluded blacks from serving and sought to continue to exclude blacks during the massive expansion that began in 1939. In part, the Air Corps justified this on the theory that blacks were not mentally competent to master the complex myriad skills needed to be effective military pilots. However, segregation and white supremacy created other organizational problems that made black military pilots even more problematic than black serving in other roles on the military. Even if the Air Corps accepted that the black population of the United States could produce enough men qualified to be military pilots, it had serious doubts that enough black enlisted men could be found to keep those pilots flying. Each pilot, who was a usually a commissioned officer, had to be supported by roughly a dozen enlisted men who served as mechanics, armorers, and supply troops and in administrative roles necessary to keep the pilots flying and fighting. However, the Air Corps believed that it could not find enough black enlisted men with the mechanical and intellectual skills needed to man these positions, and having white enlisted men serving in support of black officers was unthinkable.

These doubts on the part of the Air Corps had some basis in fact. Although demographics were changing, most blacks still lived in the rural South and had attended segregated schools, if they had attended school at all. Southern schools in general were of lower quality than northern schools, rural schools tended to be of lower quality than urban schools, and black schools were of lower quality than white schools. With these educational shortcomings, most blacks on average scored below their white counterparts. Still, Air Corps policy was to simply issue a blanket denial of allowing blacks to enter the Air Corps rather than attempting to find sufficient black men to form black aviation units, even while it struggled to find enough qualified white men for the units already authorized. Still, had the Air Corps given more than a superficial look at blacks and aviation, it would have seen a vibrant interest in aviation among African Americans.

Despite lower access to education and with less ability to draw on higher finances, blacks mirrored the interest that whites showed in aviation, and some blacks managed to overcome obstacles to flying. While blacks had been specifically excluded from the U.S. Army Air Service during World War I, at least one African American, Eugene Bullard, served as a pilot in the French air force during that war, flying combat missions and shooting down at least one German aircraft. A black woman, Bessie Coleman, learned to fly in France and became the first African American to hold a pilot's license in the United States in 1922. A few years after Coleman was killed in a crash in 1926, another black pilot, William Powell, formed the Bessie Coleman Aero Club in Los Angeles, which staged the first all-black air show in 1931. Powell, who had graduated from the University of Illinois with a degree in electrical engineering, had been turned down by the Army Air Service in 1922 solely because he was black. Powell then found that most civilian flying schools were also closed to him based on skin color. Frustrated, he went to France in 1927 to obtain flying lessons but had to return home before completing the course because of financial limits. He was able later to obtain training in aeronautical engineering at Warren College of Aeronautics in Los Angeles and was accredited as a commercial pilot by the State of California. Still, he soon found that a fully qualified black pilot would not be hired by white-owned airlines or by the government. Finding all doors into the small and tight world of white flyers closed to him, he instead began to train black pilots, seeing in aviation a great opportunity for black improvement (Pisano, 2001).

While the Los Angeles area quickly became a center of black aviation, as it was for aviation in general, the Chicago area also held a sizable number of black aviation enthusiasts, centered in the Challenger Air Pilot Association.

Cornelius Coffey and his wife Willa started a flying program at Robbins, Illinois, which was later moved to the Harlem Airport and operated as the Coffey School of Aeronautics. Despite these examples, getting the larger American society and especially the military and the federal government to recognize that blacks could and did fly remained difficult. In 1931, the Air Corps had responded to a request from the NAACP that blacks be allowed into the Air Corps by saying that blacks were not interested in flying (Homan & Reilly, 2001). In May 1939, before World War II broke out in Europe, the *Chicago Defender* and the National Airmen's Association paid for two black pilots, Dale E. White and Chauncey E. Spencer, to fly from Chicago to Washington, D.C., to meet with civil rights leader Edger G. Brown and then with a rather obscure senator from Missouri, Harry S. Truman, to emphasize the desire of African Americans to participate in the American obsession with flying. By 1940, approximately 100 African Americans held a civilian pilot's license (Francis, 1997). When the United States began its massive expansion of the military beginning in the fall of 1939, the desire of blacks to fly, serve in combat, and see black officers became focused on the Army Air Corps.

The army was in an awkward position on racial matters. Regardless of the racial views of its leaders, the American military had a long and cherished tradition of subordination to civilian authority. Most officers in the Regular Army never voted, not from any written prohibition on their doing so but rather from custom in order to preserve absolute neutrality in political matters. Added to these professional ethos was the reality of the American political process; Congress decided the military budget and passed the rules for the military to follow, and the army was loathe to offend congressmen. With southern congressmen often having long tenures in Congress, partially as a result of the de facto one-party system of the South, many important committees in Congress were headed by southerners. For the army to push a progressive agenda on racial issue, for which it had no enthusiasm anyway, would have made it powerful enemies in Congress, something the army did not want to do for professional and practical reasons—since Congress controlled the military budget, running afoul of Congress was to be avoided at all costs.

The 1940 mobilization plans called for blacks to be drafted at roughly the same percentage as their percentage of the general population, about 10 percent. However, the Marine Corps and the Army Air Corps, both of which saw themselves as elite parts of the military, resisted efforts to force them to accept blacks. General Arnold, Chief of the Air Corps, feared the "impossible social problem" of black officers interacting with white enlisted men.

Even if the Air Corps could train a complete compliment of black mechanics, fuel handlers, and all the other support troops needed to man an airfield, the realities of combat would still impose situations deemed impossible by Arnold and many others. Suppose that a black pilot was forced by mechanical problems to land at another airfield, one manned with whites. By military customs and courtesies, the black pilot, an officer, would have to be saluted and addressed as "sir" by the white enlisted men. Such a situation was unthinkable to many whites.

When civil rights organizations pushed for the acceptance of blacks into the Air Corps, they found unexpected allies within the rest of the army, although each side had different motives. The army as a whole had to absorb its quota of blacks, that is, its share of the 10 percent of selectees who were black. With the Air Corps, which was a large part of the army, not taking any blacks, other parts of the army had to absorb more than what they felt was their fair share. The army assigned most blacks to units and branches where they would perform manual or menial labor and would have little potential to actually fight. The Army's Quartermaster Corps, which dealt with supply, was 15 percent black, while the Corps of Engineers was 25 percent black (MacGregor, 1989). Most of the black soldiers assigned to the engineers, regardless of their intelligence or education level, were assigned to perform manual labor. When the Air Corps finally agreed to accept blacks, it was hardly a victory for civil rights and not a giant step toward creating black pilots. The Air Corps created nine squadrons of black men, but instead of aviation squadrons, these were service and labor squadrons assigned to perform grounds-keeping duties, laundry, food service, and other menial jobs. While some soldiers, black as well as white, liked to cook and enjoyed working in food service, most of the other tasks assigned to blacks were more backbreaking, mind-numbing, and enjoyed by few if any soldiers. For educated black men, the limited opportunities caused by racial segregation and simple bigotry were especially humiliating. But while the Army Air Corps tried to ensure that blacks remained in subservient positions, small groups of black men and a few black women began training in the CPTP to become pilots.

References

Army War College, Office of the Commandant. "Memorandum for the Chief of Staff: Subject: The Use of Negro Man Power in War." Washington Barracks, DC, October 30, 1925 (available at the Air War College Historical Research Agency).

Coffman, Edward M. *The Regulars: The American Army, 1898–1941.* Cambridge, MA: Harvard University Press, 2004.

Dobak, William A., and Thomas D. Phillips. *The Black Regulars, 1866–1898*. Norman: University of Oklahoma Press, 2001.

Dodson, Howard, and Sylviane A. Dioue. *In Motion: The African-American Migration Experience*. Washington, DC: National Geographic, 2004.

Donaldson, Gary A. *The History of African-Americans in the Military*. Malabar, FL: Krieger, 1991.

Edgerton, Robert B. *Hidden Heroism: Black Soldiers in America's Wars*. Boulder, CO: Westview, 2001.

Francis, Charles E. *The Tuskegee Airmen: The Men Who Changed a Nation*. Boston: Branden Publishing, 1997.

Homan, Lynn M., and Thomas Reilly. *Black Knights: The Story of the Tuskegee Airmen*. Gretna, LA: Pelican Publishing, 2001.

"Memo, Chief of the Air Corps for G-3, 31 Ma 1940." Quoted in Morris J. MacGregor Jr., *Integration of the Armed Forces, 1940–1965*. Washington, DC: Center for Military History, 1989.

National Museum. http://www.nationalmuseum.af.mil/factsheets/factsheet.asp? id = 8475 (accessed December 1, 2010).

Pisano, Dominick A. *To Fill the Sky with Pilots: The Civilian Pilot Training Program, 1939–1946*. Washington, DC: Smithsonian Institution Press, 2001.

Trask, David F. *The War with Spain in 1898*. New York: Free Press, 1981.

Weigley, Russell F. *History of the United States Army*. New York: Macmillan, 1967.

TWO

The Experiment

Tuskegee Institute had its origins during Reconstruction (1865–1877). Reconstruction was a failed attempt to create a biracial society in the former states of the Confederacy, mainly though ensuring that black men were able to vote. White intransigence, extralegal violence, and federal withdrawal doomed the attempt, and blacks after Reconstruction were reduced to a status with some similarities to slavery. The school at the town of Tuskegee, Alabama, for the children of freed blacks began holding classes in 1881 after the end of Reconstruction. It initially opened as what was then called a normal school that trained young black men and women to be teachers for elementary schools that would provide a basic education to the children of former slaves. The school also began other types of training, specifically in agriculture to introduce more efficient forms of farming to black farmers in the region as well as vocational training. The first head of the school, Booker T. Washington, firmly believed in black self-sufficiency but also believed that blacks should not confront segregation directly. Blacks, he believed, should accommodate themselves to white-dominated society. By the late 1930s, the school had changed a lot, but it remained a center of black education, in part from the celebrity of its first principal. Washington was known nationally and became the de facto spokesman for black Americans following the death of Frederick Douglas in 1895.

In the mid-1920s, under Tuskegee's second principal, Robert Moton, the school began offering college courses and began granting bachelor's degrees in 1927. Because of Moton's lobbying, the town of Tuskegee was selected as a site for a federal hospital for black veterans. Moton also helped ensure that the veterans' hospital would be staffed by black doctors and nurses (Jakeman, 1992). During his tenure, a pivotal moment linking the institution and flight occurred when alumnus John Robinson, later to become involved in aviation in Ethiopia, landed a small plane that he had

Laboratory at Tuskegee Institute in Alabama, about 1902. (National Archives)

flown from Chicago in May 1934 on a small oat field at the school's farm. The occasion was the 10-year anniversary of the graduation of Robinson's class. Robinson's flight and landing at the school excited the local black community, and even whites took notice. Robinson urged the school to create an airfield and offer flight instruction. Moton, however, was not enthusiastic about beginning a risky and expensive new program, but Moton was old and near the end of his long career. His successor would look on aviation differently. Robinson's flight came in the depths of the Great Depression, and institutional survival, not expansion, was the rule. Still, that September, Moton agreed to have the school participate in an aerial tour of the Americas by two black pilots, with their plane, the *Booker T. Washington*, christened on the campus. The fund-raising for the tour—and the tour itself—helped solidify in the public mind the links between black aviation and Tuskegee Institute. The goodwill flight made it only to Port-of-Spain, Trinidad, when the plane was damaged beyond repair attempting to take off from an unimproved field (Jakeman, 1992). Despite the anticlimactic ending to the flight, the tenuous linkage between Tuskegee and aviation continued.

While the goodwill flight did not bring the publicity to black aviation that backers hoped it would, inevitable changes at Tuskegee made the involvement of that institution in flight more likely. Moton, now in his 70s, had been in poor health for a few years. Most of the people involved with the institute understood that Moton's tenure as president of Tuskegee was coming to an end. In early 1935, the Board of Trustees met to choose a new president. The result surprised many people, for the board picked Frederick Douglas Patterson, the director of Tuskegee's School of Agriculture. Patterson, in his mid-30s, held a doctorate in veterinary medicine from Iowa State College and a PhD in bacteriology from Cornell University. Unlike his predecessor, Patterson understood the rising interest of African Americans—and all Americans—in flying. He saw flying as part of the future, and he wanted to ensure that Tuskegee Institute was part of that future.

Shortly after Patterson was named president, Robinson left the United States to accept a commission as a colonel in the fledgling Ethiopian air force, where he created a training program to train Ethiopian military pilots. Ethiopia was the last African nation still under an indigenous ruler and had never been colonized, and its independence was seen as a sign of hope for a free and independent Africa. Italy, under the rule of Benito Mussolini, known as *Il Duce*, and his Fascist Party, hoped to re-create some of the glories of the Roman Empire and sought colonies to help buttress the image of Italy as a great nation. But few areas of the world at the time were not either great powers or colonies of great powers. Ethiopia was relatively close to Italy and not under the rule of a European nation. Robinson's service in Ethiopia during the Italian invasion that began on October 3, 1935, made Robinson the hero to most African Americans. The black press followed his struggle against the invaders in minute detail. Most stories mentioned that he had graduated from Tuskegee Institute. Ethiopia needed modern arms and technicians rather than soldiers, but little tangible assistance came from the antifascist nations. Ethiopian Emperor Hallie Sallasie pleaded for assistance from the international community at the League of Nations, but trade sanctions against Italy soon collapsed.

Despite the efforts of Robinson and others, the 19 planes and 50 pilots of the Ethiopian air force were no match for the experienced and large Italian air force, and on May 9, 1936, Italy formally annexed Ethiopia. Robinson was out of the country when the end came on his way to the United States to raise funds and so avoided internment or execution by the Italians. When Robinson returned to the United States, he was able to accept an offer made earlier by D. L. Washington, the head of Tuskegee's Department of Mechanical Industries, to serve on the faculty. When news of Robinson's imminent return to the United States reached Tuskegee Institute, Patterson reaffirmed the offer. The plan was to use the prestige and public interest in Robinson to establish an aviation program at Tuskegee. Patterson made explicit that the exclusion of blacks from the Air Corps was indefensible and that if the Air Corps allowed black pilots, the Tuskegee program would benefit greatly (Jakeman, 1992). Tuskegee hired a public relations firm to publicize Robinson's return to the United States, his achievement, and to firmly link Robinson with the new aviation program at Tuskegee. Robinson would be feted not only in Harlem, New York, but also in his native Chicago, where massive black crowds cheered the 31-year-old aviator who had done much more than talk about defending the last independent African kingdom. Robinson was heralded as the black answer to Charles Lindbergh, whose solo crossing of the Atlantic in 1927 had so captured the imagination of Americans a decade earlier. Robinson spent the late spring and early summer of 1936 touring the country and raising funds for the aviation program. At the end of June, Robinson visited Tuskegee and negotiated with G. L. Washington over the establishment of the flying school. His agreement hammered out with Washington specified not only Robinson's status at Tuskegee but also the amount and type of support Tuskegee would give to the new flying program.

However, after leaving Tuskegee Institute, Robinson apparently grew less enthusiastic about the agreement and returned it unsigned. He was unhappy with the lack of control over funds that were being raised in his name. In addition, the lack of financial commitment from the institute caused him to doubt the sustainability of the new program. He increasingly wanted the school to support a separate flying school over which he would have control, while the institute wanted a program under the control of the institute but one that would be responsible for its own economic viability. In the end, the two sides could not resolve their differences, and Robinson instead opened his own flying school in Chicago. In the fall of 1936, he made some overtures toward Tuskegee with the aim of moving his flying school to Tuskegee, but nothing came of the proposal. Despite the tentative steps taken by Tuskegee toward establishing a civilian flying school, no such program would be established until the federal government became involved in 1939.

That Tuskegee would be the site of the federal government's first black pilot training program in the Civilian Pilot Training Program (CPTP) was by no means certain. The presidents of other Negro colleges, specifically

Hampton and Wilberforce, lobbied for the selection of their schools for the program as soon as the program was announced, while Patterson remained silent. Not until March 22, 1939, when Congress specifically included authorization for the establishment of a CPTP at black colleges under Public Law 18, did Patterson begin to lobby for the selection of Tuskegee Institute. In letters sent to Robert H. Hinckley of the Civil Aeronautics Authority and Secretary of War Harry H. Woodring, Patterson formally offered the use of the facilities of Tuskegee Institute for training black pilots and aviation mechanics. In the letter, he pointed out that the school had a long tradition of training black men in mechanics and that the institute had ample shops and potential sites for building landing strips. The fame of Robinson and the links between Tuskegee Institute and the aborted tour of the Americas by the *Booker T. Washington* had firmly linked Tuskegee with aviation, and so the institute was a logical choice for a branch of the CPTP. The main drawback was that neither Tuskegee Institute nor the town of Tuskegee had an airfield. Initially, the CPTP at the institute would have to use a municipal airfield in Montgomery, which was more than two hours away by highway.

The CPTP at Tuskegee Institute received its certification on October 15, 1939, and ground classes began that December. The first flight training began in January 1940. The first class of 20 students included two women. All trainees admitted into the program had to be at least 18 years old, an American citizen, enrolled in Tuskegee Institute, and hold a student pilot license (Homan & Reilly, 2001). Shortly after the program began, the school began searching for an airfield closer to the school. A private landing strip existed a few miles south of the town of Tuskegee. The strip was on rented land and was operated by three white flyers for personal use. After negotiating with the lease holders and landowner, the school obtained permission to use the strip for the CPTP, and in February 1940, the Civilian Aviation Administration certified the landing strip for use, provided that a few improvements were made. The landing strip was designated "Airport Number 1" or, more commonly, "Kennedy Field" after the man who originally held the lease to the land (Jakeman, 1992). The use of the rented landing strip was only a temporary measure, and the school soon built its own landing strip on land that the institute owned a few miles northeast from the main campus. The new landing strip was named Moton Field, an ironic name, as Robert Moton had been lukewarm at best over establishing a civilian aviation program at Tuskegee. One drawback to placing the civilian training program for blacks at Tuskegee—and it was a serious one—was that a single location for training blacks to fly was hardly adequate and smacked of tokenism rather than a serious effort to ensure that the nation had a suitable reserve of civilian pilots to draw on in an emergency. However, programs for blacks to earn a civilian pilots license were soon begun at several other black institutions.

On March 25, 1940, Mr. George A. Wiggs came to Tuskegee to administer the standard examination to the CPTP students at Tuskegee. Tensions were acute because low scores not only would be an embarrassment to the college but, most likely, also would be used to justify ending all black participation in the program. However, the results were excellent, with all students passing on the first attempt, with an average score of 88. For Wiggs, it was the first time that all students in the CPTP in a southern state had passed. For G. L. Washington, who ran the CPTP at the institute, the scores were testimony not only to the hard work and abilities of his students but also to the quality of the instructors. He specifically mentioned the assistance he had received from the faculty at Auburn College in providing top-notch instruction (Jakeman, 1992).

The CPTP at Tuskegee Institute was also fortunate to have C. Alfred Anderson, who was called "Chief," become one of the main flight instructors. Chief, who was black, built a reputation for his fairness and technical proficiency. He had held a pilot's license since 1929 and had been instrumental in establishing the CPTP at Howard University. Dr. Patterson had convinced Chief to come to Tuskegee to head the CPTP program there. While he was not easy on the trainees—the dangers of having poorly trained men flying airplanes were too great—he encouraged the trainees and taught them well. Under his tutelage, many blacks would earn their civilian pilot's license. But earning a civilian pilot's license did not make a man a military pilot, nor would it guarantee him a place in an Air Corps training program. All it meant was that the graduate of the CPTP had a license to fly small private airplanes. In theory, such private pilots could later be drawn on by the military in the event of a national emergency requiring rapid expansion of the Army Air Corps, but the Air Corps still did not allow black pilots. Political pressure and the scope of the danger facing the United States would soon change that position.

In the late summer of 1940, the United States undertook a measure never before done in its history—it instituted conscription in peacetime, to begin that fall. Conscription, also called "the draft," used local committees, known as *draft boards*, which consisted of prominent local men who were charged to evaluate each young man's health, intelligence, role in the economy, and familial obligations before placing him in a category. Conscription was selective, not universal. Concurrent with the induction of young men into the armed forces was the mobilization of the entire National Guard and the reserves of each branch of the military. National Guard and Organized Reserve units would absorb most of the selectees, as drafted men were called, for training.

Black leaders and their white allies hoped that the emergency would spur the administration to end racial discrimination in the military and in the awarding of government contracts. They would have liked to see the military integrate and black Regulars, Guardsmen, Reservists, and selectees be given the same opportunities as their white counterparts. But the administration was not ready to take what was then seen as such a radical step. In response, though, to black pressure, the administration did take specific steps to address black concerns. An African American, Campbell C. Johnson, was appointed to serve as an adviser to the director of Selective Service. In October 1940, concurrent with the beginning of Selective Service, Stephen Early, President Roosevelt's press secretary, released the administration's seven-point plan for the "fair and equitable utilization of blacks" for defense. The plan stated the following:

1. Negroes will be drafted in proportion to their population ration— about one to every eleven men.
2. They will used in every branch of the service.
3. Negro reserve officers will serve with outfits which already have negro officers.
4. They will be given a chance to earn reserve commissions when officers' schools are set up. (But except for the established National Guard units, black units would be officered by whites.)
5. They will be trained as pilots and aviation mechanics.
6. Negro civilians will have an equal chance with whites for jobs at arsenals and army posts.
7. Negro and white soldiers will not serve in the same regiments. (Edgerton, 2001, p. 129)

While this list of policies regarding blacks in the military was hardly progressive and disappointed many blacks and white liberals, it did set the basic framework by which blacks would serve during World War II, and it gave black leaders something like a promise from the White House that they could refer back to when the military or the administration tried to avoid fulfilling any of the seven.

In many ways, this tepid list was as much about restricting blacks as guaranteeing them an equal role in defense efforts, but the points that gave blacks a shimmer of hope, especially the fifth one, would prove problematic for the administration to implement. The administration was sensitive to political pressure that could be brought to bear by the growing black electorate and their liberal allies outside the Jim Crow states, particularly in the Northeast. At the same time, the administration was vulnerable to losing support in the white Democratic South, and because of Jim Crow, the white Democratic South was the only voting bloc that mattered in the South. The tiny number of blacks in the South who did vote had remained loyal to the Republican Party—the "Party of Lincoln"—since Reconstruction, but under Franklin Roosevelt, the Democrats had been increasing their share of the black vote, and with the population of blacks in the North who did vote growing, Roosevelt was keenly aware of his tenuous hold on black support. The Republican Wendell Willkie was running for president against Roosevelt in part on an antiracism platform, and Roosevelt feared that losing the black vote in the North to Willkie might cost Roosevelt the election in November 1940.

Part of Roosevelt's courting of the black vote involved his appointment of William H. Hastie, dean of the Howard University Law School, as a civilian aide to the new secretary of war, Henry Stimson, specifically to ensure equitable treatment of blacks in the army. Stimson, who took office on July 10, 1940, was unhappy with the arrangement, but Hastie came with excellent credentials. He had graduated magna cum laude from Amherst College and took his law degree at Harvard University. He later served as a federal judge. Hastie would find his position frustrating, in part because his nominal superior, Stimson, was fundamentally opposed to most of the promises the administration had made regarding blacks in the military. Secretary of War Stimson was adamantly opposed to the idea of black pilots, black officers, and even of blacks in combat units. He argued that he "saw the same thing happen twenty-three years ago when [then president] Woodrow Wilson yielded to the same sort of demand and appointed colored officers to several of the Divisions that went over to France, and the poor fellows made perfect fools of themselves and one at least of the Divisions behaved very badly." Stimson had actually only served in France very briefly during World War I, with a white division, and had in all likelihood very little interaction with black officers during that war (Edgerton, 2001). But his attitude demonstrates how deeply ingrained prejudices against blacks were and how the much sway the old stories had over whites in power. Stimson's views also amply demonstrate the sort of negative paternalism many whites held about blacks in the military and in society at large.

As in World War I, the army again adopted a generalized test that supposedly tested the intelligence of new soldiers and that would allow the army to place most new soldiers into a position where they could give the most suitable service. The test, the Army General Classification Test, actually tested the quality of education the recruit had received and familiarity with middle-class culture more than innate intelligence. As in World War I, blacks on average scored lower than whites. However, blacks from a similar educational background as whites scored similar to whites. But racists looked at racial averages, not the scores of individuals. The results of the tests were used to buttress the argument that blacks should be employed only in labor battalions. Stimson himself admitted that the army "adopted rigid requirements for literacy mainly to keep down the number of colored troops" (Edgerton, 2001, pp. 133–34). Under the segregated system, even highly intelligent and highly educated black men would be expected to serve in the military by performing mindless physical labor or even in menial service roles, such as cooking, cleaning, or serving food to white troops. The very best black men—or at least the lucky few—might serve as lieutenants or captains, always serving in command of other black men and under the overall command of white men. What made the whole system even more frustrating for blacks was the obligatory nature of it; most black men who served during the war had been drafted, and, once drafted, black men fell under military laws, and thus any displays of annoyance or protest could be punished under military laws as insubordination or even mutiny.

For whites like Stimson, preventing blacks from serving in combat units or as officers protected them from roles in which they were ill suited by nature, in the same manner that a responsible adult kept children from difficult or dangerous situations. Stimson, who like Hastie had taken his law degree from Harvard, said that admitting that blacks were not intelligent enough to be military pilots or in the armor corps or especially to serve as officers, pained him greatly (Edgerton, 2001). Simpson's brand of racist paternalism was prevalent among whites who saw themselves as fair and even liberal and would in many ways be a barrier even more difficult to overcome than the outright and open hatred of bigots. But unlike most racists, Stimson was the civilian head of the army and thus had a powerful influence over the role of blacks in the army and the Army Air Corps. Hastie soon found relations with the paternalistic racist difficult, and the two would repeatedly clash.

With the secretary of the army opposed to allowing black pilots, the possibility of seeing black military pilots looked dim. But other forces were also at work. Despite Secretary Stimson's insistence that blacks should not serve as officers or be allowed into the Air Corps, he was subordinate to President Roosevelt, and thus his wishes could be overridden. When President Roosevelt committed to seeing African American pilots in the

Air Corps, Stimson had to yield. The president's motives were varied, but political considerations were probably paramount. The president came from the old economic and political elite of the Hudson River valley in New York; he had no long-term political or social relations with blacks. But he was a canny politician and knew that in some key races in the Northeast and the Midwest, the black vote would be crucial. He also had to show his liberal white allies some concrete gains for blacks. In addition, his wife, Eleanor, was much more of a social activist and was prone to pricking the Jim Crow system and racism in general. Stimson himself blamed Mrs. Eleanor Roosevelt, the First Lady of the United States, for what he termed her "intrusive and impulsive folly" in stirring up criticism of the army's segregation policies (MacGregor, 1989). While the ultimate reasons for the president's decision will always remain obscure, with his backing, the establishment of black flying units was almost certain.

Under pressure from the president, the Air Corps relented from its total ban on black pilots and in late 1940 began laying plans for a black flying unit, although its size and type remained uncertain at first. But whatever size or mission the black flying unit had, the Air Corps planned for it to be separate from the larger Air Corps, to minimize any possible interactions between white enlisted men and black officers. That meant that the Air Corps would need not just black pilots for the new unit but also black mechanics, military police, supply soldiers, paymasters, and myriad other specialists—both officer and enlisted—to fully man the new unit. The Air Corps was planning to create a new, separate mini air force for blacks. Judge Hastie, for his part, was opposed to much of the Air Corps's initial plans for the employment of blacks in separate units. He believed that establishing segregated units for blacks, including the establishment of a new, separate base for training black airmen, would be not only humiliating to blacks but also wasteful. The Air Corps already had an extensive system of training bases and no need to construct new facilities just for blacks (Scott & Womack, 1994). However, while Hastie understood that segregated air combat units were far less than ideal, he was pragmatic enough to realize that before seeing integrated combat units, blacks would have to prove themselves in segregated units. By January 1941, Hastie dropped his opposition to the plan for separate air combat units. If accepting segregation was the only way to ensure seeing black commissioned officers flying combat missions, then Hastie could swallow the establishment of black units, although these were, for him, only an important step to the larger goal of an integrated Army Air Corps and, indeed, an integrated military. Hastie did warn Stimson that the black press would be critical of the plan for a segregated training base near Tuskegee. With Hastie's hesitant acceptance, the War Department could announce the creation of black combat aviation units with apparent unanimity.

Undersecretary of War Patterson announced on January 16, 1941, that the Army Air Corps would create an all-back pursuit squadron. The announcement was a bit of a surprise and not only because the squadron would be black. While the Air Corps was usually seen as the most glamorous of the military services, pursuit flying was also the most glamorous role in the Air Corps and the most demanding and most deadly. Most observers both inside and outside the Air Corps assumed that if a black flying unit were to be created, it would be a transport unit, in a sense re-creating the traditional role of blacks in the quartermaster corps—serving as truck drivers and loaders for transportation companies—adapted for the air. But the twisted logic of segregation made such units difficult. Moving supplies, whether by ground or by air, brought transport soldiers into contact with many different units. In ground transportation companies, the officers were usually white, with the enlisted men black, so the "socially impossible" situation of having black officers interacting with white enlisted men could be avoided. But with black pilots flying cargo aircraft, such situations would be inevitable.

In theory, an all-black pursuit squadron could avoid most situations that would place black officers over white enlisted men. Black pilots could be trained at a separate airfield and then deploy to theater. When flying missions against the enemy, the black pilots would take off from their own forward bases, engage the enemy in the air, and then return to their own base. The situation feared the most by white supremacists—having black officers around white enlisted men—would be avoided. Whatever the objections to the idea of black pilots by men like Stimson, the president apparently made clear to the Air Corps that he expected the "experiment" to succeed, and the Air Corps had to ensure that it did. The question remained as to whether the Air Corps was actually committed to the "experiment," as it was termed, of a black fighter squadron or if instead the Air Corps was simply bowing to political pressure and fully expected the experiment to fail before any black military aviation unit got into combat. But word got out that the Air Corps was looking for intelligent, young, healthy black men with the potential to undertake pilot training, and suitable black men responded.

Despite the direction of President Roosevelt to create an all-black flying unit, opposition within the Air Corps and society as a whole remained strong and not just from white supremacists. The National Association for the Advancement of Colored People (NAACP) opposed the idea of a completely black pursuit squadron because such an organization would further entrench the pattern of military segregation, which the NAACP wanted ended. The National Airmen's Association adopted a resolution stating that they would rather be "excluded than segregated" (Osur, 1976). But if many black leaders opposed the idea of a new black squadron, even more whites opposed it. In addition to the desire to keep blacks in a position subordinate to whites, a situation that black combat pilots would seriously challenge, many whites believed that blacks were simply unable to master the complex skills needed to fly. Despite the handful of black pilots who had been proving that belief wrong since World War I, most white Americans had never seen or heard of a black pilot. The First Lady of the United States was about to change that situation.

Mrs. Eleanor Roosevelt had long supported civil rights, for which she was loathed by many whites and respected by many blacks. While attending the 1938 Southern Conference on Human Welfare in Birmingham, Alabama, she had refused to follow the state's segregation laws that required blacks and whites to sit on opposite sides of the auditorium. After being informed by a policeman that she could not sit on the black side of the auditorium, she chose instead to put her chair in the aisle. She again showed her support for blacks when she visited Tuskegee Institute on March 29, 1941. Mrs. Roosevelt was a trustee of the institute and had come to the campus to see the Infant Paralysis Clinic (Scott & Womack, 1994). But she also used the visit to bring attention to the training of black pilots in the CPTP. When meeting with Chief Anderson at Kennedy Field, she asked him, "Can Negroes really fly airplanes?" Chief assured her that they could and offered to take her for a ride. Her Secret Service detail opposed her accepting the offer and contacted the president by telephone. President Roosevelt told the agent that "well, if she wants to do it, there's nothing we can do to stop it."

With the president's tepid permission, Mrs. Roosevelt climbed into the back of Chief's Piper J-3 Cub, and they took off. Chief flew her around for about a half an hour, and then they landed back on Kennedy Field. After they landed, Mrs. Roosevelt said to Chief, "I guess Negroes can fly," and the two posed for pictures (Ace Pilots, 2010). Much of the incident was likely staged by Mrs. Roosevelt and Chief Anderson for the press that was sure to be there. What Mrs. Roosevelt did was to publicize that blacks could fly and that a white woman, the First Lady no less, could trust the flying skills of a black man. While the episode gave further evidence to white supremacists who loathed Mrs. Roosevelt—it showed that she was a "nigger lover" and advocated racial equality—it also showed that the movement for black pilots had a strong supporter in the White House. Mrs. Roosevelt would continue to show her support for the Tuskegee Airmen in more tangible ways, helping to raise the funds to establish Moton Field.

On March 19, 1941, orders were issued to for the activation of the 99th Pursuit Squadron and Air Base Detachment, to be manned almost entirely by black men, on or about April 1, 1941, at Chanute Field, Illinois (Order 320.2). The squadron was actually activated a bit early, on March 22. The 99th at that time was mostly a paper organization, but within the bureaucracy of the army, having the squadron in official existence meant that men could be trained as pilots and mechanics for positions in it. The original 14 enlisted men assigned to the 99th—clerks, cooks, supply, and a first sergeant—were transferred from the two black infantry regiments

First Lady Eleanor Roosevelt supported the Civilian Pilot Training Program and the War Training Service. She is pictured here in a Piper J-3 Cub trainer with C. Alfred "Chief" Anderson, a pioneer black aviator and respected instructor at Tuskegee Institute. (U.S. Air Force)

in the Regular Army, the 24th and the 25th Regiments (Order 320.2). Thus, the first men to serve in the 99th Pursuit Squadron were former "Buffalo Soldiers," linking the past with the future. The original commander was Captain Harold R. Maddux, who was white; the question of who would command the squadron once it became operational remained unclear. Normally, a squadron commander, ideally a lieutenant colonel, would be an experienced pilot, but no black man in the Air Corps had long experience as a military pilot, and no black man held the rank of lieutenant colonel. The only black line officer in the Regular Army aside from Brigadier General Benjamin O. Davis Sr. was his son, Captain Benjamin O. Davis Jr. Although Captain Davis had applied for the Air Corps before, he had been turned down because of his race. Now with a black squadron in existence, he was the obvious candidate to command it. But first, he would have to master the complex skills of a pilot and prove himself as a leader and a pilot to the highest-caliber black men in the nation, who were also starting to get letters accepting them into the Air Corps cadet program. The Air Base Detachment was established on May 1 and after completing its individual and collective training would join the 99th. The Air Corps apparently saw the eventual scope of the black pilots greater than the single squadron then in existence. The 99th had positions for about 33 pilots, but the program was designed to produce about 100 black pilots annually. Even given attrition of pilots to be expected in combat, Tuskegee would produce far more pilots than the 99th could absorb. The Air Corps was already laying the groundwork for the expansion of the 99th Pursuit Squadron into at least a group.

In keeping with this concept of creating a separate and isolated all-black mini air force within the Air Corps, the army made a conscious decision to establish a new army airfield for the training of the black pilots. The CPTP courses offered at some black colleges gave many potential black military pilots their initial competence with flying an airplane, but a proper military program was needed to turn civilian pilots into military officers and military pilots, and such a program, the Air Corps believed, would best be conducted at a military base, not at a civilian college. Many black leaders argued for a site at which to train black Air Corps pilots in Chicago, which had a large black population and links with early black civilian aviators. Chicago also had a sizable black middle class from which most black officers would be drawn. While race relations in Chicago were often tense and sometimes violent, it had few of the overt Jim Crow denigrations found in much of the South. The army, however, had different criteria for where to establish the new base for training black pilots. In general, the army preferred to have training bases in along the southern tier of the nation to allow more time training in relatively benign weather and had decided that a new black training facility would be built in southern California, Texas, or Alabama. Judge Hastie supported the California location and specifically argued against placing such a base in Texas or Alabama precisely because he knew the hostility and danger that would be faced by black servicemen in those locations (Francis, 1997). His recommendations, however, would not be the final word on where to place the new base.

Finding a location to place a black unit or base was usually problematic. The real situation that the army wanted to avoid was having black officers in charge of or even around white enlisted men. So the Air Corps decided against training the black pilots at an existing base and instead chose to build a new base just north of the town of Tuskegee, about 40 miles east of Maxwell Field. Maxwell Army Airfield in Montgomery, Alabama, was home to the capstone Air Corps Tactical School. The choice was both good and bad. Tuskegee was, of course, home of Tuskegee Institute. The school by this time had its own small airfield, Moton Field, as well as the use of Kennedy Field, and had been part of President Roosevelt's CPTP. Moton Field was not large enough to serve as an Air Corps training base, but the airfields, plus the facilities of the college, would allow initial training to begin quickly while construction of a modern military airfield was completed near the campus. On June 7, 1941, the War Department approved of the use of Tuskegee Institute as a primary flying school. The local black population around Tuskegee was thrilled at the idea of the finest young black men in the nation coming to the area to train. The president of Tuskegee, Dr. Patterson, and G. L. Washington had lobbied hard for basing the training program for black military aviators near Tuskegee. The school's dormitories, classrooms, and messing facilities would all be available for the military to use while the nearby army airfield was under construction.

Still, finding a place in the United States that would be less tolerant of an influx of blacks than southern Alabama would have been difficult. General Marshall later stated that his decision to send northern blacks to the South for training was "one of the most important mistakes I made in the mobilization" (Coffman, 2004, p. 409). The white people of the town of Tuskegee held a city council meeting on April 23, 1941, at which they drafted a petition to the state's senators complaining about having a black air base located in their area (Homan & Reilly, 2001). Interactions between blacks and whites in the area had reached a status quo based at heart on the threat of violence. Whites tolerated blacks as long as blacks "kept their place," which meant that blacks remained subservient to whites and provided labor. They did not attempt to vote. The black college students at

Tuskegee were generally left alone as long as they remained around the campus and did not bring a lot of outside ideas into the region. Ideally, the college would teach young blacks skills that would make them better able to serve white people. Blacks who attempted to change this status quo were normally dealt with by the law—sheriffs' departments and courts were white, the laws they enforced were written and adopted by whites, and the law upheld white supremacy. Self-confident, educated black men— the very type of men who was drawn to combat aviation—would definitely bring a lot of new ideas to the region and upset the status quo. As dangerous as the area was to local blacks, it was even more so to black men who were unfamiliar with rigidness and inherent violence of the system.

Beginning during World War I and continuing through the interwar years, blacks in the United States had been undergoing a profound demographic change. The old stereotype of blacks as uneducated rural southern farm labor still had a lot of truth to it in 1917. However, the Great Migration of blacks—first to southern cities and then to northern cities—had a profound impact on African Americans. But white images of blacks were slow to change, and much of the military leadership responsible for the organizing and training of black soldiers in World War II worked from assumptions about blacks formed in World War I. During that war, very few blacks had more than a grade school education, and most had even less than that. By one estimate, 97 percent of southern blacks—and most blacks were southern—had no formal education beyond grade school. The much smaller number of blacks from the North was hardly better educated, with 86 percent having only a grade school education or less. By World War II, the numbers had changed dramatically, with 67 percent of southern blacks lacking education beyond primary education, while among northern blacks the change was more impressive, with only 37 percent having a primary school education or less. At the same time, the percentage of blacks who came from the North had risen from 20 percent in World War I to 32 percent in World War II (Coffman, 2004).

As a result, blacks who were able to pass the stringent requirements for aviation training tended to come from areas of the country without the strict legal and social limitations placed on blacks that existed in the South. Blacks from outside of the South were, of course, aware of Jim Crow, and most had long lived with the sting of discrimination throughout their lives but were not raised with the same admonitions passed down through the generations that informed southern blacks how to live if they wanted to avoid being beaten or killed for transgressions against the status quo. For such men, entering the rural South was physically dangerous.

The military was aware of the danger but responded to it by attempting to control black soldiers tightly, hoping to avoid violence between black soldiers and white civilians that could erode congressional support and bring negative publicity to the military. The army tried to keep blacks as isolated from the local white population as much as possible and enforced a military version of Jim Crow that many blacks in the military found perplexing as well as degrading and contrary to what they had been taught their status as officers or even soldiers of the U.S. Army meant. In almost all cases of clashes between black soldiers and white civilians, the army sided with the white community, and blacks learned from the Spanish-American War and World War I that the military expected black soldiers to avoid offending local whites at all costs and to take the abuse from whites when it occurred, and should black soldiers strike back, official military reprisals against black soldiers could be almost as deadly (Cosmos, 1998; Coffman, 1968). Despite these dangers, the Air Corps believed that the advantages of the Tuskegee location outweighed the potential problems. With the decision to build an entirely new air base to support training of the black pilots, the Air Corps had become increasingly committed to the success of the "experiment."

Congress authorized the construction of what would become Tuskegee Army Airfield in the Military Establishment Appropriation Bill, allotting $1,663,057 for the task. The building of a completely new base was not unusual at the time, as the army was building many new camps and bases throughout the nation or taking over existing municipal airports and converting them into army airfields. What was unusual about the construction of what would become Tuskegee Army Airfield was that the army awarded the contract for building the base to the black-owned firm of McKissack and McKissack, Inc., of Nashville, Tennessee. Augmented by army engineer troops and men in the federal Works Project Administration, construction began almost immediately, on July 12, 1941. Former cornfields and cotton fields, plus an old graveyard, were soon converted into runways and a cantonment area. Within six months, work on the base had been completed enough to allow the beginning of operations. But until that time, the army would conduct training on Tuskegee Institute's campus, using Kennedy Field and Moton Field to their limits.

On July 19, only a week after construction started on the new base, the first class began their preflight training on the campus. The class consisted of 12 aviation cadets and Captain Davis. As ranking officer, Davis also served as the commandant of cadets. Captain Noel Parish, who was white, was in charge of the training. Parrish had previously served as an instructor for the Air Training Command at Randolph Field outside of San Antonio, Texas, and was later picked by Arnold to be the deputy commander of the civilian contract school program at Glenview near Chicago. The commander at Glenview did not think that blacks should be trained as pilots and refused to support the program. Parrish was unusual for an Air Corps officer in that he supported the idea of training black pilots and allowing them into the Air Corps. When Tuskegee was chosen as the location for the new base, Parrish, newly promoted to captain, was given the assignment of getting the training program established. Such an assignment could be the end of a career, and Parrish knew it. Should the program fail, he would be held responsible. On the other hand, should it succeed, racists in the Air Corps would see him as a supporter of racial equality and blame him for helping to break down the racial barrier. Still, Parrish was liberal enough to understand that blacks had legitimate desires, and he took his new mission very seriously (Coffman, 2004). By August 21, that first class entered military flight training (primary), and on November 8, that first class, now reduced to seven trainees, entered military flight training (basic). The trainees moved to Tuskegee Army Airfield, which had become operational but just barely. The men lived in tents until the proper barracks were completed, and the flight line consisted of a single usable runway. Classes were held in one of the few completed buildings, but often several classes had to share the building. Still, despite the hardships, the ongoing construction on the base was a good sign.

Cadet training is never easy. During the eight months the Army Air Corp took to turn a civilian with a pilot's license into an Air Corps officer and military pilot, the discipline was rigid in the extreme, with cadets subjected to constant irritants and harassment, but it was all to a larger end. The cadets at Tuskegee wanted to be officers and military pilots, and being awarded that distinction never came without a struggle. Men who could not withstand the constant pressure in training would probably not be able to stand the pressure of combat, so the system sought to identify those men and remove them. Part of the method the army used to train cadets to be officers was to put them in positions of leadership over other cadets and expect them to perform; thus, cadets a month or two more advanced in the program could become the living terror to cadets with less time in the program. Charles Dryden recalled his introduction to cadet training when, hot and sweaty from his travels and hoping for a shower and change of clothes, a man about his height but stockier and wearing heavily starched and creased khakis, highly polished belt buckle, and shoes shined to a mirrorlike finish approached his group. The man welcomed the new cadets to

Tuskegee by stating, "All right Dummies, let's get with the program! Get the lead outta your butt. Get your bags out of the bus and line up right here in front of the cadet barracks. Move it!" Cadet Dryden had just learned that he was in the army. The man would introduce himself as "Aviation Cadet George Spenser Roberts of class 42-C. My friends call me 'Spanky.' To you I am 'Mister Roberts.' To me you are 'Dummies'" (Dryden, 1997, p. 36). Cadet Roberts would lead many of the cadets in combat one day, and he was both learning to be an effective leader and helping to turn civilians into U.S. Army Air Corps officers.

While the cadets sweated though their training and tests at Tuskegee, the rest of the 99th Pursuit Squadron began to take shape on Chanute Field, Illinois. On November 5, 1941, the 99th Pursuit Squadron moved from Chanute Field to Maxwell Field, Alabama. The 99th stayed at Maxwell only five days until it moved to Tuskegee Army Airfield and Second Lieutenant Clyde H. Bynum, who was also white, took command. Commanders in this period were in a sense holding the 99th until it became functional, at which time Captain Davis would presumably take command and bring it to combat. On the same day that the 99th moved to Tuskegee, the Air Base Detachment followed in its footsteps and moved from Chanute to Maxwell (Haulman, 2010). Lieutenant Bynum was replaced by Captain Alonzo S. Ward as commander on December 6, the day before the Japanese attacked the American naval base at Pearl Harbor, Hawaii, bringing the United States into World War II.

The attack on Pearl Harbor on December 7 and subsequent declaration of war against the United States by Japan led to reciprocal action by the United States the following day. Germany and Italy soon followed Japan in declaring war, and the United States became fully committed to World War II. The entrance into the war meant that the training at Tuskegee had become deadly serious, and cadets realized that their completion of the training would almost certainly mean they would face the enemy in aerial combat. However, the Air Corps training was already so stressful and serious that the entrance of the United States into the war had little immediate effect on the training. The entrance of the United States meant that the military would need all the pilots who could be trained and could not afford the luxury of training military pilots simply to satisfy a political constituency. If that is what some people—black or white—assumed was going on at Tuskegee, they were wrong.

Actually, the concept of black fighter pilots was about to undergo an expansion. On December 27, the 100th Pursuit Squadron was constituted, with activation to occur as soon as Tuskegee Army Airfield could accommodate the new squadron (Orders AG 320.2, 1941). Tuskegee was growing fast, even with its initial construction still ongoing. On January 5, the Air Base Detachment moved from Maxwell to Tuskegee. Renamed the 318th Air Base Squadron on March 13, the Air Base Detachment was the organization that would provide the pilots and grounds crews of the 99th with the support needed to run an air base, providing food, quarters, and pay and even ensuring that the mail was delivered. If Tuskegee Army Airfield was getting crowded, it was going to become even more crowded for a while. On March 21, 1942, the 92nd Maintenance Group (Reduced) (Colored) was activated. The 92nd contained the 366th and the 367th Material Squadrons. Other black ground units were stood up that September; the 1000th Signal Company, the 1051st Quartermaster Service Group Aviation Company, the 1765th Ordnance Supply and Maintenance Company (Aviation), and the 1901st and 1902nd Quartermaster Truck Companies (Aviation). The Army Air Forces, as the Air Corps had been redesignated in early 1942, was serious about creating an operational mini air force manned completely by blacks. In order to prevent a white enlisted man from ever coming under the authority or even in contact with black officers, the Army Air Forces had to create all the organizations needed to keep the planes of the 99th and any other squadrons of black pilots flying.

While the black aviation cadets underwent their training on Tuskegee Army Airfield, other black officer candidates were going through a very different training program at Officer Candidate School (OCS), the only really integrated institution in the army. The Air Corps needed nonflying black officers as well as pilots, and deciding on a location for their training was less controversial. Assistant Secretary of War for Air Robert A. Lovett had assured Judge Hastie that OCSs would be integrated, but the Army Air Forces' Technical Training Command announced in 1942 that it would establish a segregated OCS for black officers. For Hastie, this was the final betrayal. He had always sought integration and the elimination of segregated units. Lovett's announcement came as another betrayal, and he could take no more. The resignation did get the attention of the administration, and the Technical Training Command changed its policy, and beginning in 1943, black officer candidates attended integrated training at the Army Air Forces OCS at Miami Beach, Florida. Despite this integrated training, black men who graduated from OCS were severely limited in their postings after commissioning, and most were initially assigned to Tuskegee or Godman Field, where Tuskegee Airmen underwent collective training (MacGregor, 1989). But black officer candidates at OCS would not be in charge of white enlisted soldiers, and black graduates of OCS went off to black units and thus preserved the status quo.

Trainees gaze intently as their civilian instructor covers in meticulous detail the elaborate functioning of the fuel system in an aircraft engine, Tuskegee Army Airfield, Alabama. (Library of Congress)

The 99th was about to get its first pilots. The first class, reduced to the five who surmounted the grueling training, graduated from the Tuskegee Advanced Flying School on March 7. Four of the cadets—Mac Ross, Lemuel R. Curtis, Charles H. DeBow Jr., and George S. Roberts—were commissioned into the Army Air Forces as second lieutenants, while Captain Davis was transferred from the infantry into the Air Forces (99th Fighter Squadron). The Army Air Forces had black pilots. However, a squadron needed more than five pilots, and the squadron needed to train together before it was ready for deployment, but other classes were under way, and an important milestone had been reached. One June 1, Lieutenant Roberts assumed command of the 99th, which, along with all pursuit squadrons in the Air Forces, had been redesignated as a fighter squadron two weeks earlier. Roberts was the first black man to command a combat unit in the Air Forces, and although the squadron was still far from combat ready and the command was still more of an administrative nature at that point, it was still an important milestone ("99th Fighter Squadron").

More and more classes of cadets were in various stages of training, with graduations and commissioning ceremonies held roughly every five or six weeks. As the 99th filled its positions for pilots and the 100th began to absorb pilots, the Air Forces, on July 4, constituted the 332nd Fighter Group, with the 301st and 302nd Fighter Squadrons. The 332nd and its subordinate units were not actually activated until October 13, 1942, but the structure was in place for expansion of the "black air force." Other organizational changes would come before any of the Tuskegee Airmen were committed to combat, but the changes were necessary to move a new unit from organization and training to combat. The 99th Fighter Squadron was attached to the III Fighter Command on August 19. Three days later, newly promoted Lieutenant Colonel Davis became the commander of the 99th. Colonel Davis was the man who would take the 99th to war ("99th Fighter Squadron").

Training was not without its risks. On September 12, the Tuskegee Airmen lost their first man to a crash when Lieutenant Faythe A. McGinnis died on a routine flight. But such incidents were not uncommon, and more men would die in crashes during training. Despite all the progress made in airplanes in the decades since the Wright Brothers first flew, flying was still a dangerous business, and all pilots accepted the risk of death. Deaths in training were not uncommon in the military, and the pace of training seldom paused when such tragedies occurred. With the 99th almost ready to deploy, one death in an accident was a lesson for all but could not derail the schedule. The army had planned to deploy the 99th Fighter Squadron to the nation of Liberia, an independent republic on the coast of West Africa, to help defend it. Liberia had been created by the American Colonial Society in the 1820s and settled by free black Americans (many of them former slaves), and their descendants still controlled the republic. But by September, when the 99th was declared ready for combat, the danger to Liberia had passed. Instead, the pilots and ground crews of the 99th remained on Tuskegee, training and waiting to deploy.

References

Ace Pilots. http://www.acepilots.com/usaaf_tusk.html (accessed December 1, 2010).

Coffman, Edward M. *The Regulars: The American Army, 1898-1941*.Cambridge, MA: Harvard University Press, 2004

Coffman, Edward M. *The War to End All Wars*. Madison: University of Wisconsin Press, 1968.

"Constitution and Activation of the 100th Pursuit Squadron." Orders AG 320.2 (12-8-41).Maxwell Air Force Base, AL: Air Force Historical Research Agency.

Dryden, Charles W. *A-Train: Memoirs of a Tuskegee Airman.* Tuscaloosa: University of Alabama Press, 1997.

Edgerton, Robert B. *Hidden Heroism: Black Soldiers in America's War.* Boulder, CO: Westview, 2001.

Francis, Charles E. *The Tuskegee Airmen: The Men Who Changed a Nation.* Boston: Branden Publishing, 1997.

Haulman, Daniel L. "Tuskegee Airmen Chronology." Maxwell Air Force Base, AL: Air Force Historical Research Agency.

Homan, Lynn M., and Thomas Reilly. *Black Knights: The Story of the Tuskegee Airmen.* Gretna, LA: Pelican Publishing, 2001.

Jakeman, Robert J. *Divided Skies: Establishing Segregated Flight Training at Tuskegee, Alabama, 1934–1942.* Tuscaloosa: University of Alabama Press, 1992.

MacGregor, Morris J. *Integration of the Armed Forces, 1940–1965.* Washington, DC: Center for Military History, 1989.

"99th Fighter Squadron History, March 1941–17 October 1943." Maxwell Air Force Base, AL: Air Force Historical Research Agency.

Osur, Alan M. *Blacks in the Army Air Force during World War II: The Problem of Race Relations.* Washington, DC: Office of Air Force History, 1976.

Scott, Lawrence P., and William M. Womack Sr. *Double V: The Civil Rights Struggle of the Tuskegee Airmen.* East Lansing: Michigan State University Press, 1994.

THREE

Deployment

AFTER THE 99TH FIGHTER GROUP completed collective training, the Army Air Forces delayed its deployment to combat, leading to speculation that the Air Forces never intended to deploy the unit and had expected it to fail in training. But the 99th completed its training, and the commander of the 99th, Lieutenant Colonel Benjamin O. Davis Jr., was deadly serious about leading the 99th in combat. Lieutenant Colonel Davis already stood out in the Regular Army. His father, Brigadier General Benjamin O. Davis Sr., was the army's first and only black general officer. But the younger Davis had no easy route to becoming an officer in the army. His career thus far had shown an incredible ability to persevere despite a hostile environment. As the only black cadet at West Point, he had been ostracized by the other cadets in a shameful display of racism, with no white cadet speaking to him except in an official capacity for his entire four years. Such treatment was not uncommon at West Point; the corps of cadets had a long tradition of encouraging cadets deemed unworthy to resign from the academy and go home. Davis had been selected to receive this treatment solely because he was black. Yet despite his complete social isolation while a cadet, he never complained about it, and his father never found out until after graduation. Davis stuck it out for four lonely years and graduated in 1936, ranking 35th out of 276 cadets in his class. He was only the fourth black man to graduate from the U.S. Military Academy. He applied for pilot training before graduation, for which he was mentally and physically qualified, and his class ranking should have guaranteed him his first choice of branch. However, the Chief of the Air Corps turned down his application because the Air Corps had no black flying units, and none were planned (Fletcher, 1989). Apparently, the idea of a black West Point graduate serving in an existing unit alongside white pilots was unthinkable. The experience was deeply disappointing to Davis, and he branched infantry, his father's branch, instead.

The Regular Army still had the four black regiments, two of which were infantry, so he would have opportunities to serve as an officer, albeit in charge of segregated units. He never gave up his desire to fly, though, and the announcement that the Air Corps would create an all-black pursuit squadron revived that dream in him.

Davis turned out to be a good although not great pilot. But he had other qualities that the commander of the first black squadron needed. He understood the army, and his career had taught him when to acquiesce and when to push back. Perhaps more than anyone else, he understood that the 99th Fighter Squadron was an experiment and that many people both within the military and without wanted and expected that experiment to fail, and he would do everything he could to prevent that from happening. He had to walk a fine line between supporting his men and remaining subordinate to

Captain Benjamin O. Davis Jr. of Washington, D.C., climbing into an advanced trainer at the basic advanced flying school at Tuskegee Army Airfield, Alabama, January 1942. (Library of Congress)

his superiors. That the 99th and the whole Tuskegee Airmen succeeded is probably due to his leadership as much as any other factor. And the 99th would need solid leadership as deployment to combat drew closer.

After a spending a winter and part and into the spring of 1943 wondering if the Air Forces actually intended to employ the 99th to combat, orders were cut on April 1, 1943, directing the 99th to depart Tuskegee Army Airfield and move to Camp Shanks in Orangetown, New York, from where the 99th would depart for overseas deployment. Camp Shanks, just north of New York City, was known to soldiers as "Last Stop U.S." because it served as the main embarkation camp for soldiers deploying to Europe or Africa. The officers and men left Tuskegee on April 2 via train and headed north. The 99th would spend only a few days at Camp Shanks, and on April 15, they boarded the S.S. *Mariposa* for the trip across the Atlantic. The *Mariposa* was a cruise ship that had been adapted to serve in the war as a troop transport. The ship carried about 4,000 soldiers in all, of whom about 400 were blacks in the 99th and its supporting units, and the others white. Lieutenant Colonel Davis served as executive officer of all troops on board, black and white, and assumed his position with an ease that his years of experience had conditioned him for ("Historical Record," 1943).

As the ship pulled away, the members of the 99th had feelings similar to those of soldiers departing through the centuries: the excitement and novelty of an ocean voyage, curiosity about their destination, and, of course, the unspoken realization that they might never see their homes again. Added to their musings were the threats of modern war—air and submarine attacks. The air and naval supremacy of the United States and Great Britain by that point in the war had made the threat of attacks by enemy surface ships or aircraft remote, but the possibility of a submarine attack was both very real and dangerous, and, while on the transports, lifeboat drills filled much of the time. The *Mariposa* reached its destination in North Africa at the port city of Casablanca without incident on April 24. The weather was warm and clear that day, and the men on ship were anxious to get back on land. They watched the locals who came out to the side of the ship and dived for coins tossed overboard. Eventually, smaller ships came out to the *Mariposa* and ferried the men to shore. Once on shore, they marched about three miles to their encampment and ate a dinner of C rations—the standard combat ration for American forces (Homan & Reilly, 2001).

The part of Africa that the men of the 99th were setting foot on was the French colony of Morocco. Morocco, home to an ancient Arab-Berber civilization that had once ruled most of West Africa and even Iberia in southwestern Europe, had been divided between France and Spain in the late

19th and early 20th centuries. When France surrendered to Nazi Germany in the spring of 1940, the French Empire theoretically continued to be ruled from France, and colonial governments owed allegiance to the puppet government established in the resort town of Vichy, France. French colonial officials were, however, largely on their own. In areas of France's far-flung empire where the Germans, Italians, or Japanese operated, local French colonial officials tried to work with the Axis to maintain the facade that the French were still in charge. When the British and Americans invaded North Africa in Operation Torch in November 1942, French colonial forces put up mostly token opposition, then switched allegiance and became loyal to the Free French movement headed by French General Charles de Gaulle. Since landing in North Africa, the British and Americans had been fighting against Germany's *Afrika Korps*. That battle was almost over by the time the 99th arrived, but the army normally tried, if possible, to introduce newly deployed units in relatively quiet sectors before moving them into more serious fighting. For the 99th, participation in the last phase of the North African campaign would be their shakedown period before entering combat in the skies over Europe.

The 99th did not stay long in the outskirts of Casablanca. On April 29, they arrived at the camp that would serve as their first true overseas base, at Oued N'ja, about 10 miles west of the city of Fez, Morocco. The camp was rudimentary in the extreme, with just a dirt airfield. The men were housed in tents and ate from field kitchens. They had taken a large step down from the now seemingly pleasant barracks at Tuskegee Army Airfield, but they understood that they were in a war, not on a pleasure excursion. While the enlisted men got busy turning the area into something approximating a base and readying the aircraft, the pilots began flying their new P-40s from the base's dirt landing strip. On May 5, Lieutenants James T. Wiley and Graham Smith became the first men in the 99th to land their airplanes on African soil ("Historical Record," 1943). The P-40 Warhawk had just entered frontline service, and the pilots of the 99th were pleased to receive a new fighter. The P-40, built by Curtis-Wright, had been a controversial airplane because of its limited firepower and poor protective armor. It could fly at about 300 miles per hour, climb to around 32,000 feet, and carried from four to six .50-caliber machine guns and could also carry a single 500-pound bomb. While not a perfect fighter, it was new and available, and the men of the 99th were happy to have it. Major Philip Cochran came to the 99th to instruct them in flying the new aircraft and to teach them more about the ins and outs of aerial combat. He also sought to imbue them with a strong desire to fight. Cochran had a cocky attitude and was a bit of a legend in the Air Forces, as the character "Flip Corkin" in the comic strip "Terry and the Pirates" had been based on him. Although Lieutenant Colonel Davis outranked Major Cochran, when Cochran first came on post, he demanded that Davis come to him, and he treated Davis as a subordinate. Or at least he tried to, but Davis, as a Regular Army guy, was not about to allow that sort of insubordination to pass. The men of the 99th saw Cochran's attitude as a sign of his disrespect toward black officers, but Cochran had a long reputation in the Air Forces for paying little attention to rank. In one famous exchange, he got into a shouting match with General Henri Giraud of the Free French over the general's complaint of a lack of air cover during a recent fight. The pilots of the 99th suspected that Cochran was there to evaluate them as much as he was there to train them. On his first training exercise, he took four pilots on a practice mission that consisted of a game of follow the leader, with Cochran seeing if they could keep up. Since Cochran had earlier commanded a unit that did dive-bombing, he had them practice that mission and was impressed enough with their abilities that he proclaimed the men of the 99th to be natural dive-bombers (Homan & Reilly, 2001).

Despite the primitiveness of the facilities and the important tasks at hand, many men would later remember their time at Oued N'ja as some of their most pleasant in the war. The white pilots and enlisted men of the nearby fighter-bomber squadron were cordial, and the town of Fez proved quite welcoming. On May 9, some of the pilots of the 99th participated in

P-40L-15 42-10461 Josephine of First Lieutenant Charles Bailey, 99th Fighter Squadron, Madna, Italy, January 1944. Pilots were allowed to name their airplanes and paint the name on the nose. Most named them after a woman. (U.S. Air Force)

a parade in Fez celebrating the liberation of Tunisia. The African American singer Josephine Baker, who had spent many years living in France away from the sting of American racism, visited the 99th and introduced the pilots to the local French and Arab families (Francis, 1997). Baker had become a naturalized French citizen in 1937, and while the Nazis had generally left her alone, she remained loyal to her adopted country and became active in the French Resistance. The French in general had few of the racial animosities of white Americans and were happy to see anyone willing to fight Germans. While racial tensions existed in the Free French Forces, French officers treated officers of other nations as brother officers, and the men of the 99th found their reception by the Free French a welcome change from their normal interactions with most whites.

The American military had a policy regarding veteran pilots that was the opposite of what the Germans and Japanese did. In the American military, the best, most experienced pilots who lived through their tour of combat were rotated out of frontline combat units and became trainers for the next group of airmen who were about to enter combat. Most air forces kept their best pilots at the front lines fighting until they too were killed, making a long-term decline in the quality of pilots all but inevitable. But the Army Air Forces believed that the benefits to be gained by having the best combat pilots train new pilots outweighed the drawbacks of not having the best remain on the front lines. While in Morocco, a Major Keyes and a Captain Fechler, two white pilots with wide combat experience, were assigned to train the pilots of the 99th, putting them through constant and rigorous unit training to make them ready to enter combat. The enormous investment in training was not unique to the 99th, and if conditions permitted, the Army Air Forces sought to allow every unit that deployed to be as ready for its initial entry into combat as possible.

A fighter squadron such as the 99th did not fly and fight on its own, it was part of a larger unit called a *group*. A group was the Army Air Forces' equivalent of a regiment and contained normally three or four squadrons and was commanded by a colonel. The group was part of a *wing*, which was part of an air division and so on. Before enough black fighter squadrons deployed to form an all-black group, the 99th was attached otherwise white groups, the first being the 33rd Fighter Group, where the 99th was designated as "T," or "Trooper," squadron. The 33rd, under the command of Colonel William M. Momyer, was part of the 12th Air Support Command. During the first actual mission flown by the 99th, on June 2, the perception of racism raised its ugly head. While white airmen could be racists, as was amply demonstrated throughout the war, there were other unofficial customs and traditions of the military that could seem like racism. Most prominent was that men in units that had been through a lot of combat tended to treat newcomers with disdain. Until a new unit—and the men in it—had proven itself in combat, the "new guys" were often treated with a mixture of contempt and disrespect or as the butt of jokes. However, the same treatment was often meted out by racists against black soldiers, and where one ended and the other began was often hazy. Except for Lieutenant Colonel Davis, the men of the 99th were all relatively new to the army, and their segregated training experience left them ill prepared for some of the unwritten customs of the service, and they were an unknown quality to most of the white pilots. When the first four pilots from the 99th were to go on a combat mission with the 33rd Fighter Group, their premission briefing, later recalled by Span Watson, consisted of being told, almost as an afterthought, "You boys keep up" (Homan & Reilly, 2001, p. 85). The mission consisted of a patrol over the Mediterranean Sea and occurred without incident ("Historical Record," 1943). The pilots of the 99th would remain suspicious of Colonel Momyer, and eventually he would express his true feelings about the idea of black pilots.

Racial segregation robbed both black and white pilots of the important rituals of postflight storytelling and rough fun that built camaraderie and allowed the flow of acquired wisdom. The pilots from the 99th joined the white pilots of the 33rd Fighter Group for the premission briefings and the postmission critiques but spent no time with them in any social settings. Still, as the 99th became more experienced and eventually blooded, they did notice a difference in their interactions with other American pilots. Lieutenant Charles Hall, who later made the first confirmed kill of the 99th, returned home in part to publicize bond drives and told the black newspaper the *Pittsburgh Courier* that in combat, race or part of the country from which a man came did not matter; instead, "it is the way he flies that counts. Race theories get blasted out of a pilot's mind in the first burst of flak" (Homan & Reilly, 2001, p. 95).

The 99th remained at Oued N'ja for just a month, and on May 31, the 99th moved by rail and truck to Tunisia, to Fardjouna, on the Cape Bon peninsula. Tunisia, like Morocco, was a French colony, but it was in the most northern parts of Africa and was within striking distance of Italy. The Cape Bon peninsula juts out into the Mediterranean in the northeastern part of Tunisia and is the place where Africa comes closest to the major Italian island of Sicily. The 99th was based at a former *Luftwaffe*, or German air force, base. The men of the 99th were surrounded by the wreckage of war, as the airfield was scattered with pieces of destroyed German aircraft. But they would have little time to dwell on the wreckage left by the Germans, as they would quickly have to settle in and return to flying. They spent the first part of June 1943 attacking gun emplacements on Pantelleria Island, a relatively small island between Tunisia and Sicily, in the middle of the Strait of Sicily. Pantelleria belonged to Italy and had been heavily fortified by the Germans to protect the southern approaches to Italy. The 99th averaged two missions per day against targets on the island. Before any Allied invasion of Italy and to ensure Allied sea lanes through the Mediterranean Sea, the island had to be taken. The operation, dubbed *Corkscrew*, called for an intense bombing operation to reduce the island's defenses in preparation for an invasion by British soldiers, which came on June 10. While the mission of attacking gun emplacements was not the more glamorous aerial combat that the Tuskegee Airmen had originally envisioned themselves performing, it was important, dangerous, and real combat. The emplacements they were attacking were defended by enemy soldiers who shot up a lot of flak in an attempt to knock out the 99th. In essence, they were performing dive-bombing missions, just as Major Cochran had claimed them so naturally suited for. Attacking the gun emplacements meant diving down to about 3,000 feet and dropping a single 500-pound bomb on the target. The skies had been mostly cleared of enemy aircraft, so they had little worries about being attacked from the air while on a dive, but they worried about the flak and the ever-present danger of mechanical problems. Dive-bombing put a heavy stress on the aircraft, and failure at the wrong time meant a quick death as the plane rammed into the unforgiving earth.

But along with the dive-bomber missions, the 99th, still attached to the 33rd Fighter Group, began flying the missions that it would become famous for—bomber escort. While the P-40s of the 99th carried a single 500-pound bomb, the medium bombers they would be escorting carried a much larger load, but experience had shown that they required fighter escort to protect them from attacks by enemy fighters. The first escort mission was escorting a squadron of Douglas A-20 Havoc attack bombers on June 9, 1943. The A-20 was a two-engine medium bomber in wide use against targets behind the front lines. While the U.S. Army Air Forces had some, most in the theater belonged to the British, who called them the Boston Bombers. As the bombers were making the bombing run, four German Me-109 Messerschmitt fighters, one of the best fighters Germany produced during the war, unexpectedly attacked the Americans. Here was what the African American airmen had been training and preparing themselves for—facing the enemy in aerial combat. Instinct took over, and fighting spirit and aggression replaced mission plans (Francis, 1997).

Five of the fighters of the 99th broke with the formation and pursued the Germans, while eight of the pilots in the 99th stayed with the bombers. The actions of the five—Lieutenants Charles Dryden, Leon Roberts, Lee Rayford, Spann Watson, and Willie Ashley—were a serious breach of flight discipline (Francis, 1997). The Air Forces stressed formation flying, and on a bombing mission, each bomber and fighter was supposed to remain in position. Fighters had some freedom to maneuver to engage enemy fighters but were supposed to remain with the formation and return to position as soon as practical. The five who took off had broken rules—and serious rules at that. Of course, African Americans had long had their fighting spirit—their desire to close with an enemy—questioned, and now with their first real contact with the enemy, they were to be criticized for being overly aggressive. The incident would come back to haunt the 99th.

The next day, two planes from the 99th, along with two from the 59th Fighter Squadron, were escorting a squadron of 12 B-25 Mitchells, which were also medium bombers, on a mission to Pantelleria, when the formation was attacked by 10 German fighters, a mixture of Me-109s and Fw-190s. The Americans were outnumbered, but fortunately a squadron of British Spitfires appeared and drove off the Germans, and the Americans continued with their mission. On the way back from the island, the Germans attacked again, and, as had happened earlier, the American formation held together while the British drove off the Germans. The British and the Americans were working closely together in the air and on the ground. As a sign of the strength of the alliance and perhaps also the curiosity that some British had about this new black fighter squadron, King George VI of Great Britain paid a visit in late June to Grombalia airfield, where he reviewed some 50 enlisted men from the 99th assembled for the occasion ("Historical Record," 1943).

The men of the 99th were realizing the dream held by so many for so long—they were serving their country and fighting in the high-tech, high-stakes world of aerial combat. But few had the time to reflect on their lot—there were daily missions and a war to be won first. The Army Air Forces made incredible demands on pilots and ground crews, and the 99th felt the strains even more because of a choked system for producing replacement pilots through the segregated training system. The high operational tempo of the 99th, however, continued without a pause. Each day, the men flew various missions each of which, although usually lasting under two hours, required planning, briefings, mechanical checks, and debriefings afterward. On June 15, the 99th flew four missions (99th Fighter Squadron). Each mission required the pilot to suit up in heavy lined lambskin jackets and pants—whatever the ground temperature, the temperatures in the sky were often frigid. The pilot had to breathe through a mask hooked to a tube with oxygen to counter the effects of the thin atmosphere at high altitudes. While strapped in his seat, wearing bulky clothing, helmet, and mask, he had to conquer his fears and master his aircraft and always be ready to fight. One benefit of all the gear and equipment that each pilot wore was that pilots in the air were judged solely by their performance—the appearance of a pilot was completely obscured. Unless another pilot—whether Allied or enemy—had specific knowledge of the unit markings on the aircraft, few if any realized that the pilots were African Americans, although the Germans would later learn to identify which planes were flown by the Tuskegee Airmen. The performance of the aircraft and the skill of the man flying it were the sole arbitrators of who lived and who died in aerial combat. Each mission took a heavy toll on the pilots mentally and physically, and, of course, every mission could be a pilot's last. The enormously high selection criteria to be a military pilot made sense. The 99th flew more bomber escorts, patrol missions, and searches. On June 18, on the second mission of the day, six planes from the 99th flew a short, by then routine mission over Pantelleria. First Lieutenant Sidney Brooks spotted a flight of Germans off to the northeast. Within minutes, the German formation of eight Me-109s escorting 12 twin-engine bombers, with another 10 German fighters higher up, engaged in combat with the men of the 99th. Four of the German fighters moved to attack the Americans.

Despite being outnumbered, the 99th held its own. One P-40 flown by Lieutenant Lee Rayford took machine gun and cannon fire to its wing and tail, but the pilots from the 99th believed that they had damaged three of the German fighters, although none were seen to crash ("Historical Record," 1943). All six of the 99th airplanes made it back to their base in Tunisia, where pilots and ground crews could start counting holes in their craft. The incident was the first time the 99th had engaged the Germans in aerial combat. Lieutenant Colonel Davis was pleased. While they had only possibly inflicted damage on three of the enemy aircraft, the men of the 99th had given "a good account of themselves," and all came back safely ("Historical Record," 1943). For Davis and his men, it was a good start and something to build on. The missions of the following days were similar to the ones before it and had none of the excitement of June 18. The morning mission of June 21 would be different. It was an escort mission, with four fighters from the 99th escorting a squadron of 12 A-20 bombers. After dropping their bombs on target, the bombers headed back to their base. However, four German Me-109s had taken off from an airfield on the island

and were in pursuit. The P-40s turned on the Germans and engaged them with their machine guns, driving them off. After the skirmish, the men of the 99th returned to the formation for the trip back to Tunisia (Homan & Reilly, 2001).

The missions continued into July, although at the end of June, the 99th Fighter Squadron moved to El Haouria at the tip of the Cape Bon peninsula and was attached to the 324th Fighter Group under the command of Colonel William K. McNown (Haulman, 2010). The 99th patrolled the coasts and seas and performed bomber escort duties. In addition to Pantelleria, they also escorted bombers to other locations on Sicily: Milo, Sciacca, and Trapani. The British and Americans were getting the ready to invade the island of Sicily and then Italy proper. The bombing missions were generally designed to weaken the ability of the German and Italian forces to fight back against the invasion forces. Although the 99th was getting used to the routines, pilots knew that each time they took off could be their last. Many of the target areas were heavily defended by air defense artillery, and sometimes the flak the enemy put up could be enormous. They also flew with an eye on constant lookout for enemy fighters. Still, like soldiers throughout the ages—and more so like military pilots—they did not dwell on the dangers of their jobs or on the possibility of a violent death. Instead, they concentrated on the elements of air combat that they could control— their personal readiness and the mechanical reliability of their aircraft— and not on elements over which they had no control. Some even longed to spot the enemy, to give chase, and to dominate. The desire to engage with the enemy and shoot him down—the army had instilled in these men that all-important aspect of being a warrior, and the men of the 99th longed for their chance to strike at Hitler's minions.

The success of the 99th Fighter Squadron was only starting to change opinions about the potential of black men to serve as officers, as fighter pilots, and as warriors. Even Secretary of War Stimson, who had been an outspoken opponent of the "experiment" to train and employ black pilots, praised the 99th for its performance over Pantelleria (Homan & Reilly, 2001). The 99th Fighter Squadron was later awarded its first Distinguished Unit Citation for its contributions to the success of the operation to take Pantelleria. But with the fight for the relatively small and isolated island of Pantelleria over, the Allies were focused on taking Sicily. In the initial fighting for Sicily, air support would come from bases in North Africa, and the 99th would become increasingly committed to the fight for Sicily and then for all of Italy. On July 2, the 99th had 12 planes in the air in the early morning for a mission to escort 12 B-25 bombers on a mission to bomb targets on Sicily. As the formation approached Sicily from the southwest, four Me-109s and several Fw-190s made a pass at the formation. Both sides exchanged fire, and apparently minor damage was inflicted on planes from each side. After the bombing run on the runways of an enemy military airfield at Costelvestrano, as the formation was heading back to their bases, the Germans returned. Two of the Fw-109s made a run at the bombers. For one of the German pilots, the mission would be his last. Lieutenant Charles B. Hall, then on his eighth mission, got a confirmed kill on one of the Fw-190s when his machine gun fire found it target, and the enemy fighter was observed spinning into the ground in southwestern Sicily. Another German fighter was billowing smoke as it headed toward the ground, although no one saw it actually crash. Hall was low on fuel and worried about getting back to base. As he approached an American formation after the fight, he was mistaken for an incoming enemy fighter and had to flee from American fighters before some quick radio calls got the situation straightened out. Still, Lieutenant Hall had the 99th's first confirmed kill and another possible kill. Hall was greeted enthusiastically on his return to base and was congratulated by Generals Eisenhower, Spaatz, and Doolittle (Homan & Reilly, 2001).

The celebratory mood engendered by Hall's victory was tempered by the loss of two pilots, Lieutenants Sherman White and James McCullin, who suffered a midair collision over the sea just off the southwestern coast of Sicily. Still, the Tuskegee Airmen had drawn first blood—they had grappled with the enemy and mastered him. Lieutenant Colonel Davis was aware that with neither he nor his flight commanders having any previous combat experience—a situation rare if not nonexistent in other squadrons—long and intensive training had been key to the success of the 99th so far. Having that training pay off in enemy kills meant that the 99th was coming of age. The leaders and men of the 99th had little time to reflect on these matters, however, as the war continued and they needed to stay focused on the deadly serious tasks at hand.

July 3 was what was becoming a typical day. Twelve pilots from the 99th joined with 44 other pilots from the 324th Fighter Group to escort 24 medium bombers that were hitting targets in northwestern Sicily. As the formation approached the coast of Sicily, near the target area in the northwest, five enemy fighters appeared from below. Some fighting occurred, but apparently none of the fighters on either side suffered damage. Flak over the target area was heavy, however, and two of the bombers went down. That afternoon, at 3:15 P.M., 11 pilots of the 99th took off for the afternoon mission, which was to join up with another 24 fighters and escort

12 bombers on a mission to attack the small port town of Sciacca on the southwestern coast of Sicily. Again flak was heavy, and eight Me-109s were soon closing in on the formation. As two came at the 99th's planes, Lieutenants Herbert Cark and Herman Lawson each scored a probable hit ("324th Fighter Group"). Such days were increasingly the norm for the 99th—it was becoming an experienced combat unit.

The next day, 11 planes of the 99th joined with 24 from G squadron to escort 24 A-30s in a bombing raid on the air base at the town of Milo on Sicily. The 99th escorted the bombers in the second run over the target. During the actual bombing run, enemy opposition had been scarce. Two Fw-190s made a run at the first wave but were chased away. By the time the planes returned to base, two hours had passed—two hours like most hours spent on a mission for pilots, some routine, some boredom, some excitement. For the afternoon mission, 12 P-40s from the 99th joined with 36 planes from other squadrons to escort 35 A-20s to a repeat attack on Milo, this time with more flak and an attack by three Me-109s (Homan & Reilly, 2001).

After weeks of the air campaign, the British and Americans were ready to launch a ground invasion of Sicily, and the pace increased. From July 10 through July 12, as the Allies were landing at Licata, the 99th flew missions along the landing beaches, keeping the enemy aircraft at bay and preventing them from strafing or otherwise disrupting the landings. On a mission on July 11, after Lieutenant Willey had to return early because of mechanical problems, the rest of the 99th provided aerial cover for about a half an hour, keeping a dozen or so Fw-190s away from the ships and the landings. The enemy was seen but did not engage. However, the antiaircraft fire was heavy in the area, and Lieutenant George R. Bolling was hit. As his plane spun into the sea, he was able to eject and cling to his small life raft. Lieutenant William Campbell flew cover over his brother-in-arms until the rescue craft arrived and plucked him out of the water ("99th Fighter Squadron," 1943).

Such mishaps were part of being a fighter pilot. Every soldier in war understands that death can come from many sources—getting shot, blown up, disease, accidents, friendly fire, and other causes. But flying had its own dangers only tangentially related to the war. In normal civilian flying, pilots usually keep their craft as far from other aircraft as possible. In military flying, pilots normally flew close together, keeping tight formations to either maximize collective defense or to mass firepower in the attack. The seemingly limitless skies could get crowded in a battle zone, greatly diminishing the margin for error. Through the remainder of July and into August, the routines of war continued for the 99th. They flew patrol missions, ground attack missions, and escort missions for both bombers and transport ships. They strafed and bombed enemy convoys, trains, and troop concentrations, always keeping an eye out for enemy fighters. Minor reorganizations were also a part of the existence of the 99th, and on July 19, the 99th was again attached to Colonel Momyer's 33rd Fighter Group (Haulman, 2010).

On July 23, three replacement pilots reported into the 99th, the first that the 99th had received since leaving Tuskegee. A few weeks later, on August 11, while assembling for a patrol mission, two P-40s, flown by Lieutenants Samuel M. Bruce and Paul G. Mitchell, collided in midair. While Lieutenant Bruce was able to eject and parachute down safely, Lieutenant Mitchell was not, either being knocked unconscious in the collision, trapped inside, or he attempted to recover his aircraft all the way down, and he died when his plane smashed into the ground (Francis, 1997). Such were the dangers of flying. Ground crews put out the fires, pushed the wreckage aside, and turned over the remains of dead pilots to graves registration soldiers, who would either transport the remains home or bury them in massive cemeteries in theater. Officers from the pilot's unit would "sanitize" the dead man's personal effects—removing any items that might cause pain or embarrassment for loved ones at home—and mail them to the dead man's next of kin. The surviving pilots had little time to reflect on the tenuous hold on life and the constant presence of death. They had missions to complete and a war to be won. Like most pilots, they pushed thoughts of death away for the present and concentrated on the things they could control—themselves and their aircraft. The Allied invasion of Sicily, while not perfect, was reasonably successful, and the 99th and the whole 33rd moved to new bases on the island. From Sicily, the Allies prepared for the invasion of Italy proper.

With each setback for the Axis, the Italian people were becoming increasingly disillusioned with the war and the alliance with Nazi Germany. While Italian Fascism glorified the nation and the people of Italy, it had little of the virulent anti-Semitism or racism of Nazism. As Italian forces were pushed back from Ethiopia and then North Africa and even Sicily and as the losses on the Russian front mounted, the Italian people and many in their government began to work toward extricating their nation from the mess that the fascist dictator Benito Mussolini had gotten Italy into. The Italian government sought to avoid turning the homeland into a battlefield between the Allies and the Axis. The difficulty was that the Germans had expected the Italians to attempt to negotiate a separate peace with the Allies, and German soldiers had been stationed throughout Italy, ostensibly to help defend it but also to seize Italy in the event of the Italians switching sides. While Mussolini, known as *Il Duce* to his admirers, seemed to have total control of Italy, in reality Italy was still a monarchy, and Mussolini in theory served only at the pleasure of the king. The break came on July 25, 1943, when the Grande Council of Fascism relieved Mussolini of his official post as prime minister, and King Victor Emmanuel III asked General Pietro Badoglio to form a new government, which almost immediately began secret negotiations with the British and Americans. While these negotiations were under way, the fighting continued to consolidate the gains on Sicily and to prepare for the invasion of the mainland. On July 28, the 99th established itself at Licata on the southern coast of Sicily. The change in location did not mean a change in mission, however. They performed air patrols over beaches, escorted bombers, and flew cover over ships at sea. They performed ground attack missions, strafing railroads, convoys, barges, and troop concentrations. The war was moving forward on the ground while at the same time the concept of the Tuskegee Airmen was also moving forward although not without opposition.

The 99th Squadron had, since deploying to North Africa, flown as part of otherwise white air groups, mostly the 33rd, which was under the command of Colonel Momyer. The deployment of the 99th to theater was part of an experiment to see if black men were suitable to serve as fighter pilots. The unit and the men in it were under close scrutiny both by those who wanted to see them succeed and by those who wanted to see them fail. The 99th was the pioneer unit, and if they performed successfully, then the 99th Fighter Squadron was to be joined by three other black fighter squadrons to create a black fighter group. The other three squadrons—the 100th, the 301st, and the 302nd—were undergoing their final unit training at Selfridge Field just north of Detroit, Michigan. The 332nd had been at Selfridge since March 1943, when it had left Tuskegee to complete its unit training. With the success of the 99th, the next phase of the "experiment," deploying a black fighter group, was about to begin.

The 332nd Fighter Group had been activated on Tuskegee Army Airfield on October 13, 1942, along with the 301st and 302nd Fighter Squadrons. The 100th Fighter Squadron, which was already in existence, was assigned to it ("General Orders No. 14"). As with the 99th earlier, originally a white man had been assigned to command the 332nd during its initial formation and training. The 332nd did not get its first black officer until November 12, when a chaplain, Lieutenant Charles W. Walker, was assigned ("332nd Fighter Group"). Colonel Davis, provided that he survived and succeeded in commanding the 99th, would assume command and take the 332nd to combat. Davis had wanted to be an Air Corps officer since his days at West

Point, and now he doing just that. But in the segregated Army Air Forces, he had tied his future to the success of the 99th and later the 332nd, and conversely the success of the 99th and the 332nd was tied to him. Since the American military was opposed to the idea of black officers commanding whites, the size of the black units in the Air Forces needed to grow if Davis was to make more rank. Most pilots were either first or second lieutenants. A flight commander, normally with three other aircraft under him, was normally a captain, and a squadron commander was a lieutenant colonel. For Davis to make full colonel, he would need to command a group. He was one of three black Regular Army officers in the entire army other than a few chaplains, and one of the other officers was his father, and the other, who had recently graduated from West Point, was still in fight training. Davis was the senior of the now two black West Point graduates in the army. As with the 99th as a whole, he was under constant scrutiny, in part because he was being groomed for higher rank and positions. Had he not been able to complete the pilot training, failed as a squadron commander, or been killed, the position of commander of the 99th probably would have been given to a white Regular Army Air Corps officer with extensive flying and leadership experience, or it would have been given to a black officer with a reserve commission and far more limited command and military flying experience. Neither option was desirable and would have made the success of the 99th less likely. But under Davis's leadership, the 99th had met every challenge, and now he was selected to command the new group.

When Davis returned to the United States to take command of the 332nd, command of the 99th was given on September 2, 1943, to Captain George Spencer "Spanky" Roberts, who had commanded the 99th briefly shortly after it was first created and before Davis assumed command. Captain Roberts had been in the first class of pilots to graduate from Tuskegee and in the time since had served in most positions in the squadron. He was as experienced a pilot as the 99th had and was serving as the operations officer just prior to taking command. He was a good choice but did not have the experience in dealing with white superior officers that Davis had. The change in command was noticed by elements within the Air Forces who opposed the Tuskegee Airmen. During the month, German fighters would strafe the base on five consecutive days. Luckily, no one was injured in the attacks. However, the Tuskegee Airmen would that same month suffer an attack of a different sort, one that called into question their very existence as army fighter pilots. Colonel Momyer had never been welcoming to the pilots of the 99th, and after Lieutenant Colonel Davis left, Colonel Momyer made his move to discredit the 99th and, by extension, the entire "experiment" with black pilots.

Major George S. "Spanky" Roberts at the controls of
a P-51 Mustang. Roberts was the first African American accepted for U.S. Army pilot training. He later
commanded the 99th Fighter Squadron and the 332nd
Fighter Group. (U.S. Air Force)

Colonel Momyer attacked the Tuskegee Airmen through a report on
the combat efficiency of the 99th Fighter Squadron. His report began on
a positive note, observing that the 99th had excellent "general discipline
and ability to accomplish and execute orders promptly." After that, his report became almost completely negative, with Momyer claiming that the
99th "seemed to disintegrate" when attacked, "showed a lack of aggressive
spirit," avoided defended primary targets to attack undefended secondary
targets, and "have failed to display the aggressiveness and desire for combat that are necessary to a first-class fighting organization. It may be expected that we will get less work and less operational time out of the 99th
than any squadron in the group." Momyer specifically referred to the
incident on June 9—their first escort mission—when four fighters of the
99th left the formation to pursue the enemy ("Combat Efficiency," 1943).

So, while criticizing them for their lack of fighting spirit and aggressive-ness, he also was able to chide them for being overaggressive. Momyer's real motives and prejudices were laid bare when he recommended not only that the 99th be converted into a noncombat unit but also that all black fighter squadrons, meaning the three undergoing final training in Michi-gan, be converted into something other than combat units and their aircraft given to white units.

There was a germ of truth to the negative reports—the men of the 99th were exhausted and did seek a respite, but the reason had nothing to do with any lack of aggressiveness or desire to avoid combat. Instead, the fault lay with the Army Air Forces and the inefficiency of the segregated struc-ture of the service. The army had several airfields for training white pilots but allowed initial black pilot training only at Tuskegee. As a result, the 99th consistently received fewer replacements than typical white squad-rons, meaning that each black pilot flew on average more missions than his white counterparts. In other fighter squadrons, about four replacement pilots would arrive each month, but limited training capacity at Tuskegee Army Airfield and the need to build a pool of pilots stateside in order to stand up the other proposed squadrons for a planned all-black fighter group meant that fewer replacements arrived at the 99th. White fighter pilots nor-mally rotated back to the States after flying 50 missions, but most of the pi-lots in the 99th flew between 70 and 80 missions before being rotated back home. The 99th carried few if any "extra" pilots at any time until the final months of the European war, meaning that for most missions all pilots who could fly did fly. The heavy mission load and the shortage of pilots in the 99th began to take its toll. While in Sicily, Lieutenant Colonel Davis had re-quested that the 99th be given a period of rest. However, regardless of what-ever shortcomings the 99th might have had and regardless of the factual basis for the report, Momyer illustrated the unthinking and reflexive racism so prevalent in American culture of the period. If one black fighter squadron had deficiencies, then all must have the same deficiencies and be removed from combat. Some white combat units also had problems, and many units were found to be problematic or deficient in efficiency, but no one ever sug-gested that all white combat units should therefore be abolished.

That Colonel Momyer waited until Lieutenant Colonel Davis was away throws suspicion on his motives. But he had bided his time to strike at the 99th. He had attempted to keep the 99th from being attached to the 33rd Fighter Group, and when it was attached, he had a long reputation among the officers of the 99th for playing games intended to make the pilots of the 99th look foolish, such as rescheduling briefings to an earlier time without informing the pilots of the 99th so that they arrived for briefings after the briefing had ended (Homan & Reilly, 2001). When the other squadrons took part in the invasion of Italy proper, the 99th was relegated to remain on Sicily supporting operations there so that the other squadrons of the 33rd had better combat records than the 99th. The 99th flew missions escorting naval convoys, providing reconnaissance, and attacking occasional ground targets. While these missions were important to the war effort, they gave the 99th little opportunity to prove its mettle against Axis pilots and brought racially charged criticism from opponents both inside and outside the military who wanted to see the experiment in black pilots fail. The report was endorsed by Major General Edwin J. House, commander of the 12th Air Support Command of the 12th Air Force, and on September 16 was sent to Major General John K. Cannon, the deputy commander of the Northwest African Tactical Air Force (Lee, 1966). From Cannon, the memo was given to Lieutenant General Carl Spaatz, commander of the 12th Air Force. General Spaatz sent the report on to General Arnold, the commanding general of the Army Air Forces, who had long opposed the idea of black air combat units. General Spaatz included his own note, saying that he while he had "full confidence of the analysis" in the report, he also noted that he had personally inspected the 99th Fighter Squadron on several occasions and always found their ground discipline and general conduct excellent and added that they had been trained very well (Haulman, 2010). By October 13, the report went to the War Department's McCloy Committee for review.

Complaints about ill treatment of black soldiers from some political leaders were becoming more common, and the army became concerned about rising racial tensions on several posts. Black soldiers chaffed when post commanders disregarded army regulations on equal treatment and applied local community standards on army posts, especially strict segregation. The War Department had become caught between its own customs and traditions and the changing nature of American society regarding issues of race. The General Staff had recommended that a permanent committee to deal with issues related to the use of black troops be formed. Secretary Stimson agreed, and on August 27, 1942, he created the Advisory Committee on Negro Troop Policies (Lee, 1966). The committee became informally known as the McCloy Committee, after its chairman, Assistant Secretary of War John J. McCloy. The committee at first simply collected information regarding black soldiers but soon became involved in the issue of how black troops would be used.

The report, bearing General House's signature, was what opponents of black pilots, black officers, and blacks as American warriors had wanted—"proof" that again society had tried to employ blacks in the serious business of combat and blacks had again failed. The "experiment" could be judged a failure, and the 100th, 301st, and 302nd converted to something other than air combat units, and plans for the establishment of a black bomber group scrapped entirely. Black soldiers assigned to those units could be reassigned to construction, supply, or engineer units, and all could go back to the way it was and the way white supremacists thought it should be, with blacks in subordinate positions performing menial tasks, both inside and outside the military. *Time* magazine ran a short article on the 99th Fighter Squadron in its issue of September 20, 1943. While the article noted that the squadron "seems to have done fairly well," the writer was apparently familiar with the House report, for it also mentioned that the 99th might be taken off the front lines and reassigned to performing coastal patrols. While the article was not totally negative about the fighting qualities of black soldiers, it noted that no theater commander wanted them in large numbers and that "there is no lack of work to be done by Negroes as labor and engineering troops—the Army's dirty work." The article attributed the creation of black combat units to the pressure from the black press and from the sense of fair play inherent in Americans but implied that the creation of black combat units—not just the 99th Fighter Squadron or even black pilots but all black combat units—was a noble experiment but that blacks could better serve in the war by doing hard, dirty labor and leaving the fighting to white men. Still, the article also mentioned that given the inefficiencies in a segregated training environment, the true potential of the black pilots might never be known ("Experiment Proved?" 1943).

When Lieutenant Colonel Davis found out about the report, he was justifiably angry. However, his wife, who was not a serving army officer, was equally or even more outraged and not just by the report itself but also at *Time*'s coverage of it. In her letter to the editor that *Time* published on October 18, she took the magazine to task for publishing a story of innuendo based on "unofficial reports." She told *Time*'s readers that according to her husband, the 99th compared favorably with six other squadrons in the same area, flying the same aircraft, and performing similar missions. The only difference with the 99th was that it was manned by black men. She pointed out that the story, based on dubious sources, had done much to undercut the morale of not only black pilots in the 99th but also the entire black population of the United States and implied that such a morale killer was not in the best interests of winning the war. In a reply to Mrs. Davis's letter, the editor of *Time* reiterated the article's stance that if the record of the 99th was "only fair," then segregated training and operations were at least partially to blame ("Letters," 1943). However, while Mrs. Davis defended the honor of the 99th to readers of *Time*, her husband would be the one who had to officially defend the record of the 99th Fighter Squadron and, by extension through the bizarre logic of racism, all African American fighting men and women. The situation added an additional level of needless of stress on the Tuskegee Airmen. These black officers were among the most highly skilled and intelligent black men in America—indeed, among the most intelligent and highly skilled of all men in America—yet they often found themselves under the command and subject to the prejudices of white men of more modest abilities. Lieutenant Colonel Davis could shield them to some extent, but he was Regular Army, and in carrying out his duties he would always be a professional, even if that meant at times appearing to ignore slights against his men, but Davis knew how to walk the thin line that his position demanded.

Lieutenant Colonel Davis would need all of his skills at working with the system when he was called to testify before the War Department's Advisory Committee on Negro Troop Policies to answer questions about the proficiency of the 99th Fighter Squadron. Davis defended the record of the 99th and recommended that it remain a frontline fighter unit. Davis testified that his men had received less training before being sent to theater than white pilots, but he was also able to demonstrate statistically that the 99th had been consistently improving. His testimony must have been convincing because the committee took no action to remove the 99th from the front. However, perhaps not coincidently, the 99th was removed from attachment to Colonel Momyer's 33rd Fighter Group.

Despite this seeming tide of opposition to the continued existence of the 99th Fighter Squadron and therefore all black air combat units, the 99th also had its supporters. The army had invested a lot into the "experiment," and powerful men within the army and government were not going to allow the end of the "experiment" so easily based on one faulty report. General Eisenhower, for one, thought that Colonel's Momyer's allegations were false. The Army's G-3 (Operations) commissioned an official study of the performance of the 99th to try to get a real assessment of their flying and fighting prowess; the study was eventually completed as "Operation of the 99th Fighter Squadron Compared with Other P-40 Squadrons in MTO," the Mediterranean Theater of Operations. The findings of the G-3 investigation backed Lieutenant Colonel Davis's testimony—the 99th Fighter Squadron performed on a level similar to other units: at the high level the Army Air Forces expected of all its combat units (Homan & Reilly, 2001).

During these trying months, with their courage, competence, and manhood publicly questioned and their unit under threat of being reassigned away from combat or disbanded, the pilots and men of the 99th Fighter Squadron continued to fight the war in Italy. Despite all the insults, racially charged allegations, and slights, the 99th had maintained a level of efficiency on par with similar units manned by whites. As Captain Roberts said, "We have not turned out to be super-duper pilots—but as good as the U.S. Army turns out. That's important. Because we had one handicap: people assumed we were not producing because we were Negroes. Our men have been under a strain because of civilian attitude. It is remarkable that they have kept up their morale" (Homan & Reilly, 2001, p. 100). That they were able to keep up their morale under such circumstances was a minor miracle. The Army Air Forces had enormously high standards for its combat units. The stakes were too high to allow weak commanders or poorly performing units to continue. Yet, despite all the obstacles, the 99th was able to perform at a level similar to other units. With the continued existence of the 99th allowed for the time being (and, by extension, other black flying combat units), the 99th Fighter Squadron would soon undergo major changes as the 332nd Fighter Group was about to become operational.

References

"Experiment Proved?" *Time*, September 20, 1943, pp. 66–68.

Fletcher, Marvin E. *America's First Black General: Benjamin O. Davis, Sr., 1880–1970*. Lawrence: University Press of Kansas, 1989.

Francis, Charles E. *The Tuskegee Airmen: The Men Who Changed a Nation*. Boston: Branden Publishing, 1997.

"General Orders No. 14, October 18, 1942." Maxwell Air Force Base, AL: Air Force Historical Research Agency.

Haulman, Daniel L. "Tuskegee Airmen Chronology." October 22, 2010 (http://www.afhra.af.mil/shared/media/document/AFD-100413-023.pdf).

"Historical Record of the 99th Fighter Squadron." May 24, 1943. Washington, DC: Air Force Historical Research Agency.

Homan, Lynn M., and Thomas Reilly. *Black Knights: The Story of the Tuskegee Airmen*. Gretna, LA: Pelican Publishing, 2001.

Lee, Ulysses. *The Employment of Negro Troops*. Washington, DC: Government Printing Office, 1966.

"Letters to the Editor." *Time*, October 18, 1943, pp. 8–9.

"Combat Efficiency of the 99th Fighter Squadron." Memo of Major General Edwin J. House to Major General J. K. Cannon, September 16, 1943. Washington, DC: Air Force Historical Research Agency.

"99th Fighter Squadron History, March, 1941–October, 1943." Maxwell Air Force Base, AL: Air Force Historical Research Agency.

"324th Fighter Group Operational and Intelligence Summary, Operations for July 3, 1943." Maxwell Air Force Base, AL: Air Force Historical Research Agency.

"332nd Fighter Group History, October 1942–1947." Maxwell Air Force Base, AL: Air Force Historical Research Agency.

FOUR

The Tuskegee Airmen Meet the Challenge

THROUGH THE BLACK PRESS, African Americans throughout the United States followed the roles and treatment of blacks in the military during the war. Most blacks as well as whites wanted to see the war end quickly and victoriously, but blacks also wanted to see that blacks were treated fairly by the military. They hoped that the war would also bring new opportunities to blacks and that the example of the overt and murderous racism of Nazi Germany would make white Americans uncomfortable with racist polices in the United States. They were particularly concerned over continued efforts to relegate blacks in the military to performing unskilled labor under the control of whites—efforts often couched in terms of paternalism, efficiency, and even patriotism. The continuing gross underrepresentation of blacks in the officer corps was a constant source of concern. Some developments had given hope to blacks, however, as the Marine Corps finally began to create black units in the summer of 1942; the first group of 12 back naval officers were commissioned on March 17, 1944; and stories of black valor in action against the enemy were becoming more common. Despite the increased profile of some black officers such as the Tuskegee Airmen, the overall status of black officers in the military remained tenuous, and segregation seemed more entrenched than ever. In the army as a whole, the situation for blacks remained bleak. By 1942, only one out of about 300 black soldiers was an officer, compared with about one in 10 for white soldiers (MacGregor, 1989). While the overall lower average education levels of blacks explain a little of this statistic, segregation and racist policies and assumptions explain most of it. Black officers could not be posted to units with white enlisted men, although white officers could be and were posted to units with black enlisted men. Because black officers were not normally allowed to outrank white officers in the same unit, many black soldiers understood that black officers were somehow not full-fledged officers, undercutting the authority of black officers over their own men. For a white officer, assignment to a black unit often carried with it a stigma, and whites who were assigned to black units usually tried to avoid the assignment. As a result, black units often received white officers whom no other units wanted. The army staff retained a tendency from World War I of assigning white officers from the South to black units in the belief that southern whites had better abilities to deal with blacks. Most white officers so assigned treated their soldiers with a mixture of paternalism and contempt, and black soldiers, especially those from outside the South, found this attitude of white officers revolting. The Tuskegee Airmen, however, held a special place of hope and pride in the black community; they were the "Black Knights," and blacks at home would fiercely defend their honor.

The Tuskegee Airmen were the cream of black manhood, but they were only a relatively small percentage of all blacks in the Army Air Forces. By 1943, about 2,000 black men had graduated from the Civilian Pilot Training Program and its wartime successor, the War Training Service, and most had entered the Army Air Forces, but only a small percentage of them had qualified as army pilots (National Museum, 2010). The Army Air Forces had 77,500 blacks serving, although most were still serving in menial positions. To absorb its quota of black selectees, the Army Air Forces created hundreds of truck companies, security battalions, and other organizations that allowed the Air Forces to employ black men at its bases in menial tasks (MacGregor, 1989). Despite this depressing situation, the Tuskegee Airmen, by their performance, gave lie to the myth that blacks were unsuited to serve as officers or in highly skilled positions. As the combat record of the 99th Fighter Squadron increased, opponents of the idea of using blacks in leadership and combat roles had fewer arguments. The men and officers of the 99th Fighter Squadron were mostly from middle-class backgrounds and tended to be highly literate and so were aware of their importance to the black community in the United States. Black newspapers as well as national magazines were sent overseas to black units, and the Tuskegee Airmen in North Africa and later in Italy were able to follow developments at home and see how they were portrayed in the newspapers. The existence of the black fighter squadron had been well publicized, and while some whites were curious about them, most blacks saw them as heroes. Members of a boys' club in Philadelphia made Christmas gifts for the airmen and in return received letters from the 99th, which the boys cherished. In their letters, the Tuskegee Airmen stressed the importance of service to others ("Historical Record," 1943). Such interactions with people back home underscored the status of the Tuskegee Airmen as role models. They were always keenly aware that they carried the hopes and pride of millions. The missions over Italy continued into the late summer and early fall of 1943. On September 3, Italy and the Allies signed an armistice requiring the Italians not to oppose Allied landings on the Italian mainland. The agreement was kept a secret for a long as possible to prevent the Germans from finding out and moving to disarm the Italian armed forces and seizing control of the country. The same day, British forces crossed the narrow Straits of Messina between Sicily and the "toe" of Italy in Operation Baytown. Because of the armistice, the landing was unopposed. The armistice became public on September 8, and the next day two more unopposed landings occurred: Operation Avalanche at Salerno and Operation Slapstick at Taranto. The Germans, as soon as they figured out what was going on, began taking control of as much of Italy as they could, but the Allies were already ashore and consolidating their holdings. Despite the armistice, Italy became a battlefield as the Allies began to battle their way up the Italian peninsula against a determined German foe that had dug in and was prepared to make the Allies pay dearly for every foot of ground.

On September 14, 1943, the 99th escorted a large formation of 24 A-30s and 12 B-25 Mitchell bombers on a raid on Nola, Italy (Homan & Reilly, 2001). During this period, they continued to perform patrol missions, keeping the skies above Allied ground operations free of enemy aircraft. While enemy aircraft were occasionally spotted in the distance, the enemy stayed away, and the men of the 99th were unable to score any more aerial victories. After two months in Licata, the 99th moved to Termini Imerese for two weeks and then to Barcellona Pozzo di Gotto, where they stayed for a month, and finally, on October 17, they established themselves at Foggia Air Field No. 3 on the eastern side of the Italian peninsula ("Historical Record," 1943). Their frequent moves were normal as the front moved forward. The Army Air Forces tried to keep fighter and ground attack units as near to the front as possible to cut down on time needed to fly from their airfields to the fighting. From Foggia, the 99th Fighter Squadron attacked ground targets and provided close air support for Allied troops.

Concurrent with the move to Foggia was the reattachment of the 99th Fighter Squadron from the 33rd Fighter Group to the 79th Fighter Group, which was commanded by Colonel Earl E. Bates ("Historical Record," 1943). Again, the 99th Fighter Squadron was the only black squadron in an otherwise white group, but for the men and officers of the 99th, the change was dramatic. Unlike Colonel Momyer, who they always suspected did not like blacks and who was quite open with his disdain for the 99th, Colonel

Bates welcomed them to the 79th and made them feel part of his team. The 79th Fighter Group, like most fighter groups, normally contained three squadrons, and the 99th became the fourth squadron of their new group. The atmosphere was different, but the missions were similar—bombing, strafing, patrolling, and escorting. The pilots of the 99th bombed bridges at Lariano, the docks at Francariella, shipping at Guilanova, and gun positions at Furci ("War Diary," 1943).

Signs of increasing acceptance of the 99th were occurring. On November 1, 50 P-38s flown by white pilots were serviced by the ground crews from the 99th ("99th Fighter Squadron History," 1943–1944). A few days later, on November 5, a milestone occurred; for the first time, pilots from the 99th Fighter Squadron were rotated back to the United States. Lieutenants William A. Campbell, Span Watson, and Herbert V. Clark became the first Tuskegee Airmen to complete their tour in combat and move on to other assignments. The men were not discharged, though—their next assignment would be in training the next group of Tuskegee Airmen in the latest realities of aerial combat against the Germans. Two days later, Major General Cannon, who had earlier endorsed Colonel Momyers's derogatory report on the 99th, visited the base and awarded Air Medals to several of the pilots of the 99th for their bravery and skill in the air. On November 22, 1943, the 99th Fighter Squadron moved again, this time to a base at Madna, Italy, to keep up with the retreating Germans. Colonel Bates showed that the first impression the pilots of the 99th had of him was correct; by January 1944, he had pilots from the 99th flying mission as part of otherwise white squadrons ("99th Fighter Squadron History," 1943–1944). Bates seems to have seen the pilots of the 99th as pilots first and used them as he would any other combat pilots.

Through December 1943 and well into January 1944, the 99th flew missions in support of the British and American drive up the Italian peninsula with the goal of taking the Italian capital of Rome. "Rome, Berlin, Home" became a rallying cry, as the men, most of who were after all citizen-soldiers, not career airmen, realized that they would not all be going home to their loved ones until every Axis nation was beaten. The path home was through the enemies' capitals. They flew almost every day, hitting targets between the Trigno and Sangro rivers and performing bombing missions on the towns of Palena and Sulmona. By mid-January, the 99th was based at Capodichino Airfield, which was near Naples on the east coast of Italy. From there, they flew missions in support of the large Allied landings at Anzio. On January 27, the squadron was flying what started as a routine patrol providing air cover for an Allied fleet near the Ponziane Islands. During that morning's mission, the pilots of the 99th would score eight kills and two probable kills when a group of 15 Fw-190 German fighters moved in to attack the Allied ships. Lieutenants Howard Baugh, Clarence Allen, Robert Diez, Willie Ashley, Henry Perry, and Leon Roberts were credited with kills, while another four Germans fighters were damaged in the fight. This tally demonstrated the increasing skills of the pilots in the 99th—they were becoming a deadly adversary for the pilots of the Luftwaffe. But the victories came at a price—Lieutenant Samuel Bruce was killed in action when his P-40 crashed near Nettuno Beach, while another pilot parachuted to safety ("War Diary," 1943). While such tragedies were disturbing and saddened the other pilots, they could not dwell on them—they were part of the nature of being fighter pilots. But a good day's work did not mean respite. The war in Italy was increasingly grim, and men on the ground died in droves to move the front a few yards forward.

As good as the toll extracted from the Germans had been on January 27, such days would not be unique. The Germans were fighting a desperate air campaign to slow or even stop the Allied advances in Italy. American intelligence believed that the Germans had committed more than 100 Fw-190s and Me-109s to the campaign. The 99th was heavily involved in the fighting above Anzio and Nettuno beaches, where some of the heaviest fighting the Allies had yet encountered was ongoing. The very day after Lieutenant Bruce was killed, the 99th flew another mission above Anzio. A few minutes before noon, a group of four Me-109s and at least three Fw-190s approached from the northeast. In the ensuing fight, Lieutenant Diez scored another kill, making two kills in two days, when he found an Fw-190 that had gotten separated from the others. Diez maneuvered behind the German and opened up with his machine guns. The German managed to bail out of his dying aircraft before it slammed into the ground ("99th Fighter Squadron History," 1943–1944).

When a pilot was credited with a kill, it meant that he had destroyed an enemy aircraft in the air, and the fate of the enemy pilot was not part of the equation. A kill had to be confirmed to count, meaning that either a camera mounted in the aircraft or the pilot of another aircraft had to witness the crash of the enemy aircraft. Under the rules of war, shooting at enemy paratroopers before they reached the ground was accepted, but shooting at crewmen or pilots who bailed out of crippled aircraft was not allowed. The German was allowed to parachute to the ground with the hope that he would be captured by ground forces and held prisoner until the war was over, but it held the risk that the enemy pilot might eventually find his way back to his own side and fly again. If the downed pilot attempted to fight once he hit the ground, then he was again a legitimate target for kill-ing. Not shooting at a pilot who had bailed out was a generally accepted and followed practice, although sometimes the Tuskegee Airmen did re-port Germans firing at American pilots who had bailed out. Germany could make new aircraft easier than it could produce new fighter pilots, how-ever, German industry was hard pressed to keep producing aircraft, and as the land area that Germany controlled continued to shrink, getting the raw materials to produce high-tech aircraft became increasingly difficult. Each German plane destroyed was a step in an eventual Allied victory. Pilots in the 99th noticed a decline in the quality of German pilots. Lieutenant Bailey later said that when they would fly up next to a German airplane and get a look at the pilot, he would more often than not look like a schoolboy rather than a man. They also were seeing more enemy aircraft on the ground, the Germans lacking the fuel or pilots to use them (Homan & Reilly, 2001).

During the same scrap in which Diez got his second kill, Lieutenant Lewis Smith also scored a kill. He ran down an Fw-190. That German was not as lucky, and he died when his aircraft smashed into the ground and erupted in a ball of flames. Lieutenant Charles Hall claimed two kills, one Me-109 that burst into flames after Hall's machine guns found the engine of the enemy craft, and an Fw-190 that spun into the ground after Hall man-aged to fire a few bursts into its rear. By the time the enemy air onslaught was over, the 99th could tally an impressive 12 kills, three probable kills, and four enemy aircraft damaged. The victories were not without cost, as one pilot from the 99th, Lieutenant Bruce, had been killed, and three other airplanes had suffered damage. During the same two-day campaign, "Flip" Cochran's squadron was credited with five kills, a British squadron with nine, and another British squadron with one. Nothing proved the efficiency of a fighter squadron more than grappling with the enemy and destroying him, and the 99th had shown its ability to do just that.

With more and more pilots of the 99th Fighter Squadron being credited with confirmed kills, the pressure was on for the others. To be a pilot who had been with the 99th since the start and not have a credited kill became a psychological burden. Pilots envied those with multiple kills and longed for the day when they too would earn the bragging rights that came with having a confirmed kill. Despite the noticeable decline in the quality of Luftwaffe pilots, Allied airmen could not count on easy pickings. Experienced and skillful enemy pilots still existed, and every mission could still be a pilot's last. On February 5, Lieutenant Elwood Driver was part of a flight of six planes from the 99th—one of the original seven that had taken off had to abort the mission and return to base because of engine troubles—to patrol the skies off the Ponziane Islands. About halfway through the 45-minute patrol of the area, a flight of 10 Fw-190s attacked, hitting the 99th from the east so that the sun covered their initial advance. Lieutenant Driver was able to come down on one of the Fw-190s and let loose his machine guns on it. When last seen, the German fighter was burning as it flew out to the sea. It was the 13th enemy aircraft shot down by the 99th. Lieutenant Elwood T. Driver earned his bragging rights that morning, but other pilots from the 99th were not so lucky; Captain Clarence C. Jamison and Lieutenant George T. McCrumby were listed missing after the engagement, but Jamison, who had to belly land on a field between lines after getting hit, was able to get back to friendly lines and hitched a ride back to the airfield at Capodichino ("War Diary," 1943).

While the pilots of the 99th Fighter Squadron obviously faced the greatest dangers, no one in a war zone was ever completely safe. The ground crews and support troops who were also part of the Tuskegee Airmen legacy served heroically by keeping the complicated machines flying and keeping the unit running smoothly so that the pilots could concentrate on their deadly duties. While the 99th had about 40 officers, most of whom were pilots, it also had about 250 enlisted men ("Historical Records," 1944). While the enlisted men did not fly, reminders of the danger of wartime service were all around—ruined buildings, shell holes, and the threat of air attack. To make the area more dangerous, areas that had previously been fought over often had large amounts of unexploded ordinance—bombs that failed to detonate—laying around or buried. Additionally, retreating troops sometimes left behind land mines and booby traps, hoping to slow down an advancing foe. First Lieutenant Thomas Malone, who was part of the 366th Air Service Squadron, found out how dangerous ground service could be when his truck ran over a land mine left by the Germans, and he was seriously wounded. His wounds were so grievous that he had to be evacuated back to the United States and recovered at the Army Convalescent Hospital in Coral Gables, Florida (Homan & Reilly, 2001).

Despite such tragedies, the missions continued. Just two days later, on the morning of February 7, the pilots of the 99th added three more kills to their total when, during another mission over Ponziane Beach, eight planes from the 99th got into a fight with 12 Fw-190s. Lieutenants Wilson Eagleson, Leonard Jackson, and Clinton Mills each got a confirmed kill that day. Jackson saw the pilot of the plane he shot down bail out before it crashed, but the enemy pilots of the other planes were not as lucky, and they died in the flaming wreckages of their planes. All eight of the 99th's planes returned safely, although one had suffered damage (Haulman, "Tuskegee Airmen

Crew Chief Marcellus G. Smith of Louisville, Kentucky, works on an airplane at an airbase in Ramitelli, Italy, March 1945. Crew chiefs were highly skilled enlisted men and were in charge of all members of a ground crew for a particular airplane. (Library of Congress)

Chronology"). The reputation of the 99th was on the rise. Even General Arnold, the head of the Army Air Forces who had opposed the creation of black combat units in the Air Forces, sent a message to Lieutenant General Ira C. Eaker, the commander of operations in the Mediterranean Theater, which included Italy, praising the 99th for its performance since the landings at Nettuno two weeks earlier (Homan & Reilly, 2001).

February started much as January had been—daily missions to escort, patrol, strafe, or bomb. Most of the mission were directed against stubborn German resistance on the small island of Ponza itself, about half a dozen miles off the east coast of Italy. The mission on the morning of February 21 would, however, end tragically differently from most previous missions, when the engine on Lieutenant Alwayne Dunlap's P-40 began burning over a beach area, apparently from mechanical problems. Although Captain Hall told Dunlap to bail out, Dunlap attempted to land the burning machine on the beach but was killed when the crippled machine stalled and crashed after he overshot the beach. Later that morning, 22 enemy aircraft approached the landing beaches at Anzio. The 99th and the Germans exchanged fire and did some dogfighting on each other, but each side broke off with no confirmed kills, although an unidentified plane apparently crashed in the distance and was seen to explode. Another German plane was seen flying low and trailing back smoke, but its crash was not confirmed ("99th Fighter Squadron History," February–April 1944).

While the men of the 99th were racking up more victories in the increasingly bitter combat on the Italian front, the other three black fighter squadrons—the 100th, 301st, and 302nd—were declared ready for deployment to Europe. They formed the all-black 332nd Fighter Group, to which the 99th was expected to be reassigned as soon as the other squadrons were brought up to speed. On January 3, the three fighter squadrons of the 332nd, along with the 96th Service Group, departed Hampton Roads, Virginia, on four ships and, like the 99th before them, began their voyage overseas from which some would never return (Haulman, "Tuskegee Airmen Chronology"). But unlike the voyage of the 99th almost a year earlier, the 332nd was under the command of a proven combat leader—Lieutenant Colonel Benjamin O. Davis Jr. The convoy made short stops in North Africa and Sicily before docking, and the 332nd and its subordinate units debarked in the ports of Bari, Taranto, and Naples, Italy. The 332nd was initially posted to Montecorvino Air Base, just south of Naples. The 332nd was issued a different aircraft than the 99th, the Bell P-39Q Aircobra, which, with a top airspeed of 368 miles per hour, was much faster than the P-40, which had a top speed of about 300 miles per hours. As the 99th had done before them, the newly deployed squadrons would be given a shakedown period, flying missions where enemy contact was possible but not likely. By February 19, planes from the 100th Fighter Squadron were flying air cover for naval vessels and performing similar missions. Enemy fighters were glimpsed in the distance, but they did not come in for an attack. Similar duties would occupy the 332nd through the end of February, as the men in the new squadrons became more adjusted to flying in the sometimes crowded skies of a combat zone. Despite the training that all aircrews were given in aircraft identification, in the high speed and confusing world of aerial combat, sometimes both fighters and gunners on bombers fired at aircraft from their own side by mistake. Telling enemy fighters from friendly fighters coming straight into a bomber formation was difficult, and many men manning machine guns on bombers opted to be safe and treat any unknown aircraft as an enemy until they became sure it was friendly. Fighter pilots were advised to approach bomber formations from the side rather than head-on so that bomber crews could see the side of the fighter and better identify it as friendly.

Although the three new squadrons were gaining more and more experience, they were still performing mostly rear-area missions and had few opportunities to perform the one service that counted above all others when tallying up the skill of fighter squadrons—shooting down enemy aircraft. They occasionally saw enemy airplanes in the distance, but seldom did the Germans venture that far from their own lines to grapple with Allied pilots. On March 17, some members of the 302nd Fighter Squadron were called to check out a suspected enemy bomber sighted in their area. The six P-39s caught the lone Ju-88 (a German medium bomber), made a positive identification, and engaged it. Despite the attempts by the German pilot to hide in some clouds, one American emptied his machine guns into the Ju-88. The large German plane started smoking and headed out to sea. While this was a successful mission, since no one saw the enemy airplane crash, it could be counted as only a possible kill ("War Diary," 332nd Fighter Group, March 1944).

The next day, the 100th Fighter Squadron lost one of its own when Lieutenant Clemenceau Givings's P-39 had mechanical problems, caught fire, and crashed into the Gulf of Gaeta ("War Diary," 332nd Fighter Group, March 1944). Such incidents could play havoc with the morale of ground crews. When an airplane was lost in combat, the ground crew would mourn the dead pilot, but they took satisfaction that he went down fighting and accepted that death at the hands of an enemy was one of the major risks of combat flying. But mechanical problems were something the ground crew might have been able to avoid. When a plane went down from mechanical problems, especially when it crashed and the pilot was killed, ground crews could spend the rest of their lives second-guessing themselves—"Was that engine tuned just right?," "Did I tighten that bolt properly?," "Did I miss something I should have noticed?" An investigation was usually conducted, but with any evidence most likely sitting in the middle of a pile of wreckage or at the bottom of the sea, most investigations consisted of questioning the ground crew and rechecking the maintenance records. Unless the investigation uncovered shoddy maintenance or poorly skilled mechanics, the crash would remain a mystery, and the members of the crew were either assigned to other crews that were short personnel or assigned to a new aircraft and pilot. Such are the necessities of war.

The Ju-88 that engaged on the 17th turned out not to be an isolated incident. The Luftwaffe was apparently engage in a short campaign to bomb Allied rear positions supporting the Anzio beachhead and the allied drive toward Rome. Through March, the pilots from the 332nd would continue to spot the lumbering bombers. Planes from the 302nd recorded another probable kill of one on March 28, when two pilots gave chase to a German until they expended all their ammunition. By the time they broke contact, the right engine of the bomber was pouring smoke, but no crash was observed ("War Diary," 332nd Fighter Group, March 1944). The rest of the spring would continue in a similar fashion for the three new comers in the theater—they flew patrols, responded to reports of enemy aircraft sightings, and in general became more and more accustomed to the rhythms of combat. On April 3, two P-39s scrambled to intercept some suspected enemy bombers, only to discover that the possible enemy planes were actually a group of three American B-25 medium bombers. The pair later spotted a strange aircraft near Mount Vesuvius and fired a burst of machine gun fire before being informed by radio that the odd aircraft was an American P-51 Mustang (Homan & Reilly, 2001).

Despite the existence of the all-black 332nd Fighter Group in theater, the 99th Fighter Squadron remained for a while attached to otherwise white fighter groups. On April 1, 1944, the 99th was reassigned to the 324th Fighter Group and moved its base of operations to Cercola, a few miles inland from Naples. Other changes were also coming. Major George "Spanky" Roberts, who had commanded the 99th since Colonel Davis left to take command of the 332nd Fighter Group, also left the 99th to assume duties with the 332nd, and Captain Erwin B. Lawrence assumed command of the squadron. About the same time, the study commissioned by the army during the controversy engendered by Colonel Momyer's report was completed. To the surprise of no one in the 99th, it found that the 99th was a "superb tactical fighter unit" and that statistically no difference existed between it and similar fighter squadrons in the Mediterranean Theater. The standards for fighter squadrons in the Army Air Forces were incredibly high, and the 99th Fighter Squadron, the first all-black fighter squadron in the U.S. military, had shown that black pilots were equal to the task.

In May 1944, major changes came to the Tuskegee Airmen fighting in Europe. The 332nd Fighter Group transferred to a new airfield at Ramitelli, Italy, on the east coast of the peninsula, and fell under the 306th Wing. The 99th Fighter Squadron was finally assigned to the 332nd Fighter Group but remained separate from it, remaining attached to the otherwise white 324th Fighter Group. On May 10, the 99th moved to a new base at

P-47D-16 42-75971 of Second Lieutenant Lloyd Hathcock, 301st Fighter
Squadron, Ramitelli, Italy, May 1944. It was one of the first Thunder-
bolts received by the 332nd. (U.S. Air Force)

Pignataro, Italy. Davis was promoted to full colonel, the normal rank for
the commander of an air group. Some squadrons were equipped with the
P-47 Thunderbolt, which was one of the best fighters of the war. The P-47
could reach speeds as high as 428 miles per hour and had better protection
for the pilot. The P-47 was also equipped with external fuel tanks, which
greatly extended the range of the fighter. Since the additional fuel tanks
were located outside the fuselage, they hampered performance. While en
route on a mission, the P-47 would draw its fuel from its external tanks. If
the formation were attacked by enemy aircraft, the P-47 pilot would jettison the external tanks and switch to his internal fuel tanks and then engage
the enemy fighter. But despite the new organization, basing, and aircraft,
the missions for the time being were similar to what they had been since the
332nd arrived in theater—mostly patrols, convoy escort, with some ground
attack missions and a few scrambles for suspected enemy aircraft—but
few German aircraft were spotted. The work was exhausting and could
also be dangerous, especially the ground attack missions. The pilots of
the 332nd often had to attack German gun positions with either machine
guns or 500-pound bombs. The German positions were often built on top of
houses and protected by antiaircraft artillery. On May 26, while attacking
one such German position, Lieutenant Woodrow Morgan's aircraft was hit
so bad that he had to crash-land, although he was able to do so at a nearby
army airfield and walk away from the crash. Lieutenants Robert Diez's and
Henry Perry's aircraft both sustained damage from ground fire, while Alva
Temple's aircraft suffered serious damage, with both wings hit, the elevator
system knocked out, and the tail damaged, yet he was still able to bring his
crippled craft back to base (Francis, 1997).

Despite such days of incredible danger and feats of flying prowess,
the days often blurred into each other. On June 2, the 99th reached two

milestones—500 missions flown and one year since its first combat mission ("99th Fighter Squadron History," June 1944). The Italian front moved forward very slowly, and the war seemed to have bogged down in the rugged terrain of Italy. But Italy was about to lose importance in the overall war as the Allies began a long-planned invasion of Western Europe. The leaders of the U.S. military in particular believed that the Allied armies had to enter Europe through France or the Low Countries and somewhere in Western Europe come to grips with the German army and destroy it. After repeated delays, the day of the invasion came on June 6, 1944, when a massive sea and air invasion by U.S., British, and Canadian forces began on the Normandy beaches of northwestern France. Suddenly, the Italian Theater was a secondary effort. For the pilots of the 99th and the 332nd, this change in the direction of the war did not mean that they would see a diminishing of their mission load. One of the characteristics of airpower was the ability of the airplane to fly great distances and over obstacles that would block armies on the ground. While the Alp Mountains at the northern end of Italy made Italy a poor route for attacking Germany from the south by land, they posed little challenge to Allied fighters and bombers striking targets deep in Germany.

With the changing face of the war, the 332nd was to be integrated into frontline missions, mostly the bomber escort missions for which the Tuskegee Airmen would become famous. The leadership of the Air Forces had always been lukewarm about using airpower for missions such as ground attack, convoy escort, and patrol. They saw such missions as a waste of the true value of airpower, which was to bring an enemy nation to its knees through attacks on key elements of its infrastructure. The best mission for airpower was to use bombs to destroy factories, railroad yards, electrical power generation facilities, dams, oil refineries, and other key elements of a modern economy. All other uses of airpower might bring short-term results, but in the long term they lengthened the war, and General Arnold wanted a return to the focus on strategic bombing. Flying from its bases in Italy, the 15th Air Force would be able to strike targets deep within German-controlled Europe and bring the German capacity to make war to an end. On June 7, the 332nd Fighter Group flew its first real mission, a fighter sweep in the Ferrara-Bologna area of occupied northern Italy (Haulman, "Table of 332nd Fighter Group"). But this first mission was only to whet the appetite of the pilots of the 332nd, and the next day the 332nd would fly its first bomber escort mission, a type of mission that would be the most common mission flown by the 332nd. General Arnold had wanted Army Air Forces units to be aggressive in their campaign against the Luftwaffe, and Colonel Davis was ready to give Arnold what he wanted. German fighters were thick in the air as the formations entered the skies over the Third Reich, and Davis ordered his men to pursue and kill the German fighters.

The Tuskegee Airmen had come a long way from early political pressure to allowing black men a chance to earn a commission and their pilot's wings. They had pushed through the opposition to the very idea of black fighter pilots, and now they were a frontline American combat unit, fighting the enemies of the United States in the skies over enemy nations and occupied nations. The earlier missions in North Africa, Sicily, and Italy had been tough, deadly, and necessary, but flying bomber escort missions for heavy bombers over Germany was definitely the big leagues—this was the what the leaders of the Air Forces meant by "airpower." The Tuskegee Airmen had arrived, and the Luftwaffe was getting a lesson in the fallacy of Nazi ideology about racial superiority of the "Aryan" Germans—a lesson that would reverberate throughout the U.S. military and back to the United States.

Pilots of the 332nd Fighter Group pose at Ramitelli, Italy. From left to right: Lieutenant Dempsey Morgan, Lieutenant Carroll Woods, Lieutenant Robert Nelson Jr., Captain Andrew D. Turner, and Lieutenant Clarence Lester. (U.S. Air Force)

The mission of June 9 was the biggest the Tuskegee Airmen flew to date. Along with numerous other fighter groups, the 99th Fighter Squadron and the 332nd Fighter Group took off in the morning to escort five heavy bombardment wings—the 5th, 47th, 304th, 49th, and 55th—in a strike against oil refineries near Munich in southern Germany (Haulman, "Table of 332nd Fighter Group"). Because of the late arrival of four bombers at the rendezvous location, the formation was spread out over the skies as it moved north. As the formation crossed the northern area of Italy, before crossing the Alps, German fighters flying out of Udine, near the Yugoslav border, flew up to attack the formation. Colonel Davis called over the radio for his men to engage, and they responded with gusto, punching off their wing tanks and moving in to attack the Germans. In the opening phase of combat, Lieutenant Frederick D. Funderburg tangled with a pair of Me-109s, and when the scrap was over, two Messerschmitts were in the water and at least one German pilot was dead. Lieutenant Robert Wiggins was able to put some rounds into a German aircraft, although the German was apparently able to escape. Lieutenant Wendell Pruitt fired three bursts into a Messerschmitt, and the plane went down in flames, although its pilot was able to bail out before his plane crashed into the ground. Lieutenant Charles M. Bussey led a formation of eight into a flight of four Me-109s. When one German got on the tail of Lieutenant Melvin Jackson, Lieutenant William W. Green and Bussey were able to fill the enemy plane with enough machine gun fire that it came apart and the pilot was forced to bail out before the mangled enemy craft smashed into the ground and exploded. Lieutenant Jackson became entangled in a dangerous dogfight with a Messerschmitt but through some skillful flying managed to get behind his opponent and fill the German aircraft with so much machine gun fire that the German pilot was barely able to clear his wrecked plane as it burst into flames. In all, the Tuskegee Airmen got five kills that day, and the bombers got through to hit their targets. Still, the price was high. In the 332nd, Lieutenant Cornelius G. Rogers was killed in the fighting. Colonel Davis was awarded the Distinguished Flying Cross for his leadership in the battle (Headquarters). Perhaps of equal value was a short message the 332nd received from one of the bomber pilots praising the 332nd as the best escort the bombers had ever had.

The escort missions would continue, and the Tuskegee Airmen became more accustomed to the long missions. They were settling in to the routines of war. One pleasant surprise was the generally hospitable nature of the Italians. While Italian men, like men everywhere, did not appreciate the competition for women posed by the relatively wealthy American flyers, the Tuskegee Airmen found that the Italian women carried few of the prejudices against blacks that they had experienced in the United States. Lieutenant Felix Kilpatrick Jr. told a reporter for the *Chicago Defender* about a dance held with local women in Italy and how, after dancing with one black airman, an Italian woman turned to a white lieutenant and gave him an earful for the awful things the white lieutenant had told her about black men. Such pleasantries in war often made airmen the target of envy and taunting by ground troops, who resented that airmen usually got to sleep in beds with sheets and could spend off evenings at clubs while ground troops slogged through the mud, but such taunts ignored the high skills needed by pilots and the higher chance of death the airmen faced with every mission.

On June 13, the 301st and 302nd Squadrons escorted formation of B-24s from the 5th and 49th Bomber Wings on another mission to Munich. Despite a few mechanical problems, the mission went over with only one bomber lost to enemy fighters (Haulman, "Table of 332nd Fighter Group"). A few Me-109s made passes at the formation, and some shots were exchanged, but no damage was reported on to the fighters on either side. But not all missions would be as smooth, and in war fortunes could change from day to day. On June 24, the 332nd was assigned the mission of strafing a German airfield near Airasca, Italy. Of the 48 P-47s that initially took off, seven had to abort because of mechanical problems—an ominous start. As the group approached the target area, low clouds and glare off the ocean cut the visibility, and three P-47s became lost. Most of the group apparently became disoriented and were unaware of the low altitude at which they were flying. They were flying under radio silence to prevent the Germans from homing in on them by triangulating their radio signals, but their silence also prevented the cross talk that often allowed the group to correct errors made by one. The group leader became lost, and the formation stumbled on as the flak began to take its toll. Lieutenant Earl Sherard's plane started burning, and he had to crash-land in the sea, although he was later rescued. Soon after Sherard went down, Lieutenant Samuel Jefferson's P-47 also went into the sea. Lieutenant Charles B. Johnson's plane augured into the sea and exploded on impact, killing him instantly. The tragedy did not end with Johnson's death. Lieutenant Robert B. Tresville, who like Colonel Davis had graduated from West Point (indeed, he was the seventh black man to graduate from that school), was the leader of the 100th Fighter Squadron. He came in at too steep a dive, and though he was able to level his aircraft before he slammed into the sea, the resulting damage to his plane from the stress and g-forces made the plane inoperable, and it too crashed into the sea, taking Tresville with it as it went under. Lieutenant Tresville would never see the daughter his wife had given birth to while he was at war. After an investigation, the Army Air Forces blamed the failure of the mission on the weather, radio silence, and flying too low (Francis, 1997).

Despite such terrible days, the war and the missions continued, and better days would come. Again, the living performed the grim task of collecting the personal property of the dead, sanitizing it, and shipping it home. Replacement pilots would be integrated into the unit. A mission a day after the 332nd had suffered such losses underscored the rapid changes of fortunes in war; pilots from the 332nd scored one of the most unusual victories of the war. Twenty P-47s from the 332nd were tasked to strafe enemy troops sighted on the coastal roads at the northern end of the Adriatic Sea along the border of Yugoslavia and Italy, in an area now part of the nation of Croatia. Leaving from their airfield at Ramitelli on the west coast of Italy, at mid-morning, the planes flew almost directly north to hit their targets. The formation broke into five groups of four fighters each. As they approached the target area, three groups searched for the troops on the roads and, finding none, instead shot up the coastal areas nearby, hitting radio stations, small vessels, and in general causing havoc along the coastline. The other two groups, eight planes in all, found a more interesting target: what appeared to be a small destroyer bearing the German Iron Cross painted on its smokestack. Lieutenants Wendell O. Pruitt and Gwynne Peirson made an initial pass. The ship, seeing the American planes, attempted a series of maneuvers in an attempt to avoid the air attacks, but instead a turn allowed all American planes to hit the side of the ship at almost the same time. After unloading their ammunition at the ship, the American pilots watched the smoke begin to spread on the ship, and then they saw an explosion on the ship, suggesting that they had hit either a fuel or an ammunition storage compartment on the ship. The claim of eight pilots that they had attacked an enemy warship was met with incredulity, but the footage from Peirson's wing camera caught the attack on the ship. The ship has never been positively identified but was probably the old Italian destroyer *Giuseppe Missori*, which had been seized by the Germans after Italy switched sides and was converted in a torpedo vessel designated as the TA-22. Despite the heavy damage inflicted by the 332nd on the ship, it apparently remained afloat and was later sabotaged by Italian members of the crew in the summer of 1944 and scuttled by the Germans in 1945 (Daniel L. Haulman, e-mail to author, December 6, 2010). Still, after the attack by the Tuskegee Airmen, the operational life of the TA-22 ended. The Tuskegee Airmen, those in the 332nd Fighter Group as well as the 99th Fighter Squadron, had become dangerous foes of the Axis.

Both units manned by Tuskegee Airmen—the 99th Fighter Squadron and the 332nd Fighter Group—had become experienced combat units, and obviously the men in these units had similar experiences. Their similarities came not just from being black but also from all taking the same route through Tuskegee Army Airfield—through the same arduous selection and training process—to be able to face the Luftwaffe in the skies over Europe. But the two units had developed an unofficial rivalry. The pilots and men of the 99th had been true pioneers, created from the first graduates of the program, some even starting before Tuskegee Army Airfield had been completed. Some of the nonflying members of the unit had been the first black soldiers first to pass through their own training programs at Chanute Field and other locations. They had been in theater since April 1943, fighting their way from North Africa to the Italian peninsula. They tended to look at the other squadrons of the 332nd as a bunch of Johnny-come-latelies—following the trail that the 99th had blazed. And while the 99th Fighter Squadron had been assigned to otherwise white fighter groups and had therefore partially integrated the Air Forces, the 332nd flew as an all-black fighter group. For their part, the pilots in the 332nd did indeed look up to the more experienced pilots of the 99th but wanted to carve out their own glorious record in the air war. The 99th Fighter Squadron had indeed been the first, but sometimes it seemed as if the black press—white newspapers largely ignored both units—was unaware that there was another, larger, black combat unit in the Air Forces.

Thus, the decision from the leaders of the Army Air Forces to move the 99th Fighter Squadron under the operational control of the 332nd Fighter Group was hardly welcome news. Besides the rivalry between the squadrons, the development was also seen as a step backward, solidifying a racially segregated Army Air Forces. All the black combat units were in a single group, flying out of a single airfield. The days of mixed-race groups were over. The change in organization came on July 3, 1944, without much fanfare ("99th Fighter Squadron History," July 1944; "332nd Fighter Group History," July 1944). For the airmen in the 99th, the only good part of the change was that they would again fall under Colonel Davis—a man they all respected and probably the man best suited to bring these proud units together and make them fight as a team. The 99th began moving to the 332nd Fighter Group's airfield at Ramitelli on July 6, and Ramitelli became the only black American airfield in Europe.

Concurrent with the new organization came new aircraft: the P-51 Mustang, one of the best fighters of the war. All four squadrons got the new fighter, with the 99th turning in its P-40s and the 100th, 301st, and 302nd

P-51C-10 42- 103960 Skipper's Darlin' III of Captain Andrew "Jug" Turner, Rami-
telli, Italy, September 1944. Turner was the Commanding Officer of the 100th
Fighter Squadron. The nose and tail of the airplanes were painted red. (U.S. Air
Force)

turning in their P-47s. When they got the P-51s, they had to come up with
a distinctive marking for all planes in the group so that they could identify
each other quickly during combat and also so that bomber crews could
recognize them. The marking had to be something unique to the 332nd
and simple but recognizable. And here, through a seemingly small decision made mostly by using what was available at the time, the reorganized
332nd Fighter Group would acquire its distinctive markings and the nick-
name through which the Tuskegee Airmen would become legendary, all
from a few gallons of red paint.

According to Harry Sheppard, reminiscing many years later, the decision
to paint the tails of the planes red came out of expediency. Their planes
had been marked with several schemes—checkerboards, candy stripes,
and yellow. When the Mustangs came in, the group decided to finally de-
velop a distinct marking. When some of the men got to the supply depot at
Foggia, they found abundant cans of what was called "red insignia paint,"
which was an exceptionally bright shade of red. The men took the paint
back to their base at Ramitelli. They decided to paint the tails, empennage,
trim tabs, and nose spinners with the red paint (Homan & Reilly, 2001).
With bright red tails on their P-51 Mustangs, the 332nd soon became known
throughout the theater as the "Redtails." Many bomber crews and fighter
groups would soon recognize the 332nd by their distinctive red tails, and
the Redtails soon developed a reputation for professionalism and fighting
prowess that Allied airmen, who were often unaware of the skin color of the
men who flew those distinctively marked Mustangs, respected. Although
no one knew it at the time, the war in Europe had less than a year left. That
year would be one of hard fighting as an increasingly desperate Germany

fought savagely against the encroaching Allies. During the hard months ahead, the Tuskegee Airmen would build their reputation even higher as the sight of the Redtails brought confidence to bomber crews and struck terror into the hearts of German pilots.

References

Francis, Charles E. *The Tuskegee Airmen: The Men Who Changed a Nation.* Boston: Branden Publishing, 1997).

Haulman, Daniel L. "Table of 332nd Fighter Group Missions for the Fifteenth Air Force," no. 1. Maxwell Air Force Base, AL: Air Force Historical Research Agency.

Haulman, Daniel L. "Tuskegee Airmen Chronology." Maxwell Air Force Base, AL: Air Force Historical Research Agency.

Headquarters Fifteenth Air Force August 31, 1944. "General Orders Number 2972 Award of the Distinguished Flying Cross." Maxwell Air Force Base, AL: Air Force Historical Research Agency.

"Historical Record of the 99th Fighter Squadron." May 24, 1943. Maxwell Air Force Base, AL: Air Force Historical Research Agency.

"Historical Records." 332nd Fighter Group, March 1–31, 1944. Maxwell Air Force Base, AL: Air Force Historical Research Agency.

Homan, Lynn M., and Thomas Reilly. *Black Knights: The Story of the Tuskegee Airmen.* Gretna, LA: Pelican Publishing, 2001.

MacGregor, Morris, J. *Integration of the Armed Forces, 1940–1965.* Washington, DC: Center for Military History, 1989.

National Museum. http://www.nationalmuseum.af.mil/factsheets/factsheet.asp?id = 8475 (accessed December 1, 2010).

"99th Fighter Squadron History," July 1944; "332nd Fighter Group History," July 1944. Maxwell Air Force Base, AL: Air Force Historical Research Agency.

"99th Fighter Squadron History." November 1943–January 1944.Maxwell Air Force Base, AL: Air Force Historical Research Agency.

"War Diary, 99th Fighter Squadron." November 1, 1943. Maxwell Air Force Base, AL: Air Force Historical Research Agency.

FIVE

A Separate Black Air Force

THE REORGANIZED 332ND FIGHTER GROUP, with four fighter squadrons and supporting units and its base at Ramitelli, had become its own little black air force. In that regard, it surpassed the situation at Tuskegee Army Airfield. All functions of an air base—maintenance, communications, medical, clerical, and weather—were handled by black soldiers. This situation insulated most members of the 332nd, especially the enlisted men, from the everyday indignities most blacks in the military faced, but it was also a perpetuation of the strict military version of "separate but equal." While any shortcomings of the 332nd could be used against all black combat units and black officers, success could also be used to buttress the idea that blacks worked best in segregated units. Despite such risks, the officers and men of the 332nd continued to serve—performing their assigned missions with professionalism and aggressiveness that increasingly marked them as a top-notch outfit. German intelligence had picked up on the existence of the American fighter group manned by blacks, even if the appearance of the pilots was obscured while in the cockpit. The Germans started to refer to the black American fighter pilots as the "black birdmen," or *Schwartz Vogelmenschen*. Through the end of the war, German pilots would learn to respect and even fear these fighting men whom Nazi ideology held should never be educated.

The 332nd flew combat missions almost every day, with some duties becoming routine. On July 6, with the airmen of the 99th Fighter Squadron adjusting to their new surroundings, the other three squadrons performed another escort mission for the 47th Bombardment Wing on a mission to hit targets in northern Italy. The mission went off without any difficulties; no enemy aircraft were encountered ("Narrative Mission Report no. 8"). On July 12, the same three squadrons performed a similar escort mission for the heavy bombers of the 49th Bombardment Wing. This time, the

Tuskegee Airmen attending a premission briefing in Ramitelli, Italy, March 1945. Photo by Toni Frissell. (Library of Congress)

pilots of the 332nd spotted several enemy fighters in the distance as the formation approached the target area. On the return trip, the enemy fighters attacked. When one group of Fw-190s attacked the bombers, Lieutenant Harold E. Sawyer scored another kill when he was able to get behind one enemy fighter and open up with his machine guns. A few minutes later, squadron commander Captain Joseph Elsberry saw 16 Fw-190s making a run to hit the bombers. He ordered his men to drop their external fuel tanks, and the squadron turned to meet the attacking Germans. The Germans turned away from their attack and attempted to flee. Elsberry scored one probable and three definite kills in the ensuring combat. In doing so, he became the first black American pilot to make three kills in a single day. He would not be the last, nor would these kills be his last. In all, the 332nd was credited with four kills that day, but it came at a price: Lieutenant George M. Rhodes had to bail out of his airplane near Viterbo, while three of the bombers were lost to enemy fighters (Haulman, "Table of 332nd Fighter Group").

On July 16, the pilots of the 332nd had more opportunities to prove their mettle against Axis pilots. The 332nd, minus the 99th, was assigned to fly a fighter sweep over an area that included Vienna. The skies over a large area around Vienna were thick with flak, but the mission continued. As the formation left the Vienna area, a strange aircraft was seen approaching a stray B-24 bomber that had fallen behind the formation. On investigation, the approaching aircraft was identified as a Macchi C 205 V Vetro, an Italian aircraft considered the best Italian fighter of the war. While Italy had signed an armistice with the Allies and had later declared war on Germany, this Italian plane was definitely not friendly. It most likely belonged to the air force of the so-called Italian Socialist Republic, a puppet state created by Nazi Germany in northern Italy under the nominal leadership of Mussolini after he had had been rescued from the Italian authorities by German commandos. Two Mustangs from the 332nd were soon on the strange aircraft and filled it with American bullets. The fascist fighter then struck a mountain and exploded. The Tuskegee Airmen then spotted a second Macchi fighter, which soon joined its companion as another kill credited to the 332nd ("Narrative Mission Report no. 26").

A definite tipping point in the air war had passed. The quality of Allied pilots continued to increase, while attrition had taken a heavy toll on the quality of the German pilots. The German practice of keeping their best pilots on the front lines until they were killed contributed to the declining quality of German pilots. Germany continued to train new pilots, but each new pilot had less and less experience before facing the now seasoned veterans of the 332nd. On a mission on July 17 escorting the 306th Bombardment Wing on a mission to hit targets near Avignon, in a part of France still under German occupation, the pilots of the 332nd came up against 19 Me-109s. Three of the more aggressive enemy pilots made a move to hit the bombers. As a result, Lieutenants Ralph Wilkins, Robert Smith, and Luther Smith each scored a kill when the three enemy planes slammed into the ground. In their after-action interviews, the pilots of the 332nd spoke of the enemy's apparent inexperience and lack of aggression ("Narrative Mission Report no. 27"). On the same mission, Lieutenant Maceo A. Harris escorted one damaged bomber back to its base on the French island of Corsica, using hand signals to communicate to the bomber pilot the damage to the bomber, as the bomber's radios were out. The bomber pilot was able to successfully belly-land at a base, with only the tail gunner sustaining injuries. Apparently being posted on the French-owned island had influenced the bomber pilots stationed there, as Lieutenant Harris received a kiss on the each cheek "after the manner of the French" from the appreciative pilot and copilot of the stricken craft (Homan & Reilly, 2001).

As the summer wore on, the pilots of the 332nd scored more and more victories, taking an increasing toll on the enemy pilots. Each mission could be a physically and mentally exhausting experience for a fighter pilot, but the pilots understood that all of them would not be going home until Nazi Germany was driven to its knees. The mission on July 18 was an especially good mission for gaining aerial victories, but such days were not uncommon. Three of the squadrons—the 100th, 301st, and 302nd—were escorting the bombers of the 5th Bombardment Wing on a mission to take out the Memmingen Airdrome. As the formation passed over northern Italy, between 30 and 35 Me-109s approached. When the clash ended a few minutes, nine enemy airplanes were burning on the ground, and another was seen leaving the area with heavy damage. Having dropped their external fuel tanks, the 21 Mustangs that had engaged the enemy fighters had to return to Ramitelli, while the remaining 36 continued on with the bombers. Near the target area, a large number of German fighters were spotted, but only four Fw-190s attacked. Minutes later, two of the Fw-190s were burning on the ground, and the other two enemy fighters were fleeing (Haulman, "The Battle of Memmingen"). One of the bombers had succumbed to flak. In the day's totals, the 332nd was credited with 12 enemy kills, but it came at a high price; they lost three of their own, and 15 of the bombers were lost to enemy fighters ("Narrative Mission Report no. 28").

The 332nd spent the remainder of the summer and autumn of 1944 performing almost daily missions. Most of the missions were escorting heavy bombers against strategic targets in areas of Europe still under German control. They usually escorted bombers from the 49th, 55th, and 304th Bomb Wings. Flak took the biggest toll on bombers and escorts, but German fighters could still be dangerous. However, the pilots of the 332nd usually gave more than they took, and many German planes would go down after coming into contact with the Tuskegee Airmen. The 332nd still performed the occasional bombing and strafing mission in between bomber escort missions. On August 12, the Tuskegee Airmen were engaged in destroying radar stations along southern France in support of Operation Dragoon, the Allied invasion of southern France. The four squadrons of the 332nd split up to hit different sites at Sete, Montpellier, Marseilles, and Cape Couronne. The combat turned out to be quite hot, and six airplanes of the 332nd went down, while several aircraft made it back to Ramitelli with extensive damage. Lieutenant Richard D. Macon's engine burst into flames after taking a hit from flak. Macon passed out but somehow managed to eject and land in a farmer's field, where he was soon captured. Lieutenant Alexander Jefferson was also captured that day, as was Captain Robert H. Daniels. Jefferson later recalled that he was captured by the Germans almost immediately after he hit the ground, but Daniels had to be fished out of the sea by the Germans. Two days after being captured, they were taken first to French city of Toulon and then to Marseilles, where they boarded trains bound for Germany. During the trip, they could see firsthand the effects of the air campaign against the German transportation system. They were generally left alone by the civilians, but they did notice that many Germans stared at them, Jefferson and Daniels surmising that they were among the first black people many Germans had ever seen. During his interrogation, Jefferson, like other captured members of the 332nd before and after, was surprised to find that the Germans had a booklet about the 332nd and often knew more details about the unit than members did (Francis, 1997).

After spending a few days at Wetzlar, about 75 miles from Frankfort, Jefferson eventually arrived at Stalag Luft III, where he lived with nine white American officers in a 16- by 16-foot room While the Germans were fighting a bitter war in which millions of civilians had been killed, in general the Germans followed the Geneva Convention regarding the treatment of prisoners of war, at least in the war against Great Britain and the United States. Captured Allied airmen were turned over to the Luftwaffe, the German air force, for internment. And despite the Nazi's low opinion of blacks, the Luftwaffe's *Stalags*, or prisoner-of-war camps, were racially integrated. Enlisted men were kept separate from officers, but in one of the ironies of race relations during the war, black American pilots in Italy were segregated from white units, but as prisoners of the Nazis, American airmen were racially integrated. Jefferson later recalled that the other American officers held prisoner treated him as an equal during their captivity, with their eating and living together without any animosity. Although he knew of other black American officers in the camp complex, the way the camp was divided kept him from any direct contact. Despite some cold and hungry days, forced marches, and uncertainty over their fate as the war drew to a close, Jefferson and the others were eventually liberated by the Third Army on April 29, 1945, just days before the war ended. He and Daniels were back in the United States on June 2, 1945, and happy to have lived through the war (Francis, 1997).

Despite losses in men and machines, the 332nd continued to fight. Beginning on August 16, they attacked the Ploesti oil refineries in Romania and followed up with more attacks on Ploesti over the next several days as well as attacks on refineries at Osivecin and Kornenburg. Without oil and gasoline, the German armed forces and economy could do little, and oil facilities were a common target for Allied bombers. But the attacks came at a price; the 332nd lost one fighter to flak while escorting bombers on the August 16. As the formation approached the target, the flak was intense, and the pilots of the 332nd watched as one of the B-24s exploded ("Narrative Mission Report no. 53"). On the repeat mission the next day, nine of the bombers were lost to flak ("Narrative Mission Report no. 54"). Enemy fighters were bad, but against them a pilot had a chance, an opportunity to match skills and wits with an enemy in a deadly duel. But flak—that was feared far more. Enemy gunners on the ground simply set the flak to explode at a certain altitude where spotters had calculated the approaching Allied formations to be and fired upward, filling the skies with deadly explosions. Bombers and fighters approaching a target were locked into a pattern from which they could not deviate and had to fly through the flak screen, and the odds usually favored the destruction of some of the bombers and fighters from the insidious effects of flak. Flak was a mindless killer, and surviving it was more of a lottery than a game of skill. Only the rigid discipline imposed on pilots by the rigid training of the Army Air Forces and a man's own intestinal fortitude gave them the ability to fly through that aerial version of hell. But despite the flak, the mission continued. Fighter pilots would relish the opportunity to have a fighting chance against enemy airplanes.

October 1944 would prove to be a costly month for the 332nd, with 15 pilots from the 332nd either killed or taken prisoner during the month. On October 4, the 332nd began attacks on targets in Greece, strafing airfields at Tatoi, Kalamaki, and Eleusis. The attacks on enemy airfields worked best when the enemy was surprised and the enemy aircraft were still on the ground. The Allied fighters would sweep in and sometimes use their 500-pound bombs to destroy hangers or make holes in runways, but ideally their machine guns would destroy enemy aircraft while they remained parked on the ground. Nine enemy fighters were destroyed on the ground that day (Haulman, "Table of 332nd Fighter Group"). An enemy aircraft burning while it sat on the ground would not later have to be faced in the air. At Tatoi, Captain Erwin Lawrence succumbed to ground fire, crashing and burning on the airfield. Lieutenant Kenneth Williams was somewhat luckier, surviving a crash landing and spending the remainder of the war in a German prisoner-of-war camp.

Autumn continued with similar missions. On October 12, during a mission to strafe railroad traffic from Budapest to Bratislavia, the group destroyed nine enemy fighters in the air and 26 enemy aircraft on the ground. The next day, the 332nd flew in support of the 304th Bombardment Wing in an attack on the Blechhammer oil refinery. After the bombing run had been made, the pilots of the 332nd had some latitude to seek targets of opportunity for strafing. While strafing an ammunition dump in Yugoslavia, Lieutenant William W. Green was shot down. He was able to avoid the Germans after he landed and was eventually found by Yugoslavian anti-Nazi partisan fighters who hid him and eventually smuggled him to Soviet forces, who turned him over to the Americans. Walter D. Westmoreland, who was the nephew of Secretary Walter White of the National Association for the Advancement of Colored People, was not as fortunate. His plane went down on the way back from Blechhammer and crashed into a tree, and he was listed as missing in action for a few days until his death was confirmed (Homan & Reilly, 2001).

As autumn continued, the weather became colder and wetter. On the coastal plains of central and southern Italy, snow was rare, but the climate could still make for less-than-ideal conditions. Men who had grown up in Chicago or other cities in the northern United States did not find winter in Italy all that harsh, but in Italy they were spending the winter largely in tents rather than in solid houses or apartments. For men from the southern United States, the climate of Italy in the winter felt cold, wet, and unpleasant. The airfield at Ramitelli was a wartime post, created in haste and with little time or funds to improve the physical structure of the post. The most important element on the post was the repair facilities for the airplanes; for the living quarters of the men and officers, tents would suffice. Of course, the Tuskegee Airmen understood that their lot was far better than the infantrymen slogging across northern France at that time, but still, like humans everywhere, they attempted to use what they could find to improve their lot. Scrap wood was soon hammered into little cabins and other attempts to make the site more comfortable. Some members of the 332nd, through skill and luck and a little wheeling and dealing, were able to create relatively comfortable lodgings.

War is often a mixture of mind-numbing boredom interspersed with moments of extreme stress and even terror. In an Army Air Forces fighter unit, ground crews would spend many anxious hours beginning from when the fighters lifted off on a mission until when they returned. Crew chiefs, usually a senior enlisted man with a high level of technical expertise on the mechanics of the aircraft, led a team of skilled technicians who kept each plane in top condition. Crew chiefs often thought of the airplane as their own, with the pilot allowed to use it. While pilots, as officers, had authority over the enlisted men on the ground crew, usually a stronger, more personal bond formed between officer pilots and enlisted grounds crews, and crews would send their plane and pilot off on a mission doing all they could to ensure that everything on the airplane worked properly. Then all they could do was pass the anxious hours until the plane returned. Ground crews usually had little or no information on how a mission went until after the airplanes had returned and the pilots gave their debriefings, both official and unofficial. Time between missions could be tedious, with enlisted men catching up on tasks, sleeping, reading, or playing sports. When the returning planes were first sighted in the distance, ground crews would anxiously count the returning planes and try to identify the plane they were assigned to. On recognition of a crew's plane, they would breathe a sigh of relief and then prepare to service and repair the plane, making it ready for the next mission, which could be later that same day. Sometimes the damage to a returning airplane was extensive, meaning long stretches of work and missed sleep to make it ready for the next mission. Occasionally, a wounded pilot would be able to land his craft but would have to be gently pulled from his airplane, loaded onto a stretcher, and taken to the base hospital in the hope that the doctors could save him from the effects of shrapnel, enemy bullets, or myriad other hazards pilots faced on each mission. If the plane did not return, the crew could do little but question the other pilots about the fate of theirs; did he land at another base with mechanical problems, was he on the run behind enemy lines after getting shot down, or was he dead? The tension could be unbearable, but if the worst had happened and their plane and its pilot would not be returning, there was little for the grounds crew to do but clean their tools and wait to be assigned to another aircraft.

To break the monotony and stress, the Air Forces—and the army as a whole—encouraged sports, with top competitors from each unit competing in larger competitions. The men played outdoor sports like baseball and football when the weather permitted. Boxing proved especially popular, and the 332nd held place of pride in the late autumn of 1944, when Technical Sergeant Burnley from the 99th Fighter Squadron became the champion middle-weight fighter for the entire 15th Air Force. The army tried to provide some of the niceties of home for the men while in theater, and the 332nd was not neglected. The men got special holiday meals that tried, as much as possible given the circumstances, to replicate traditional Thanksgiving

A pilot from the 332nd Fighter Group signing the Form One Book,
indicating any discrepancies of aircraft, prior to take off, 1945.
(Library of Congress)

and Christmas dinners. The United Services Organization, better known
as the USO, brought professional entertainers from the United States to
entertain the troops, offering shows that proved especially popular. Since
most of the officers in the 332nd had at least a college degree, officers
began offering classes to the enlisted men of the group, holding classes
in foreign languages, mathematics, and current events. The program was
dubbed the *Naptha University* (332nd Fighter Group, April 1945). Despite
the sometimes pleasant distractions, in the Army Air Forces the mission
always came first, and classes, entertainment, sporting events, and the like
could always be postponed or canceled when a mission came up. Keeping
the aircraft flying was the primary reason for the ground crews to be there,
and many periods would consist of little but long hours working on the airplanes broken only by a few hours of sleep and a few bites of food.

Although the 332nd was heavily involved in the war, fighting on the front lines against the Luftwaffe, slights and insults from white soldiers continued to be part of the existence of the Tuskegee Airmen. One incident in late December 1944 underscored the entrenched attitudes that many whites had about blacks regardless of rank or service. A rare snowstorm covered much of southern Italy, while the airfield at Ramitelli remained clear. A bomber squadron that was based in southern Italy was forced to land at the base and spend a few days there until the weather cleared. Bombers carried enlisted crewmembers as well as an officer pilot, copilot, navigator, and bombardier. The 99th hosted their guests as best they could, finding sleeping spots for all and providing food for them. The post was temporarily crowded, but the men and officers of the 332nd all worked to help get through a difficult period. One of the duties of Lieutenant Louis Purnell was to censor the mail of enlisted men on the post, a common practice during war to make sure no information that an enemy could use was sent out. One letter, from a white sergeant who served as a gunner on one of the bombers particularly stood out. The writer was depressed that he was spending Christmas away from his family, and, worse, he was "at a nigger airfield, sleeping in nigger beds, and eating nigger food." Lieutenant Purnell knew that if the men in the 332nd saw the letter, there would be trouble, so he said nothing about it. A few days later, when the bombers were preparing to leave the base, he went up to the sergeant and asked the sergeant if he had forgotten anything. The sergeant answered all the questions from the lieutenant with "nos" and "yeahs," neglecting the "sir" required by military regulations when an enlisted soldier addressed an officer. Lieutenant Purnell reminded him of military customs and regulations regarding how a sergeant was to address an officer. He then mentioned that perhaps "sleeping in nigger beds, staying at a nigger field, and eating nigger food" was not so bad and then turned away. Lieutenant had been privy to read the innermost sentiments of one bigot, but he suspected that such racist sentiments were widespread in the army (Homan & Reilly, 2001, pp. 85-87). To risk their lives in a common effort as Americans knowing the hatred that existed in the hearts of some of their fellow Americans on account of skin color was a heavy burden for the Tuskegee Airmen to carry, but regardless of the prejudices of others, the officers and men of the 332nd Fighter Group continued to carry out their assignments professionally, striking terror into the hearts of their enemies, both German pilots and the upholders of Jim Crow.

Missions came almost daily, and on many days more than one mission would be flown. On November 4, the 332nd flew three missions, including one escorting the 5th Bombardment Wing in an attack on the Regensburg/ Winterhafen oil storage facility. All missions were without incident (Haulman, "Table of 332nd Fighter Group"). On November 16, they were performing a similar mission for the 304th during an attack on Munich, with two kills but one bomber lost. On November 19, the pilots of the 332nd strafed railroads, canals, and highways in the Gyor-Vienna-Esztergom area, with the loss of two planes (Haulman, "Table of 332nd Fighter Group"). The phosphorous on each tracer round allowed the pilot to follow where his bullets were going, but the burning phosphorus also caused the bullet to ignite any fuel that it hit. When a pilot strafed an oil barge or other large fuel tank, the pilot often had to pull up sharply and would spend a few terrifying moments as the exploding balls of flames poured into the sky around the attacking fighter. While the 332nd was destroying a lot of railroad cars, they were also getting credit for destroying much horse-drawn transport, a sign that the attacks on the oil industry had taken a heavy toll on German transportation. During the attack on the Danube area of Hungary, Lieutenants Roger Gaiter and Quitman Walker became prisoners of war. Gaiter later recalled that after his capture he was put with six white American airmen in a similar circumstance and marched off to captivity by German guards. Local civilians (Hungarians who were allied with the Germans) often attacked the American airmen, taking out their frustrations on the prisoners. The German guards usually did nothing to protect their prisoners, and Gaiter remembers one American captain being rendered unconscious by a thrown brick that hit him in the head. The civilians in Vienna were equally vindictive, but Gaiter managed to survive his ordeal (Homan & Reilly, 2001).

Most of the missions for the 332nd in December were supporting the 5th, 55th, and 304th Bombardment Wings, hitting targets—oil facilities—all over the Third Reich. On December 9, on a mission escorting B-17s on an attack on Brux, the formation crossed over the Regensburg area, home of the factories where the Messerschmitt fighters were built. Because of the importance of those factories to the German war effort, the area was heavily defended and a frequent target of Allied bombers. As they crossed that dangerous airspace, the pilots of the 332nd noticed a lone aircraft approaching at high speed. The strange aircraft had no propeller and could move much faster than the P-51 Mustangs flown by the 332nd. The strange aircraft was an Me-262 and was the first sighting of a jet fighter for most of the Americans. The jet zipped by the formation at a speed that none of the pilots in the 332nd had even seen before. They fired a few bursts without hitting it before the Me-262 vanished into the clouds as quickly as it had come. Two airplanes from the 332nd did not make it back to base (Homan & Reilly, 2001).

As Germany was running out of men, resources, and time, Hitler put more of his faith into what he called "wonder weapons," weapons of such sophistication that they would be able to overcome the enormous power of the Allies. One of these was the Me-262, the first practical jet fighter fielded by any nation. One of the main factors in giving any fighter an edge over another was its speed, and the Me-262 was faster by a wide margin than any fighter flown by the Allies. It carried four 30-millimeter cannons in its nose—if it got behind a Mustang and opened up, there was little chance the American would survive. The Me-262 had some weaknesses, though. The Germans could never produce it in large enough numbers to seriously threaten the air superiority that the Allies had gained by that point in the war. In addition, its two jet engines burned fuel at an incredible rate, meaning that the Me-262 could not spend a lot of time in the air patrolling or even fighting. It had to take off, find its enemy immediately, and engage. After that first sighting, other Me-262s also harassed the formation. As with the first one, they were able to avoid the bullets from the Mustangs but were not able to hang around for very long. Still, the knowledge that these vastly superior aircraft were out there struck an ominous note as 1944 drew to a close. But while the Tuskegee Airmen continued to face a stubborn and dangerous enemy over the skies in Europe, their fellow black pilots in the Air Forces back in the United States would face an equally stubborn and dangerous enemy—Jim Crow.

In part from the increased acceptance of the idea of black fighter pilots due to the success of the 332nd Fighter Group in the skies over Europe, blacks in the United States wanted to see an expansion of opportunities for blacks in military aviation. Conspicuously absent were black bomber units. With the Army Air Forces doctrinally and culturally committed to the strategic bombing as the ultimate expression of airpower, blacks wanted to be involved in this important aspect of the war effort. They wanted the 332nd to be true pioneers, the first of an expanding number of black pilots and aircrews. The Air Forces certainly had enough of a talent pool to draw from to create more black flying units. The Army Air Forces had a priority in claiming the highest-caliber men inducted by Selective Service, a situation that other branches increasingly found indefensible. While the demands on air crew members, pilots, and even ground crews required men of high intelligence and physical fitness, just why the Air Forces should also have the highest-qualified enlisted men to serve as cooks, clerks, and security forces was not appreciated by the other branches. The Air Forces maintained enormously high standards for men selected to undergo pilot training but still found itself in the awkward situation of maintaining a large backload of highly qualified black men without the facilities to train them in the segregated system.

Another problem was the lack of positions for black pilots once they completed their training. With a single black flying group, once the training pipeline through Tuskegee had filled all flying position in the 332nd and enough replacements existed to fill slots caused by death, capture, or combat veterans who rotated home, a number of qualified black pilots began to accumulate at Tuskegee. The creation of a second black group would provide a host of new positions to be filled by qualified black pilots. However, it could also be seen as a step in the wrong direction—toward the entrenchment of segregated flying units in the Army Air Forces. Blacks such as Judge Hastie and white opponents of segregation had only grudgingly accepted the creation of the segregated 99th and later the entire 332nd on the idea that they would show the military and all Americans that blacks were intellectually and physically suited for the demands of combat flying. That proven, ideally the Army Air Forces would have simply eliminated segregation within its structure and opened all positions to men based on their abilities without regard to color. Such a response would have eliminated many of the bottlenecks and inefficiencies in the current two-race structure. But the army was not yet ready for what was then seen as such a drastic change. Instead, the Army Air Forces opted to expand flying positions for blacks by the creation of a medium bombardment group, which, like the 332ndFighter Group, would train at segregated facilities in the United States before deploying to a combat theater to perform its missions, flying from mostly black forward bases. Again, the great dilemma for racists—having black officers in command of or even in contact with white enlisted men—would be avoided at all costs.

Bombardment missions differed greatly from fighter missions. While the 332nd Fighter Group occasionally performed ground interdiction missions—basically tactical bombing missions—such missions were the focus of a medium bomber group. Heavy bombers attacked strategic targets, which were in theory the elements of an enemy economy that allowed that nation to wage war. Strategic bombers flew missions to destroy factories, key transportation points, harbors, and the like. However, experiences in Germany had led the Americans and British in Europe and later the Americans alone in the Pacific to simply target cities. Medium bombers had different missions from heavy bombers. The Army Air Forces and its predecessor the Army Air Corps had never been keen on any mission aside from strategic bombing, but structural realities—the Air Forces were still part of the army—forced the Air Forces to also perform tactical bombing missions. Tactical bombing employed a variety of aircraft from small, single-seat fighter bombers up to two-engine medium bombers. The most common of the medium bombers was the B-25 Mitchell, a respected aircraft that first won fame in April 1942 when Colonel "Jimmy" Doolittle led the first bombing raid on Japan in a secret mission that launched the Mitchells from an aircraft carrier in a largely symbolic mission to disgrace the Japanese military and let Americans know their country was striking back. But most medium bomber missions were less dramatic if not less dangerous. Medium bombers normally attacked railroad lines, supply centers, concentration areas, and bridges used by the enemy closer to the battlefields. Unlike strategic bombers, the medium bombers were expected to have a direct impact on the battlefield. While such missions were not what the leadership of the Air Forces wanted, ground commanders and ground troops understood their importance.

The 477th Bombardment Group was initially constituted on May 13, 1943, and activated on June 1 at MacDill Field, Florida (Haulman, "Tuskegee Airmen Chronology"). But this early incarnation of the 477th did not include Tuskegee Airmen as pilots. The few airmen who were assigned to it were white, but it never was fully manned and never became operational. The 477th and its four squadrons were all inactivated on August 25, 1943. But the leaders of the Army Air Forces were under pressure to create more black combat units and had decided to create a black bombardment group. To train the bomber pilots, several twin-engine AT-10 aircraft were brought to Tuskegee Airfield. After initial multiengine training on the AT-10s, the cadets transitioned to the TB-25 Mitchell, which was a modified training version of the medium bomber.

While all potential Army Air Forces pilots underwent the same precadet flight training, mostly through the Civilian Pilot Training Program or War Training Service, and the same course for commissioning, much of the advanced flight training was different. Bomber pilots required a different set of skills. Whereas a fighter pilot was alone in his cockpit, a bomber pilot commanded a crew of both officers and enlisted men. A fighter pilot, once in actual combat with enemy aircraft, was expected to show initiative and aggressiveness, working perhaps in pairs, to kill enemy fighters. A bomber pilot was expected to remain in formation no matter how many enemy fighters attacked the formation or the density of the flak exploding all around. A fighter pilot fired his own machine guns or dropped his own small bombs, whereas a bomber pilot counted on the skills of his enlisted crewmen to defend the aircraft with machine gun fire and on the skill a bombardier officer to put the bombs on the intended targets. And, of course, the aircraft used for bombing were far different than fighters. Fighter aircraft were mostly single-engine airplanes able to turn, climb, and dive quickly and sharply, while bomber aircraft had two or four engines and were designed for their ability to fly relatively high and fast, carry a heavy load of bombs, and continue to fly after taking a beating from the enemy.

By December 1943, the program at Tuskegee Army Airfield was producing pilots certified in twin-engine flying, and with no black bombardment groups, such graduates would do little but sit around at Tuskegee waiting for an assignment until an actual black bombardment group was created. Finally, the 477th Bombardment Group was resurrected on January 15, 1944, along with one of its squadrons: the 616th at Godman Field, Kentucky (Haulman, "Tuskegee Airmen Chronology"). The other three squadrons—the 617th, 618th, and 619th—were activated individually in April and May, with the 618th and 619th initially based at Atterbury Field, Indiana. The 477th was assigned to the First Air Force. Apparently, the 332nd "experiment" had been judged a success, and, as Mrs. Roosevelt had declared two years earlier, blacks could fly airplanes.

The 477th Medium Bombardment Group was equipped with the B-25 Mitchell bomber, but the war ended before they saw action. (U.S. Air Force)

Despite the endorsement of the First Lady and the proven record of the Tuskegee Airmen in Europe, entrenched prejudices would continue to hamper the development of consistent, fair, or efficient policies toward black airmen. The Air Forces leadership apparently saw the creation of the 477th and all black combat units as a response to political pressure and a problem for the Army Air Forces rather than a potential source of combat power. The commanding general of the Army Air Forces, General Arnold, had only grudgingly accepted the Tuskegee "Experiment" and tried to end expansion of black units through the creation of the 477th before it actually formed (Gropeman, 1978). Unlike the record of achievement of the 332nd in combat against the enemy in the skies over Europe, the 477th would be plagued by problems, and the war ended before the 477th entered combat during World War II. Almost all the problems stemmed from the Army Air Forces' commitment to a segregated force, which created problems in training the officers and enlisted men needed for the larger crews required for bomber groups and in finding a suitable locations for group training on the bigger airplanes. Tuskegee Army Airfield was adequate, although barely, for individual training on multiengine bombers but not suitable for group training on the medium bombers.

While the limitations of the facilities at Tuskegee were problematic, equally problematic was the individual commitment of some white commanders to upholding all the traditions of Jim Crow and segregation on military bases. Highly intelligent and highly skilled black men—men who had earned commissions in the armed forces of the United States and some of whom had already served in combat with the 332nd Fighter Group or the 99th Fighter Squadron—found being expected to accept the second-class treatment inherent in segregation intolerable. After the pilots for the 477th took their individual flight training at Tuskegee, with some earning their wings and their commissions and others being retrained from single-engine airplanes to multiengine rating, they joined the 477th at Selfridge Field, Michigan, for collective training. Selfridge Field was near Detroit, Michigan. During the war years, Detroit was simmering with racial tensions, as the growth of war industries in the city had brought a large influx of black workers. In late June 1943, rumors and summer heat ignited a riot between blacks and whites that soon overwhelmed the police and State Troops, requiring the army to send in federal soldiers to quell the conflict. In one ugly incident on Selfridge, a white colonel, possibly while drunk, shot a black private on the post. His sentence after a court-martial was a reduction to his permanent rank of captain. The incident and slight punishment brought a response in the form of a letter to the editor of *Time* magazine from a group of most likely black enlisted soldiers—their names withheld—undergoing training at Chanute, stating that they would not want such a man to ever command them (*Time*, 1943). When the black airmen of the 477th reported to Selfridge, General Hunter, the commander of the First Air Force, welcomed them by reminding them that blacks were not the social equals of whites, that he would not tolerate the mixing of the races, and that only white officers would be permitted to use the officers' club. He also made it clear that he would not tolerate any "race problems" and that any black officer protesting the situation would be "classed as an agitator" and dealt with (Warren, 1995). The 477th was under the command of Colonel Robert R. Selway Jr., a regular Air Corps officer and a pilot of great experience who had formally commanded the 332nd while it was still training in the United States but who was white, something that was resented by the black pilots of the 477th. The racial tensions in the 477th continued to grow, with incidents that might have looked minor to outsiders slowly growing to a crisis point. That point was not far away.

The commitment of the Army Air Forces and the entire military to segregation caused gross inefficiencies in the training and assignment of these highly qualified black men. The Air Forces maintained a large backlog of men awaiting training at Tuskegee Army Airfield, but the Tuskegee program had limited capacity. The Tuskegee program had by the end of 1943 finally been able to produce enough pilots for the 99th and the 332nd and had built up a small surplus, but the creation of a bombardment group increased the problems with training several times over. The planes of the 99th and 332nd were single-man fighters, requiring only a pilot when on a mission. Bombers, on the other hand, required a crew of about 11, of which two were pilots, while the navigator and bombardier were also highly trained commissioned officers. Additionally, bomber crews included enlisted men serving as radioman and gunners. In order to find enough navigators and bombardiers, the Air Forces took black men awaiting pilot training and sent them for training as navigator-bombers. This situation was unusual and a poor use of talent. All candidates for flight service were given an examination that measured a potential airman's aptitude for various specialties. The scores, known as "stanine scores," were different for men with the potential to be good pilots than for those who showed an aptitude for serving as navigators or bombardiers. The Air Forces normally assigned men to either pilot training or navigator-bomber training based on these scores. But because of the backlog of black men awaiting pilot training, the Air Forces decided to train them as navigators and bombers instead. But this inefficiency was only a symptom of a flawed system.

At Selfridge, the officers and men of the 477th found the petty annoyances and indignities of Jim Crow were alive and well. Segregation of on-base facilities for officers ran counter to the army's official policies on the subject, and the contradictions in policies and practices and in ideals and realities came to a head in the 477th and called into question the commitment of the Air Forces to an increase in the number of black combat flying groups but, more important, whether the Army Air Forces and the U.S. military as a whole really accepted blacks not just as pilots but as officers as well. In theory, to become an officer meant becoming part of an elite fraternity of military leaders. A commission as an army officer came from the president of the United States, with the "advice and consent" of the Senate. A commission could be regular, which went mostly to West Point graduates, reserve, or temporary but made no reference to skin color. When an officer was on active duty, a commission was a commission. Therefore, a club on post for commissioned officers should have been open to all commissioned officers. But the army also had a tradition against social interaction between blacks and whites, and an officers' club was a social setting, and segregation was to be enforced. In the army of the period, the officers' club played an important role in bonding. Normally, a commander would go to the club after the end of the duty day, especially on the weekends, and drink. All the officers who served under him were expected to join him for drinks and not leave until the "old man" did. But with Colonel Selway and the squadron commanders drinking at the white club, this important part of the military's culture would be broken in the 477th. The army eventually sided with the black officers and reprimanded Colonel William Boyd, the commander of Selfridge Field, for not allowing black officers into the officers' club (Murphy, 1997). But the problems with officers' clubs were far from over.

On May 6, 1944, the entire 477th moved to Godman Field, Kentucky, in part to remove it from the racially charged environment around Detroit. Godman Field was not a good choice, as its short runways were unsuited for the B-25J bombers of the 477th, which made realistic training more difficult. Godman Field was part of Fort Knox, though, a large army post. Godman Field had a single officers' club, which was open to black officers. However, it was hardly an integrated club. White officers on Godman Field were allowed into the club on Fort Knox as guests, and thus de facto segregated officer's clubs were maintained. Other problems ate at the morale of the men in the 477th. The continuing shortage of personnel assigned to the 477th made many of the assigned officers doubt that the Air Forces ever intended to actually commit the 477th to combat. The 477th was supposed to have 270 officers serving on the planes, but by the middle of the spring of 1944, the 477th still had only 175 actually assigned. Probably the most troubling for the men of the 477th was that black combat veterans who came to the unit from the 332nd were not assigned to leadership positions. Some former fighter pilots, men who had real combat experience—often more than the white pilots assigned to train the 477th—had cross trained for the medium bombers. But when they reported into the 477th, they were treated little different from other pilots who came straight from their initial training. All leadership positions at the group and squadron level—and even on the base—continued to be held by white men (Osur, 1986).

Throughout much of its existence, the 477th remained plagued by a shortage of trained officers and enlisted men. The shortage of trained personnel was caused mainly by the Air Forces' refusal to open other training facilities to black pilots and navigators. The Tuskegee program simply did not have enough capacity to meet the enlarged demand. The refusal to allow black airmen to undergo initial flight training at other bases created the absurd situation of a large backload of black men qualified to begin the training, while black combat units in the Army Air Forces—the 477th Bombardment Group and even the 332nd Fighter Group—labored under a shortage of trained men.

For the next year, the 477th continued collective training, and all the while tensions in the unit continued to build, as the black pilots increasingly resented the race-based petty annoyances to which they were subjected. At the same time, the continued uncertainty over whether they would actually deploy and the poor training facilities continued to sap their morale. Despite the problems, concrete steps were taken to prepare the 477th for eventual deployment. On June 15, 1944, the Air Forces activated the 387th Service Group at Daniel Field, Georgia. The 387th would later include the 590th Air Material Squadron and the 602nd Air Engineering Squadron and was slated to provide support for the 477th (Haulman, "Tuskegee Airmen Chronology"). The 387th moved to Godman Field in January 1945 to join the 477th ("387th Air Service Group History"). The Air Forces was planning the 477th to function essentially as another mini black air force, similar to the situation for the 332nd at Ramitelli, Italy. Questions lingered, though, over the seriousness of the Air Forces on deploying a black bombardment group and over whether the Army Air Forces was more committed to upholding Jim Crow than it was to treating officers and men fairly.

References

Francis, Charles E. *The Tuskegee Airmen: The Men Who Changed a Nation.* Boston: Branden Publishing, 1997.

Gropeman, Alan L. *The Air Force Integrates, 1945–1964.* Washington, DC: Office of Air Force History, 1978.

Haulman, Daniel L. "The Battle of Memmingen, 18 July 1944." Maxwell Air Force Base, AL: Air Force Historical Research Agency.

Haulman, Daniel. "Table of 332nd Fighter Group Missions for the Fifteenth Air Force," no. 23. Maxwell Air Force Base, AL: Air Force Historical Research Agency. (See also Missing Air Crew Reports 6894, 6895, and 7034.)

Haulman, Daniel. "Tuskegee Airmen Chronology." Maxwell Air Force Base, AL: Air Force Historical Research Agency.

Hitler, Adolf. *Main Kampf.* Translated by Ralph Manheim. Boston: Houghton Mifflin, 1943.

Homan, Lynn M., and Thomas Reilly, *Black Knights: The Story of the Tuskegee Airmen.* Gretna, LA: Pelican Publishing, 2001.

Murphy, John D. "The Freeman Field Mutiny: A Study in Leadership." Unpublished master's thesis, Air Command and Staff College, 1997.

"Narrative Mission Report No. 8." July 6, 1944. Maxwell Air Force Base, AL: Air Force Historical Research Agency.

"Narrative of Mission Report No. 26." July 16, 1944.. Maxwell Air Force Base, AL: Air Force Historical Research Agency.

"Narrative Mission Report No. 27." July 17, 1944. Maxwell Air Force Base, AL: Air Force Historical Research Agency.

"Narrative Mission Report No. 28." July 18, 1944. Maxwell Air Force Base, AL: Air Force Historical Research Agency.

"Narrative of Mission Report No. 53." August 16, 1944.. Maxwell Air Force Base, AL: Air Force Historical Research Agency.

"Narrative of Mission Report No. 54." August 17, 1944.. Maxwell Air Force Base, AL: Air Force Historical Research Agency.

Osur, Alan M. *Blacks in the Army Air Forces during World War II: The Problems of Race Relations.* Washington, DC: Office of Air Force History, 1986.

"387th Air Service Group History." Maxwell Air Force Base, AL: Air Force Historical Research Agency.

332nd Fighter Group. "Personal Narrative April 1945." Maxwell Air Force Base, AL: Air Force Historical Research Agency.

Time. [Report on court martial of Colonel William T. Colman], September 27, 1943, p. 65; Letter to the Editor, October 4, 1943.

Warren, James C. *The Freeman Field Mutiny.* San Rafael, CA: Donna Ewald, 1995.

SIX

Dangerous Enemies

WITH THE SUCCESS OF THE 99TH FIGHTER SQUADRON in combat and later the whole 332nd Fighter Group, the Army Air Forces became more accepting of the idea of black pilots and belatedly sought to build public support and appreciation for these men who were risking their lives fighting for the United States. All branches of the military had units that produced films for the war. Many of the people assigned to these units had worked in the film industry in New York City and Hollywood before the war, and Selective Service put these professionals to work making films in support of the war effort. Most of these films were training films to be shown to soldiers, sailors, marines, or coast guardsmen to help train them in general topics such as map reading or avoiding venereal disease. Some were to make servicemen understand why the United States was fighting and what it was fighting for. Others were of a more technical nature and shown to men training to be specialists on specific weapons. But throughout the war, military filmmakers also produced short documentary films for the general public, highlighting and glorifying the exploits of the military and assuring parents and friends back home that their loved ones still lived by wholesome American values while far away in the war zones. These short documentaries would be shown along with newsreels and cartoons before a main feature at cinemas around the country.

In the spring of 1945, not long before the war in Europe ended, the Army Air Forces produced *Wings for This Man*, which was about the fighter pilots of the 332nd (U.S. Army Air Forces, 1945). The film built on the surprise of revealing that the fighter pilots were black, opening with scenes of aerial combat where American fighters are seen battling a Luftwaffe formation three times larger than the American formation. Only after the American planes land and the pilots emerge from their cockpits and remove their helmets is the audience made aware that the American pilots are black. The pilots are the allowed to speak for themselves, and no attempt was made to have them speak standard American English.

The film's narrator, a relatively well-known film actor named Ronald Reagan, never mentions that the flyers are black but instead refers to them as "American boys going to work" and that they had recently been "just plain citizens from Everywhere, USA." While the narration avoids mentioning racism and segregation specifically, Reagan explains that the men had to surmount enormous obstacles to create the unit and fly and fight. He noted that to build Tuskegee Army Airfield, "more than trees had to be cleared away. There was misunderstanding, and distrust and prejudice to be cleared away." The message of the film was clear—the Tuskegee Airmen were Americans fighting for their country, and the experiment in black fighter pilots was a success. Near the end of the 10-minute film, a long line of marching black airmen is shown, with Reagan saying that they represent America, where people of different races and creeds were working to defeat Japan and Germany. The voice-over states that "one thing was proved here: that you can't judge a man by the color of his eyes or the shape of his nose" and that "they were pioneers, and no pioneer has it easy."

Here was something blacks, especially blacks in the military, had long wanted to hear: official recognition and publicity for their success. The Tuskegee Airmen were presented not simply as a novelty or a sop to the black population but as pioneers in the long struggle to bring blacks into mainstream American life. They were presented as American warriors—officers successfully engaged in the glamorous and deadly arena of air to air combat. The film could hardly have been more favorable. Another sign that the Tuskegee Airmen were becoming legends came in an article in the March 10, 1945, issue of *Liberty Magazine*, first making the claim that the Tuskegee Airmen never lost a bomber they escorted, a misconception that would linger for many decades. The legend of "never lost a bomber," although hyperbola, was a reflection of the increased celebration of the service of the Tuskegee Airmen in America. Still, blacks had been celebrated for their service during the Civil War, Spanish-American War, and World War I, only to see that service denigrated and then denied soon after those wars ended. With the end of the war in Europe all but certain and no black combat aviation units engaged in the war against Japan, those pioneering efforts might have been in vain.

By the spring of 1945, the main thrust in the war against Japan had become the strategic bombing of the home islands. There, some of the harshest theories of airpower advocates were being put to the test. The Japanese military still occupied vast stretches of the Far East, with the Dutch East Indies, most of Southeast Asia, and large areas of China still under Japanese occupation. But once the Americans gained control of the Marianna Islands, they built large air bases there, and soon the most advanced bomber of the war, the new Boeing B-29 Superfortresses, began a campaign to destroy Japan city by city until the Japanese government begged for peace. As some early airpower theorists had envisioned, the massive military of Japan was unable to protect the nation from destruction from the air. Some Allied planners even dared to hope that Japan might agree to surrender without the need for an invasion of the Japanese home islands. Still, most conservative estimates saw the war against Japan lasting into late 1946 or even 1947. The medium bombers of the 477th would still be needed for missions during the grueling invasion of Japan that so many American leaders and soldiers dreaded.

Despite problems in the 477th Bombardment Group, the Air Forces still intended to deploy the 477th. The group finally reached full strength in early 1945 and had a tentative date of July 1 for entering combat. However, events in the spring of 1945 cast the future of the 477th into doubt. The commander of the First Air Force, Major General Frank O'Donnell "Monk" Hunter, under whom the 477th fell, directed that strict segregation between black and white officers be maintained. On March 5, 1945, the 477th was transferred from Godman Field to Freeman Field, Indiana, which was better suited to the medium bombers, in order to facilitate training ("477th Bombardment Group History," 1945). The 387th joined them two days later to provide ground support ("387th Air Service Group History," 1945). While at Freeman Field, friction increased between the commander, Colonel Selway, and his mostly black junior officers, who resented the commander's insistence on upholding segregation policies. Racial tensions continued to rise, reaching a crisis point in April when black officers staged the so-called Freeman Field Mutiny. The incident was hardly a mutiny in that the men involved were not using force to overthrow legal military authority but were protesting the racially segregated facilities on base.

Freeman Field had two officers clubs: Club Number 1 for trainees and Club Number 2 for instructors. This arrangement was not that unusual; many bases had similar arrangements with separate facilities for cadre, or permanent personnel on a post, and for soldiers who were there temporarily for training. This arrangement prevented fraternization between the trainees and the people who were supposed to train and evaluate them. However, in the racially charged atmosphere, with all the trainees black and all the instructors white, the base had a de facto segregated system.

That the white officers in the 477th, including Colonel Selway, were also allowed into the so-called cadre club only made the racist intent of the separate clubs overt. The black officers referred to Club Number 1 as "Uncle Tom's Cabin" and refused to use it (Homan & Reilly, 2001). As the club had formerly been used as the noncommissioned officers' club, it meant that the black club was inferior to the white club and that the noncommissioned officers no longer had a club. The trainees were incensed with this situation and apparently began planning to challenge it even before all of the black officers had arrived at Freeman.

On March 10, two groups of black officers, 14 officers in all, decided to test the segregation of the clubs by going into Club Number 2 and ordering drinks and cigarettes. Each time, the black officers were refused service, and they departed. On April 1, 1945, a post regulation stated that some buildings on post were restricted for the use of whites only. Although the order was posted on April Fools Day, it was not a joke. General Hunter was apparently following Jim Crow traditions more than army regulations, but army regulations were open to some interpretation. Army Regulation 210-10 forbade the use of buildings on post for an "officers club, mess, or other social organization of officers . . . unless all officers on duty at the post [were granted] the right to full membership." Most of the black officers in the 477th interpreted this to mean that whites-only facilities on post ran counter to the army regulation. While all recreational facilities on post were segregated, the blatant segregation of the officers' clubs became the focus of the resentment of the black officers. Black officers had earlier, in August 1944, walked into a "whites-only" section of a post restaurant on Tuskegee Army Airfield asking for service based on 1940 War Department regulations banning segregation in post exchanges and restaurants. Colonel Parrish, by then commander of Tuskegee, agreed and ended racial segregation on post (Davis, 1991). The situation at Freedman Field would be handled with a lot less common sense.

In response to the protest on March 10, Lieutenant William Ellis had been returned to Godman on April 3 after being labeled an "agitator" at Freeman. At Godman, he informed the officers still awaiting transfer to Freeman about the officers' club situation there. The officers were disgusted by what they heard and developed a plan to challenge the situation at Freeman (Warren, 1995). The challenge was organized by Second Lieutenant Coleman A. Young, who would later serve as the first black mayor of Detroit, from 1974 until 1993. In the army, he had been accepted into the pilot training program and assigned to the 477th. However, he chafed under the segregated system that he found in the army, and, true to his nature, he began organizing a challenge to it (Gropeman, 1985). Earlier, while at Midland Army Airfield in Texas, he had organized a protest over segregation at the officers' club that resulted in black officers being allowed to join the previously all-white club (Warren, 1995). The incident had, however, given Young a reputation among whites as an agitator.

The black officers realized that what they were planning was dangerous, and their actions show that they took the situation seriously. Under the Articles of War, the officers could be charged with conspiracy and even mutiny. The army as an institution tended to react immediately and harshly to any perceived group of soldiers attempting to challenge authority. Reprisals could range from dishonorable discharges to lengthy jail terms or even the death penalty, although that was not likely. Still, the stakes were high. The last of the officers arrived on Freeman Field in the late afternoon of April 5, and their plan went into operation that evening. In groups of no more than five, they would attempt to be served in Club Number 2. Word had apparently gotten to post headquarters that some of the black officers might try to enter the white club. At about 8:30 in the evening, three black officers went to the club but were turned away by Major Andrew M. White, who was in charge of the club. Apparently, Major White knew that something was afoot, and he sent a message to Colonel Selway about the incident. Selway ordered the Officer of the Day, First Lieutenant Joseph D. Rogers, to go to the club and see that the rules were enforced. As Officer of the Day, Lieutenant Rogers carried a .45-caliber sidearm in a holster strapped to his waist, wore an armband identifying him as the Officer of the Day, and held authority directly from the post commander. Whatever the rank of the Officer of the Day, to challenge or disobey him was seen as a direct challenge to the authority of the post commander. The second group of black officers of the evening, a group of 19 that included Young, ignored Rogers and went to the club. Lieutenant Rogers told them to leave. The black officers stated that they were not refusing to leave but insisted that they be told the reason they had to leave before they would do so. The situation suddenly became much more serious; a barrier had been crossed. By refusing to immediately obey a direct order, the black officers were taking a principled stance, but the ramifications were serious. Major White had the 19 arrested and sent to their quarters.

The black airmen had planned to ensure publicity for their protest. Lowell M. Trice, a reporter for the *Indianapolis Recorder*, a black newspaper, had gone onto the post earlier that day and was on hand to witness and report on the event. When Trice's presence became known, Colonel Selway ordered him barred from post and refused to meet with him

(Homan & Reilly, 2001). Selway stood on procedure, and since Trice had not gotten authorization from the Army's Bureau of Public Relations in Washington, D.C., before seeking an interview, Selway had no obligation to speak with him. Selway went even further, though, and barred all newsmen from post.

New groups of black officers kept coming, and the events at the door to the club repeated themselves. Captain Anthony A. Chiappe, commander of the 118th Base Squadron, tried to damper down the situation by assembling the men and informing them that they could bring their grievances to him in the morning and that he would bring up the issues with his superiors and that in the meantime they would stay in their barracks (Warren, 1995). Later that evening, three other officers came to the club. Two of them, Lieutenants James V. Kennedy and Roger C. Terry, were quite light skinned, and apparently Lieutenant Rogers could not immediately tell if they were black; however, perhaps surmising that they were black from the appearance of their companion, Flight Officer Oliver Goodall, Lieutenant Rogers prevented them from entering the club. Lieutenants Rogers and Terry apparently got into some sort of shoving match. This incident made the situation even more serious, as Lieutenant Rogers was the Officer of the Day, and to not only disobey his command but also get into a physical altercation with him constituted a serious breach of military discipline. The protest had not ended, though, and the next evening, a further 25 black officers, in three groups, attempted to enter the so-called instructors' club and were also arrested.

In all, 61 black officers had been arrested. In order to prevent the incident from becoming far more serious, Selway took what he saw as a prudent step and disarmed all the black military policemen on post. Whatever the advisability of that action, it reinforced the idea that whites did not trust blacks and underscored the idea that black military authority was far more limited than the authority given to whites. From the point of view of the army, attempting to enter the instructors' club was a rather minor offence. Far more serious was the disobeying of the direct orders of the Officer of the Day and the planned mass-protest nature of the incident, which smacked of a conspiracy. The black officers had in fact planned the incident before it occurred, and except for the shoving between Rogers and Terry, the protest had been peaceful. The incident had the potential to be used as fodder for those who did want to see a black bombing unit or even black officers in the military. While the 332nd had proven itself in combat, the 477th had not and was still more of an experiment. Opponents to black officers could use it to demonstrate that blacks were ill suited to be officers and needed the firm hand of a white leader to keep them in line. Or the incident could be used to argue that the black officers in the 477th were afraid of entering combat and had staged the incident in an attempt to avoid deployment—the whole "natural coward" stereotype coming back. The stakes were high, but the officers of the 477th found the continuation of Jim Crow practices on military posts serious enough to warrant the risks they were taking.

Knowing that the incident could quickly escalate into something much larger, the army attempted to ensure that no one was overreacting and tried to diminish the incident quickly. Colonel Torgil C. Wold, the inspector general for the First Air Force, investigated the incidents at the club and recommended that charges be dropped against all the officers except for Lieutenant Terry, along with Lieutenants Marsden A. Thompson and Shirley R. Clinton, who were arrested with him. Wold believed that the base regulation on the separate clubs had been poorly drafted and published and might not stand up in courts-martial. Colonel Selway, after conferring with General Hunter, accepted Wold's recommendations, and the charges were dropped against the 58 officers. However, Colonel Selway then drafted a new order on the segregation of the officers' clubs, Base Regulation 85-2, which he believed met all the requirements from the army on such regulations and would hold up.

Review of officers during the Freeman Field Mutiny, Freeman Field, Indiana. The officers in the formation had refused a direct order to sign a statement acknowledging Base Regulation 85.2. (Library of Congress)

Colonel Selway did not want to back down in the face of what he saw as a collective breach of discipline. He drafted a new base regulation on the clubs, one that would uphold the separation of the clubs and forbid trainees from entering Club 2. Lieutenant Colonel John P. Pattison, deputy commander of the 477th, summoned all the officers to the base theater on April 10, at which time he read and explained the new regulation to the assembled men. Each of the black officers was then given a written copy of the regulation. The officers were instructed to then sign a statement attesting that they had read and understood the regulation. Colonel Selway was attempting to make an airtight case if any of the officers attempted to repeat the protests of April 5 and 6. He wanted the officers to sign the statement and stay out of Club 2. For him, this whole incident was simply a distraction, but he apparently believed that his obligation to maintain discipline forced him to take drastic actions, and he saw the enforcement of segregation as his duty. For the black pilots, not only was the continued existence of a de facto segregated club system contrary to army regulations and what they understood about the status of officers, but the whole thing was deeply offensive, and they in good conscience could not acquiesce to the situation. None of the officers initially would sign the statement. One of the squadron commanders, Captain Chiappe, tried to get the officers under him to sign but managed to convince only three to do so (Warren, 1985).

Colonel Selway, after consulting with the judge advocate of the First Air Force and with the inspector general, set up a board consisting of two white and two black officers. On April 11, the board called each man before it and gave them three choices: they could sign the statement, write out their own statement saying that had not understood the regulation, or face arrest under the 64th Article of War for disobeying a direct order from a superior officer, which in time of war could theoretically be punished by death. While the likelihood that the men would be executed for failure to sign the document was unlikely, the men were fully aware of the seriousness of their actions and knew that the army had executed black soldiers during World War I and could do so again. A few signed it, some signed only after crossing out the words "and fully understand," and others signed but added a statement saying that the regulation was racially discriminatory. But 101 officers chose to stand on principle and would not sign the document.

As a result, all were again placed under arrest and confined to their quarters. The group of 101 officers was soon brought back to Godman Field to stand courts-martial, while the other 58 who had been arrested for trying to enter the club remained at Freeman. The repercussions from the incident were growing daily. The black press reported extensively on the plight of the men, and soon leading African American organizations, as well as labor unions and eventually members of Congress, began to ask questions of the army that the army was uncomfortable answering. Finally, on April 23, all the men except for the three involved in the shoving incident were released. A letter of reprimand was placed in each officer's record, but for most, the incident was over. Army Chief of Staff General Marshall apparently believed that the incident had been blown out of proportion, and continuing in the direction that things were moving would help no one. General Hunter, who had been a firm segregationist, put most of the blame for the unrest on Colonel Selway, the white commander of the 477th.

However, things were not over for Lieutenant Terry and the other two officers charged with shoving Lieutenant Rogers, who faced general courts-martial in July. Still, given the high profile of the case, the three would never be able to claim that they were not adequately represented, and the board itself was comprised entirely of black officers (Warren, 2001). A young civil rights lawyer, Thurgood Marshall, later to be the first African American to sit on the U.S. Supreme Court, directed the defense of the three, although he did not actually appear at the trial. The actual lead defense council at the trail was Theodore M. Berry, who would later be the mayor of Cincinnati. He had two assistants: Lieutenant William C. Coleman, who would later gain fame after the war as the chief defense council for the National Association for the Advancement of Colored People, and Chicago lawyer Harold Tyler. Both Thompson and Clinton were acquitted of any wrongdoing. Terry's defense was more problematic, as witnesses had seen him actually make physical contact with Lieutenant Rogers. Although he was acquitted of the charge of disobeying a direct order—the most serious charge he faced—he was found guilty of jostling Lieutenant Rogers. For this, he was fined $150, lost his rank, and was given a dishonorable discharge (Homan & Reilly, 2001). General Hunter endorsed the findings of the courts-martial but described the sentence as "grossly inadequate" (Warren, 1995).

The unrest in the 477th was a distraction from the deadly serious task of training men for war and could have been avoided had War Department policies regarding access to post facilities been followed. But the incident also demonstrated how committed many senior career officers were to upholding Jim Crow and that intelligent, educated black men were ready to sacrifice a lot in order to end a humiliating situation. The unwanted attention that the "mutiny" brought to army practices on race embarrassed the War Department. However, the 477th was too far along in its training and organization to simply disband it and reassign its personnel to other duties.

What was needed was solid leadership. The Army Air Forces realized that the man to restore pride and confidence in the 477th and take it to war against Japan was Colonel Benjamin O. Davis Jr., but first he would have to finish the war in Europe with the 332nd Fighter Group.

By the beginning of 1945, Germany was far beyond any hope of winning the war or of even dividing the Allies and signing a separate peace with each. Despite the hopelessness of their cause, the Nazis and Adolf Hitler were determined to fight until Germany itself was destroyed. But if the destruction of Germany was required to bring about the absolute surrender of Germany, then the Allies were prepared to do just that. As the year started, the Tuskegee Airmen in Europe could look back on their combat record with pride. They were credited with shooting down 62 enemy aircraft. They had destroyed many more than that on the ground. They had destroyed enemy trains, trucks, barges, and horse wagons. But the war was not over, and Germany still had some fight in it. For the 332nd, most of their missions during these weeks were in support of the 5th, 47th, 49th 55th, and 304th Bomb Wings in operations against targets in Moosbierbaum, Regensburg, Schewechat, Vienna, and other targets across Germany's crumbling empire. Credited kills of enemy aircraft were becoming fewer for the simple reason that Germany had few aircraft left to send against the bomber fleets, and even finding fuel for the aircraft Germany still had was increasingly difficult. The first aerial kill of 1945 did not come until March 16, although the 332nd had destroyed much rolling stock and airplanes on the ground ("15th Air Force General Order No. 1734").

By the end of February, the Allied bombing effort had been so thorough that few strategic targets remained in areas still under German control. The 332nd increasingly performed reconnaissance escort missions, with a few fighters escorting a single P-38 equipped to take aerial photographs. The pilots of the 332nd also found themselves again performing ground interdiction missions, as they shot and bombed rail yards, trains, troop concentration sites, and power plants. So effective were the attacks against oil facilities that motor transport on the roads was rare, and instead most people and goods in German-controlled areas moved by foot, rail, or even by horse. Increasingly, the main danger came from small-arms fire—German troops firing their rifles and machine guns at the approaching American fighters. The bomber escort missions continued, though, and the 332nd continued to lose men. During a mission to strafe trains in Germany on February 25, Lieutenant George Iles was shot down, captured, and spent the remainder of the war as a prisoner of the Germans. Lieutenant Wendell W. Hockaday was also shot down, but his fate was unknown, and he was classified as missing in action. Eventually, his status was changed to killed in action (Homan & Reilly, 2001).

As February ended and March began, the end of the war in Europe was in sight. The Red Army of the Soviet Union was smashing its way into the eastern parts of Germany, while the Americans, British, and Canadians were pounding away from the west. Allied military and civilian leadership knew, however, that the end of the war in Europe would not be the end of the war and that the war against Japan might last for another year or even longer. With Germany on the ropes, the reorganization of the Army Air Forces began. For the 332nd, the first tangible sign of the approaching end of the war in Europe and the reorganization of the military that was to follow came on March 6, 1945, when the 302nd Fighter Squadron was inactivated, leaving the 332nd Fighter Group with three squadrons. Under the system in place in the army, the deactivation of the 302nd did not mean that the pilots and ground crews of the 302nd would be reboarding ships and returning to the United States together. Instead, the American military had instituted a point system to decide who went home and who remained in the theater fighting. Points were awarded for time in the service, time spent in a combat zone, missions flown, and awards received. Those with the most points were rotated to the States, and the ones with lower point remained. Although the system was disruptive to unit cohesion and necessitated a lot of shifting of personnel, it allowed those among the living who had given the most to return first. Throughout the 332nd, points totals were tabulated, and those with the most were transferred to the 302nd to begin their trip home, and those in the 302nd with lower totals were reassigned to other squadrons in the 332nd Fighter Group.

Despite these signs that the end on the war in Europe was drawing ever closer, the war went on. Germany had little left to give but continued to resist. German aircraft were getting quite rare, as Allied aircraft moved over the skies of Germany to bomb and strafe with little opposition. On March 14, the 99th Fighter Squadron roamed over Bruck, Leoben, and Steyr strafing all sorts of railroad targets and power stations, one of four missions flown that day (Haulman, "Table of 332nd Fighter Group Missions"). The 99th, 100th, and 301st performed similar missions on the March 16. Among an impressive list of mostly railroad equipment destroyed were three Fw-190s and one Ju-52 destroyed and two Me-109s and one biplane damaged while on the ground, most likely grounded from a lack of fuel, spare parts, or pilots. Only one German fighter challenged the 301st, over the Mettenheim air base, when a single Me-109 attempted to take off and was quickly downed by a burst of machine gun fire from a Mustang ("Narrative Mission Report No. 227").

On March 24, the three remaining squadrons of the 332nd flew one of the longest combat missions of the war when they escorted a formation of B-17 Flying Fortresses in a mission to strike at Berlin, where the Daimler Benz Tank Works was the target of the heavy bombers' deadly payload. Ground crews began installing the extra-large 110-gallon external fuel tanks on the Mustangs starting late at night on the March 23, giving the Mustangs the range they would need for the long mission. The crews worked all night, but by mission time 59 Mustangs were ready. The 332nd had to fly 600 miles just to meet up with the bombers and escort them the final 200 miles to the target. Given the greatly shrunken territory that the Third Reich still controlled, the importance of the tank works to the Germans, and the symbolic importance of the German capital of Berlin, the Luftwaffe threw much of its remaining strength against the bombers in a desperate attempt to hold off the inevitable. Around 25 German fighters attacked the formations, several of which were jets. In some hard fighting, the 332nd managed to shoot down three of the jets but also lost one of their own, with three others missing and three of the bombers shot down near the target area. For its heroic service that day, the 332nd Fighter Group was awarded the Distinguished Unit Citation ("Narrative Mission Report No. 246").

On the last day of March 1945, the 332nd was assigned a mission to strafe railroad targets in the area around Linz, in a part of Germany that had previously been the independent country of Austria. While the pilots of the 332nd were tearing up boxcars, locomotives, passenger cars, and other materials Germany desperately needed to continue to wage war, a group of German fighters came in to challenge them. The first group had five Me-109s and one Fw-190. In short order, the six German planes were burning wrecks on the ground, and Major William Campbell and Lieutenants D. L. Rich, Hugh White, James Hall, John Davis, and Thomas Braswell each had a confirmed kill to their credit. In all, the 332nd was credited with 13 kills that day, although one of their own was lost ("Narrative Mission Report No. 252"). The next day, coincidently April Fool's Day, the 332nd escorted a formation of B-24s from the 47th Bombardment Wing in an attack on a marshaling area near St. Poelten. On the return flight, the 332nd encountered a group of about 16 German fighters. Four acted as decoys, while the other 12 attacked from the direction of the sun. In the ensuing battle, two pilots of the 332nd were killed, Lieutenants Walter Manning and William Armstrong. However, the Germans fared worse, and Harold Morris, James Fischer, and Manning, who was later killed in the same fight, were all credited with a single kill. Charles White, Carl Carey, and John E. Edwards were credited with two kills each, and in an amazing display of aerial prowess, Harry T. Williams knocked down three German fighters. The 332nd earned a total of 12 enemy kills that day ("Personal Narrative").

The focus on destroying the railroad infrastructure continued until the very end of the war. On April 15, the 332nd were at it again, making a wreckage of much of Germany's remaining railroad equipment. A single Me-109 came out to challenge the hardened pilots of the 332nd, and that German fighter soon joined countless other German fighters as a burning wreck on the ground ("Historical Records," April 1945). On April 26, six Mustangs from the 100th and 301st Fighter Squadrons took off on mission to escort a reconnaissance version of the P-38 Lightning in a mission over the Czech city of Prague. The P-38 was outfitted with special cameras in its nose that took high-resolution photographs that would later be analyzed for things such as the presence of German ground forces. Around noon, a strange aircraft was spotted in the distance, but it turned out to be a British bomber. A short time later, five Me-109s were spotted. In the ensuing fight, four of the German aircraft went down, with one pilot bailing out in time, and the last one a probable kill ("Historical Records," May 1945). For the 332nd, the mission was a total success. Those four unlucky German pilots had the dubious distinction of being the last enemy pilots shot down by the Tuskegee Airmen during World War II.

While most people in the war understood that the end was close, no one could tell just when the final end of the war in Europe would come. On May 4 and 5, the 332nd moved from Ramitelli to Cattolica, Italy, but the last day was fast approaching. That day finally came on May 7, 1945, and a reconnaissance mission flown on that day into Austria to test the truce turned out to be the last combat mission of the 332nd Fighter Group and thus of the Tuskegee Airmen of World War II, although that was not known at the time. The war against Japan still looked to continue for some time, perhaps a year or two more, and so while the men and officers of the 332nd could take some satisfaction from the defeat of Nazi Germany, their future remained uncertain. With the end of the war in Europe, men again thought again of peacetime, and many of the Tuskegee Airmen were eager to get back to civilian life and loved ones, to start businesses, to return to school, and to take the confidence that their experience in war had given them and ensure that this time the proud service of black men in war was not forgotten and instead would form part of the basis for bringing about some fundamental changes in American society. Men with high point totals would probably be rotated stateside to train others or be discharged.

Seven noncommissioned officers from the 332nd Fighter Group arrive at La Guardia airport on their way home, July 26, 1945. From left to right: Sergeant Leon W. Coles, John H. Turner, Sergeant Robert T. Howard, Leonard R. Brewer, Sergeant Charles Davis, Sergeant Charles D. Hensley, and Sergeant Julius C. Lovett. (Bettmann/Corbis)

In the meantime, they were still in the army, and the army expected soldiers to conduct themselves properly. The 332nd held ceremonies mark the end of the war in Europe, to memorialize the men they had lost, to award honors, and to welcome back some of the Tuskegee Airmen who had been captured during the war and had recently been released from prisoner-of-war camps. On June 8, Colonel Yantis H. Taylor, commander of the 306th Fighter Wing, awarded Colonel Davis the Silver Star Medal for gallantry in action. He also awarded five Distinguished Flying Crosses, five Air Medals, and a Bronze Star to other airmen. The ceremony also marked the departure of Colonel Davis, who was leaving to take command of the troubled 477th Bombardment Group. The next day, Major Roberts reassumed command of the 332nd. (Haulman, "Tuskegee Airmen Chronology") Fighter units such as the 332nd had to remain prepared in case rogue elements of the Third Reich attempted to continue fighting in spite of the surrender. In retrospect, there was little need for that as Germany was exhausted, and most Germans in the western part of the country believed that occupation by the British, Americans, or even the French was preferable to occupation by the Soviets. The Soviet Union had lost perhaps 20 million people during the war and was not expected to treat generously the Germans in the eastern sections that they occupied. By July, the movement of the 332nd back to the United States began, with the majority of the unit shipping home that October under the command of Major Roberts.

Aside from a very few such as Major Roberts, most of the members of the 332nd Fighter Group who boarded the transports in the summer and autumn of 1945 for the voyage home were not the same airmen who had boarded the transports back in 1943 and 1944. Throughout the war, most of the initial Tuskegee Airmen who had not died in combat had earlier rotated back to the United States in line with Army Air Forces's policy that the best, most experienced pilots be reassigned to teach flying skills to new pilots. One such man was Captain Pruitt, who with 70 combat missions under his belt, including the confirmed kills of enemy aircraft, and who attacked a German ship and held a Distinguished Flying Cross, returned to Tuskegee Army Airfield to teach. Sadly, after surviving combat against the worst the Luftwaffe could throw at him, Pruitt died in a plane crash near Tuskegee on April 20, 1945, shortly before the war in Europe ended. His funeral and burial at St. Peter's cemetery in his hometown of St. Louis, Missouri, saw a huge turnout as the black community paid homage to the dashing young hero (*Chicago Defender*, 1945). His death underscored the sometimes arbitrary nature of death for airmen, while the large numbers of people who attended his funeral showed the respect in the black community for the Tuskegee Airmen. But at the time, an ominous cloud still hung over the future; the war in Europe had been won, but the war in the Pacific was still grinding on and might continue to do so for many months if not years. Captain Pruitt's funeral might not be the last for a Tuskegee Airman during the war. The 477th Bombardment Wing was still slated to deploy to the Pacific, although changes were under way.

Despite the anticlimactic ending to the protest against the segregated officers' clubs, the incident had alerted Army Air Forces officials that all was not well in the 477th, and the group came under closer scrutiny. Realizing the toxic climate at Freeman Field, the Air Forces began to institute significant structural changes in the 477th on April 26, 1945. The constant movements, inadequate training facilities, and distractions caused by indefensible racial policies had delayed the completion of collective training, and it was not initially scheduled to deploy until July 1, 1945. However, the German surrender began a massive realignment of the American military, and the composition of the 477th changed radically. The Air Forces inactivated the 616th and 619th Bombardment Squadrons on June 22, 1945. The 99th Fighter Squadron, combat experienced and just back from Europe, was added to the 477th, which was redesignated as the 477th Composite Group on the same day the 616th and the 619th were inactivated. Perhaps most significantly, Colonel Davis had been appointed to command the group on June 21, and he actually assumed command on July 1.

Davis, the second-highest-ranking black officer in the army, with a West Point education, regular commission, and a proven record of leading aerial combat organizations, was the perfect choice to take charge of the 477th at its nadir. But Davis had a large job ahead of him and would need all his skills and leadership abilities to turn the 477th around. Besides the obvious task of reorganizing the 477th around its new mission as a composite group, he had to overcome the divisions and resentments caused by the controversy over Club #2 on Freeman. But Colonel Davis had a long record of meeting difficult challenges, and he set about readying the 477th for deployment. Davis immediately replaced white staff officers with black officers, ironically making the 477th more segregated but allowing advancement for qualified black officers. Under the new schedule, the 477th was to complete its training under its new composition on August 31 and deploy to the Far East to fight against Japan.

That deployment never came. While the 477th was undergoing its agonies over the segregated clubs and the 332nd was destroying whatever means Germany still had to fight, groups of scientist, technicians, engineers, and support personnel, 100,000 people in all, at secret sites in Washington State, Tennessee, and New Mexico, were putting the finishing touches on an experimental weapon that had the potential to change the course of the war in what was termed the Manhattan Project. The War Department, especially Chief of Staff General Marshall, was growing increasingly worried about war weariness on the part of the American public. The war in Europe had ended in May, and that victory brought a sense of euphoria but also a desire to end the Pacific war quickly. The American plans for the total defeat of Japan included operations lasting well into 1946, with the Soviets pledged to enter the war against Japan within three months after the end of the war in Europe, American invasions of the home islands from the south, and a Soviet invasion from the north. Soviet involvement would complicate the postwar situation;

such a scenario would leave the Soviets in control of northeastern China, Korea, and northern Japan. General Marshall and others also feared that increasing casualties from the fight against Japan would sap the will of the American people to bring the war to a definite conclusion, and that pressure would mount for a negotiated peace with Japan. The ferocious fight on the small Japanese island of Okinawa, at the southern end of the Ryukyu island chain south of the Japanese main islands, led American military planners to raise the level of casualties they expected during an invasion of the four main islands. Okinawa had ended only on June 30, and the costs in lives were staggering. In three months, more than 12,000 Americans had died, and 107,000 Japanese soldiers were killed, along with almost the same number of civilians. Marshall feared that the invasions of the home island, set to begin on November 1, would include all the ferocity of the Okinawa campaign, only much larger. He predicted at least 31,000 U.S. casualties in the first month, with unknown numbers after that (Walker, 2005). What American leaders were hoping for was a new weapon that would convince the Japanese leaders that victory was impossible and convince them to surrender unconditionally to the United States before the total destruction of their nation.

In the early morning of July 16, 1945, a Monday, at Site Trinity, 40 miles south of Socorro, New Mexico, the first atomic bomb exploded. The other two bombs created by the Manhattan Project were soon sent to the Pacific, and the first was dropped on the Japanese city of Hiroshima on August 6 and the second on Nagasaki on August 9. Perhaps equally important in convincing the Japanese of the hopelessness of their situation was the declaration of war by the Soviet Union on August 8, concurrent with a massive Soviet invasion of the Japanese puppet state of Manchukuo in northeastern China. On August 15, the emperor of Japan announced that his nation would accept the surrender terms. The formal surrender ceremony occurred on the battleship USS *Missouri* in Tokyo Bay on September 2, 1945. World War II was over. The 477th would not see combat.

After World War II ended, the future of all wartime organizations fell into limbo. The massive wartime military was about to undergo a massive reduction, although the postwar military would be larger than it had been in the 1930s. For a while, the 477th was retained, but its future was in doubt. On October 8, the 618th Bombardment Squadron was inactivated, leaving the 477th with one fighter squadron and one bombardment squadron. Eleven days later, the 332nd Fighter Group was inactivated, along with its two remaining squadrons (Haulman, "Tuskegee Airmen Chronology"). In March

1946, the 477th moved to Lockbourne Army Air Base in Ohio. Colonel Davis was both commander of the 477th and the base commander, becoming the first black man to command an American military post. When Tuskegee Army Airfield closed in the early summer of 1946, Lockbourne became essentially the heart of the "black air force." The arrangement did not last long, as in July the 477th Composite Group and the 617th Bombardment Squadron were inactivated, and the 99th Fighter Squadron was reassigned to the reactivated 332nd Fighter Group, along with the reactivated 100th and 301st Fighter Squadrons (Haulman, "Tuskegee Airmen Chronology"). Black combat aviation would continue, and apparently it would continue in segregated units.

References

Chicago Defender, April 28, 1945.

Davis, Benjamin O., Jr. *Benjamin O. Davis, Jr., American*. Washington, DC: Smithsonian Institution Press, 1991.

"15th Air Force General Order No. 1734."Maxwell Air Force Base, AL: Air Force Historical Research Agency.

"477th Bombardment Group History for the Period 16 Jan 15 April 1945." Maxwell Air Force Base, AL: Air Force Historical Research Agency.

Gropeman, Alan L. *The Air Force Integrates*. Washington, DC: Office of Air Force History, 1985.

Haulman, Daniel. "Table of 332nd Fighter Group Missions," nos. 221–224.Maxwell Air Force Base, AL: Air Force Historical Research Agency.

Haulman, Daniel. "Tuskegee Airmen Chronology." Maxwell Air Force Base, AL: Air Force Historical Research Agency.

"Historical Records." April 15, 1945.Maxwell Air Force Base, AL: Air Force Historical Research Agency.

"Historical Records." May 1, 1945.Maxwell Air Force Base, AL: Air Force Historical Research Agency.

Homan, Lynn M., and Thomas Reilly, *Black Knights: The Story of the Tuskegee Airmen*. Gretna, LA: Pelican Publishing, 2001.

"Narrative Mission Report No. 227." also "15th Air Force General Order No. 1734."Maxwell Air Force Base, AL: Air Force Historical Research Agency.

"Narrative Mission Report No. 246." March 24, 1945.Maxwell Air Force Base, AL: Air Force Historical Research Agency.

"Narrative Mission Report No. 252.Maxwell Air Force Base, AL: Air Force Historical Research Agency.

"Personal Narrative." April 1945.Maxwell Air Force Base, AL: Air Force Historical Research Agency.

"387th Air Service Group History for the Period February–April 1945."Maxwell Air Force Base, AL: Air Force Historical Research Agency.

U.S. Army Air Forces First Motion Picture Unit. *Wings for This Man.* Special Film Project 151, 1945.

Walker, Stephen. *Shockwave: Countdown to Hiroshima.* New York: Harper Perennial, 2005.

Warren, James C. *The Freeman Field Mutiny.* San Rafael, CA: Donna Ewald, 1995.

Afterword: The Legacy of the Tuskegee Airmen

IN THE SUMMER OF 1941, when the initial yearlong call up of the National Guardsmen, Reservists, and selectees was about half over, only 2,250 black men served in the Army Air Corps. By the end of 1942, a year after the attack on Pearl Harbor, about 72,000 black men were in the Army Air Forces. By the end of the war in 1945, that number would double to over 140,000. Of that number, only 1,559 served as officers, giving a ratio of about 93 black enlisted men for every one black officer, a rate about one-tenth of that for whites (Donaldson, 1991; Osur, 1976). The vast majority of blacks assigned to the Army Air Forces did not serve with the Tuskegee Airmen. Instead, most remained assigned to various support units where their duties more often than not were in performing unskilled labor under white leadership or performing demeaning work in laundries and dining halls. For many blacks inducted into the armed forces during the war, military service had been simply another experience with Jim Crow. There had been, however, some bright spots, and some of the brightest were the Tuskegee Airmen. The pilots, support officers, and men in the ground crews were some of the most highly trained and educated black men in America. They had succeeded despite some powerful bigots in the government and armed forces. They accepted the challenge of one of the most difficult jobs during the war—fighter pilot—and met every challenge.

The Tuskegee Airmen did what was asked of them and more. A total of around 450 Tuskegee Airmen flew in the 99th or 332nd during the war, totaling more than 800 missions. The 332nd itself flew at least 311 missions in all. They were credited with 112 kills of enemy aircraft in aerial combat—including three jets—and around 150 that they destroyed on the ground. They destroyed dozens of locomotives, hundreds of boxcars, oil cars, and miles of railroad track. They played havoc with the German transportation system. The Tuskegee Airmen earned a total of 96 Distinguished Flying

Crosses as well as many other individual awards. The 99th Fighter Squadron earned three Distinguished Unit Citations, and the 100th and 301st Fighter Squadrons each earned a Distinguished Unit Citation. By their very presence with their distinctive red tails in the air alongside formations of bombers, the Tuskegee Airmen gave confidence to American bomber crews and struck terror into the hearts of German fighter pilots. While the individual reasons each man strove to enter the training program and earn his wings so that he could face a skilled enemy in deadly combat were complex and varied, each man understood he carried the hopes and dreams of millions of black Americans. The full civil rights movement would not get under way until several years after the end of the war, but the Tuskegee Airmen were laying a solid foundation for the later black struggle for civil rights and the dismantling of official segregation. Their success in combat would show black and white Americans that blacks did not shirk the duties of citizenship and thus had a right to the privileges of citizenship. At the same time, they gave lie to the argument that blacks were somehow mentally or morally unfit to serve as leaders or in highly technical positions. The record of the Tuskegee Airmen was a powerful argument to use against those who opposed military integration in the belief that blacks could not or would not fight.

Despite the success of the Tuskegee Airmen—and all blacks who served loyally during the war—the perseverance of military segregation during World War II delayed the integration of blacks into American society for generations. Before World War II, serious divisions existed in the United States within the white population. Old stock Protestants, generally of English, Scottish, or Dutch descent, tended to look askance on newer immigrant groups, especially Italians, Irish, and Eastern Europeans. Catholics often had their loyalty questioned. Jews were targets of discrimination sometimes as violent as that meted out to blacks. But during the mass national experience of World War II and especially through shared military experience, much of the antagonism between ethnic groups and religions disappeared from American life. The shared experience of the mass military of World War II fundamentally changed the concept of who was considered an American, and while most other ethnic and religious groups were included, blacks were specifically excluded from this process (Bruscino, 2010). To be sure, other groups were also segregated in the military, but for other reasons and in smaller numbers. Japanese Americans were confined largely to a few specialized units, most famously the 442nd Regimental Combat Team. Most Puerto Ricans who could not speak English were assigned to the Regular Army's 65th Infantry Regiment or one of the two National Guard units from Puerto Rico: the 295th and 296th Infantry Regiments. But in other aspects, the U.S. military during the war was integrated—Jews, Hispanics, Chinese Americans, and other minorities were not organized into separate units but served alongside whites. But all blacks, regardless of language skills, religion, or number of generations their ancestors had been in the country, were assigned to segregated units. By design, whites did not eat, sleep, train, or fight with blacks, and thus blacks remained after the war different or unfamiliar—the "other" to most white Americans.

Despite the reservations of people like Judge Hastie who feared that the creation of new, all-black combat units would further entrench military segregation, the days of separate units for blacks were ending. The groundwork for the postwar separation of the Army Air Forces from the army had been laid during the war. Despite the overwhelming evidence that maintaining segregation in the military had been wasteful, the leaders of the Army Air Forces planned for a continuation of segregation in the independent air force. However, the smaller size of the postwar air force made plans for maintaining segregation even more difficult. When President Harry S. Truman issued Executive Order 9981 in 1948 ending racial segregation in the armed forces, the air force dropped all plans for segregated unit and began planning, albeit awkwardly, for integrating units. Early efforts at integration were clumsy, with black units simply deactivated and black personnel assigned to formerly all-white units. But in the massive demobilization and reorganization of the military following the end of the war, deactivations were the common fate of most units. Following the end of the war, the 332nd Fighter Group returned to the United States and was deactivated on October 19, 1945. The group was reactivated on July 1, 1947, when it became part of the 332nd Fighter Wing, but was again deactivated July 1, 1949, during a general reorganization of the air force. Eventually, in 1998, the designation "332nd" would be resurrected as the 332nd Expeditionary Operations Group and its lineage preserved.

Tuskegee Institute continued to provide higher education for blacks, although like most "Negro colleges," which were increasingly called "Historically Blacks Colleges and Universities" during the 1970s, Tuskegee had to adjust to a world where the top black high school graduates were courted by formally whites-only colleges and not limited to a handful of black colleges. The air force continued its association with Tuskegee Institute and maintains a Reserve Officers Training Corps program at the university, which draws heavily on the legacy of the Tuskegee Airmen.

Tuskegee Army Airfield, as with most of the air bases built for the war, closed in 1946, shortly after the end of the war. The land reverted to private landowners, and the buildings were sold, with the buyers responsible for removing them. Two of the runways from the former base operated as a private airport for a few years, but by the 1970s, the crumbling runways were closed forever as landing strips. The former army airfield is today a tangle of trees and brush, with a telltale pattern of crumbled roads and runways underfoot. Its role in World War II and in knocking down one of the keystones that held Jim Crow in place has largely been overlooked. Kennedy Field is completely gone, the area covered by a canopy of trees. Most of the curious who come to Tuskegee looking for some tangible link to the now legendary Tuskegee Airmen find themselves at the still operational Moton Field, where a marker refers to it as the site of the training of the Tuskegee Airmen.

Most of the former Tuskegee Airmen who survived World War II, like their white counterparts, went on to lead often surprisingly normal lives after the war. Some stayed in the Army Air Forces and became part of the newly independent—and racially integrated—U.S. Air Force in 1947. Many found careers in business, academia, or government. Given the high caliber of the men who made it through the program and the war, their overrepresentation in the ranks of the successful should not be surprising. In 1971, many of the surviving Tuskegee Airmen formed a national organization to preserve their legacy. In 2007, a special Congressional Gold Medal was awarded to the Tuskegee Airmen in recognition of their place not only in military aviation but also in the early civil rights movement. The Tuskegee Airmen entered into mythology, much in the way as had their forebears in the American military, such as the 54th Massachusetts Regiment from the Civil War and the so-called Buffalo Soldiers of the late frontier period. The American entertainment industry did not fail to notice the increasingly legendary status of them. In 1995, HBO Films produced *The Tuskegee Airmen*, a television movie about the Tuskegee Airmen that earned high praise. While several elements and people in the film were fictionalized, much of the core remained true to the actual experience. In 2010, Lucusfilm announced plans to release a major motion picture on the Tuskegee Airmen, *Red Tails*. Clearly, the talented young men who reported to Tuskegee, Alabama, during World War II have become national heroes.

The creation of separate black fighter and bomber units in the Army Air Forces during World War II represented a compromise between those who wanted full integration of the military immediately and those who sought to keep blacks out of the Army Air Forces, officer ranks, and cockpits completely. The Tuskegee Airmen were flesh-and-blood men with normal human frailties and strengths, but they were also among the best of the nation. Their sacrifices helped defeat Nazi Germany abroad and helped knock down a pillar of segregation at home. By proving that black men could and would fight and die for the nation in the complex and high-stakes world of aerial combat, they paved the way for the eventual dismantling of military segregation, which in turn was a seminal event in the eventual overturning of a whole system of laws and practices intended to keep blacks subordinate.

The Tuskegee Airmen came from a long tradition of black participation in the American military. They came at a critical junction of the early stirrings of black political power, the growth of airpower in war, and a world that had become increasingly dangerous. They helped defeat Nazi Germany and Jim Crow. They worked within a racist system to change that system. Their contributions to the war effort, to civil rights, and to America fully justified the hopes of so many they first carried into the skies over Tuskegee, Alabama.

References

Bruscino, Thomas. *A Nation Forged in War: How World War II Taught Americans to Get Along* Knoxville: University of Tennessee Press, 2010.

Donaldson, Gary A. *The History of African-Americans in the Military*. Malabar, FL: Krieger Publishing, 1991.

Osur, Alan M. *Blacks in the Army Air Forces during World War II: The Problem of Race Relations* Washington, DC: Office of Air Force History, 1976.

Short Biographies of Key Figures

C. Alfred Anderson
(February 9, 1907–April 13, 1996)

Nicknamed the "Chief," Anderson was born in Bridgeport, Pennsylvania. He attended Drexel Institute, the Chicago School of Aeronautics, and the Boston School of Aeronautics. He earned his private pilot's license in 1929 and a transport pilot's license in 1932. In 1933, along with Dr. Albert E. Forsythe, he became the first African American to cross the United States and return by air. He became involved in aviation instruction in black high schools in Washington, D.C., and later taught aviation at Howard University. In 1940, Dr. Patterson brought him to Tuskegee Institute to head the Civilian Pilot Training Program there. His March 1941, flight with First Lady Eleanor Roosevelt greatly publicized the ability of black men to fly and was an in important symbolic step in the creation of the Tuskegee Airmen. Chief later served as director of the Air Corps's Primary Training Program at Tuskegee Institute. He remained involved with aviation training at Tuskegee and with the Tuskegee Airmen the remainder of his life.

Henry H. "Hap" Arnold
(June 25, 1886–January 15, 1950)

Career army and air force officer. Arnold, from Pennsylvania, graduated from West Point in 1907 and initially branched infantry. In 1911, he switched to the Signal Corps, which had responsibility for aviation. He was taught to fly by the Wright Brothers and became the second military pilot in the U.S. Army. He remained in aviation, rising until he was chief of the Army Air Corps and later the Army Air Forces during World War II. Promoted to five-star rank (general of the army) in 1944, Arnold became the only air force general to wear five stars in the Air Force 1949.

Josephine Baker
(June 3, 1906–April 12, 1975)

African American singer, dancer, and actress. Born and raised in St. Louis, Missouri, she left school at age 12 and lived on the streets before going to New York City. She soon became one of the most famous entertainers in Harlem. By the mid-1920s, she was working in Paris, France, where she became known simply as "La Baker." Her fame in Europe was widespread, and she starred in films, modeled, and sang. She capitalized on what were seen as her exotic good looks, often appearing as the sexually alluring savage. During World War II, she continued to work as an entertainer but secretly used her position to smuggle information to the Free French. In 1942, she went to North Africa, and, after the Allied invasion of French North Africa, she stayed to entertain Allied and Free French troops. For her service, she became the first American-born woman to receive the French Cross de Guerre. After the war, she made appearances in the United States and supported the civil rights movement, refusing to perform at segregated venues and speaking at the 1963 March on Washington. However, her greatest fame was always in France, and she died there in 1975. She was buried with full military honors.

Herbert E. Carter
(September 2, 1919–)

Career air force officer. Born in Amory, Mississippi, Carter attended Tuskegee Institute. When World War II began, he applied for pilot training and was accepted into the fourth class of Tuskegee Airmen, from which he graduated. After deploying with the 99th, he served as the squadron engineering officer, with the responsibility for overseeing maintenance. He flew 77 combat missions during the war. After the war, he remained in the air force and completed more advanced training in maintenance, leadership, and flying. He served as the professor of military science, teaching Air Force ROTC at Tuskegee Institute from 1950 to 1955, when he left to become part of a U.S. Air Force advisory group to the German air force. He served as an instructor for German pilots making the transition to jets. He served in a number of maintenance and leadership assignments until his retirement from the air force as a lieutenant colonel in 1969, after which he accepted a position at Tuskegee Institute as an associate dean.

Bessie Coleman
(January 26, 1892–April 30, 1926)

First African American women to hold a pilot's license. The daughter of sharecroppers in Texas, Coleman completed one term at Oklahoma Colored Agriculture and Normal School before a lack of funds forced her to leave school. She moved in with a brother in Chicago. In 1920, desiring to fly after hearing stories of French women pilots from returning veterans of World War I, she went to Paris to take flying lessons. No American flying school would accept her because she was black and a woman. By the autumn of 1921, she was back in the United States with an international pilot's license. She returned to Europe for more training before beginning her career as a "barnstormer" in the United States—performing daring aerial stunts at air shows. By her very existence, she showed thousands of blacks and some whites that blacks, even black women, could fly. She died when a plane in which she was a passenger developed mechanical problems and crashed.

Benjamin O. Davis Sr.
(July 1, 1877–November 26, 1970)

Career soldier, first African American general in the United States. Davis dropped out of Howard University in 1898 to help recruit the 8th United States Volunteer Infantry for the Spanish-American War, in which he was commissioned as a first lieutenant. As with most Volunteer regiments, the 8th did not deploy during the war. He was mustered out with the 8th on March 6, 1899. Davis found that he loved being a soldier and, against the wishes of his family, decided to make a career out of it. Unable to secure a Regular Army commission after the war, he enlisted as a private in the 9th Cavalry Regiment, one of the four regiments for black soldiers in the Regular Army. He eventually reached the enlisted rank of sergeant major when he was able to secure a commission through examination. Given the segregated nature of the U.S. military, he was limited in potential assignments. Still, he saw service in the Philippines, served as military attaché to Liberia, and was professor of military science and tactics at Wilberforce University and Tuskegee Institute. Like most white career officers of the period, he also served as an adviser to the National Guard, working as an instructor in the black 372nd Regiment in the Ohio National Guard and, in a more unusual arrangement, took command of the black 369th Regiment in the New York National Guard. He was promoted to the temporary rank of brigadier general—the first black flag officer in the United States—on October 25, 1940. Approaching retirement as World War II was beginning in Europe, he retired on July 31, 1941, and was recalled the next day. He served during the war in a variety of assignments, mostly as a special assistant to theater commanders and as an inspector and adviser on matters pertaining to the use of black soldiers. He retired in 1948 after 50 years of military service.

Benjamin O. Davis Jr.
(December 18, 1912–July 4, 2002)

Career army and air force officer. Born in Washington, D.C., an early memory was of his father donning his army uniform and standing proudly in front of the family home in Tuskegee as the Ku Klux Klan marched down the street. Davis began his college education at Western Reserve, later transferring to the University of Chicago. Based on his record there, Congressman Oscar Depriest (R-IL) appointed him to the U.S. Military Academy at West Point, where he was socially ostracized by his fellow cadets. He did not tell his father of the shameful treatment he had received until after he had completed the course. He graduated in 1936, ranking thirty-fifth out of a class of 278 and earning the respect of his fellow classmates for his determination. When he accepted his commission, he became one of two black line officers currently on active duty, with the other being his father. Turned down for pilot training because of his color, he branched infantry and was assigned to the 24th Infantry, then at Fort Benning, Georgia. He was later assigned to teach ROTC at Tuskegee Institute. When the Roosevelt administration announced the creation of black combat unit in the Army Corps, Davis applied and was accepted into the training program. Since he was Regular Army, he was groomed as the likely commander of this new unit. He was one of five trainees to complete the first training cycle and in March 1942 was awarded his pilot's wings and changed his branch from infantry to Air Corps. Soon after, he was named the commander of the 99th Fighter Squadron, which he took to North Africa and brought to combat. He successfully defended the record of the 99th against racially based charges in front of investigating committees and in public opinion. In September 1943, he assumed command of the 332nd Fighter Group and led it in combat. After the war ended in Europe, he assumed command of the 477th Composite Group and helped plan the integration of the newly independent air force. He commanded the 51st Fighter Interceptor Wing during the Korean War. He became the first black general in the air force on October 27, 1954, when he was promoted to brigadier general. He became the first black two-star officer in the U.S. military when he was promoted to major general on June 30, 1959, and the first black three-star officer on April 30, 1965, when he was promoted to lieutenant general. He remained in the air force until his retirement on February 1, 1970, serving in a variety of command and staff positions in the racially integrated air force. On December 9, 1998, President Bill Clinton advanced him to full general (retired) in recognition of his long service to the nation and his key role in desegregating the military.

Eugene J. Bullard
(October 9, 1894–October 12, 1961)

African American who served as an officer in the French army, including as a pilot, during World War I. Bullard gained fame in France as the "Black Swallow of Death." Bullard was born and raised in Columbus, Georgia. He later stowed away on a ship to Scotland. He remained in the United Kingdom, working as an entertainer and boxer. He visited France as World War I was beginning and joined the French Foreign Legion in the summer of 1914. After being wounded in 1916 at the Battle of Verdun, he transferred to the *Aéronautique Militaire* and flew as a member of the Lafayette Flying Corps, which was manned by expatriate Americans, most of whom were white. After the United States entered the war in 1917, the Lafayette Flying Corps was brought into American service, but Bullard was denied service with the Americans because of his color. He continued flying for France, scoring at least two aerial victories, until January 1918, when he was returned to the infantry after getting into a fight with a French officer. He remained in France after the war, eventually opening a nightclub. Among black Americans, his service to France was seen as proof that blacks could master the skills needed to be fighter pilots. He remained in France for a while after Germany occupied France during World War II, spying on the Germans for the French underground. He later escaped France and, wounded in the fighting, eventually made his way back to the United States with his two daughters. Suffering from his injury and relatively unknown in the United States, he worked at a series of menial jobs. In 1959, the French government made him a Knight of the Legion of Honor in recognition of his service to France during both world wars.

Philip Cochran
(January 29, 1910–August 26, 1979)

Regular Army Air Corps officer and pilot. Cochran enlisted in the Air Corps after graduating from college and was able to complete flight training and earn a commission. He asked his old acquaintance from college, Milton Caniff, to design an insignia for the 65th Fighter Squadron. Milton did but also used some of the members of the 64th, including Cochran, as models for his "Terry and the Pirates" comic strip. Cochran's character was Flip Corkin. Major Cochran led a group of unassigned replacement pilots in an unnumbered squadron he dubbed the "Joker Squadron." His daring flying and colorful personality soon made him a favorite of the press corps. After North Africa, he served in Burma as a commander of the Army Air Force Air Commando Group.

W.E.B. (William Edward Burghardt) Du Bois
(February 23, 1868–August 27, 1963)

Born in Great Barrington, Massachusetts, Du Bois became the first African American to earn a PhD from Harvard (1895). Du Bois became a leading black intellectual and spokesman for black America. As an educated black man who later lived part of his life in the South, Du Bois was particularly incensed by Jim Crow, and he became one of the driving forces behind the early civil rights movement. He was one of the founders of the National Association for the Advancement of Colored People in 1909. He disagreed with Booker T. Washington's stance on accommodation with Jim Crow, instead arguing for confrontation with racists practices. During World War I, he encouraged black men to serve loyally, believing that service would lead to recognition of basic civil rights after the war, while refusal to serve would be used to justify further losses in what few civil rights blacks still had. He was deeply disillusioned by the savage repression of blacks following World War I. He supported the entry of the United States into World War II mainly because he had come to see the Soviet Union as the best hope for the future. After the war, he moved further to the left politically—joining the U.S. Communist Party in 1961. He died in Ghana, where he had gone to direct the *Encyclopedia Africana*.

Henry O. Flipper
(March 21, 1856–May 3, 1940)

First African American to graduate from the U.S. Military Academy at West Point and serve as a Regular Army officer. Flipper was born into slavery in Thomasville, Georgia. He attended Atlanta University during

Reconstruction and was appointed to West Point. Although West Point had four other black cadets when he arrived, only Flipper completed the program and was commissioned in 1877. He served in the 10th Cavalry Regiment until found guilty by court-martial in December 1881 of "conduct unbecoming an officer" and dismissed from the service on June 30, 1882. Flipper and his supporters believed that he had been set up by a new post commander because he was black. Although Flipper tried for many years to regain his commission, he was never allowed back into the army. His descendants in 1976 applied to the Army Board of Correction of Military Records. On the board's recommendation, Flipper's discharge was changed to "honorable." In 1999, Flipper was pardoned by President Bill Clinton.

Charles B. Hall
(August 25, 1920–November 22, 1971)

Army Air Forces officer and pilot. A native of Brazil, Indiana, Hall left his studies at Illinois State Teachers College in 1940 to enlist in the army. While serving as a private, he applied for the aviation cadet training and was accepted in 1941. He graduated in the fourth class of pilots from Tuskegee Army Airfield. He won fame when he became the first African American combat pilot, flying for the U.S. military, to shoot down an enemy aircraft, a German Fw-190. For this, he was personally congratulated by Generals Eisenhower, Doolittle, and Spatz. He later was awarded the Distinguished Flying Cross for leading a flight of eight aircraft on a patrol on January 8, 1944, that encountered six enemy aircraft positioning themselves to strafe Allied ground troops. In the ensuing fight, Hall shot down another two enemy airplanes, while other members of his flight shot down two others and chased away the two surviving enemy. He left the air force as a major and became an insurance agent.

William H. Hastie Jr.
(November 17, 1904–April, 14, 1976)

Jurist and government official. Born in Knoxville, Kentucky, Hastie graduated magna cum laude at the top of his class from Amherst College in Massachusetts, going on to earn a PhD in juridical studies from Harvard University. He then accepted a position as professor at the Howard University School of Law. In 1937, he broke a major barrier when President Franklin D. Roosevelt appointed him to the U.S. District Court for the U.S. Virgin Islands, making Hastie the first African American federal judge. He resigned from that position in 1939 when he accepted the position of dean of the Howard University Law School. Later Roosevelt appointed him to serve as civilian aide to Secretary of War Henry Stimson, with the specific mission to advocate for black issues in the military. He resigned from that position in protest in 1943 but was back in government service in 1946, when President Harry S. Truman appointed him to serve as the first black governor of the U.S. Virgin Islands. In 1949, Truman appointed Hastie to serve on the U.S. Court of Appeals for the Third Circuit, again the first black to serve as an appellate judge. His name was often mentioned as the likely first black judge to be appointed to the U.S. Supreme Court, but apparently President John F. Kennedy believed that Hastie was too conservative on issues other than civil rights. Hastie became the chief judge of the Third Circuit in 1971 and retired in 1974.

Daniel "Chappie" James Jr.
(February 11, 1920–February 25, 1978)

Career air force officer, first African American four-star general. Born in Pensacola, Florida, James attended Tuskegee Institute and later graduated from the Civilian Pilot Training Program at Tuskegee Institute in 1942. He worked at Tuskegee Army Airfield for a short period as a civilian flight instructor until January 1943 when he was finally admitted into the cadet program. After his commissioning, he remained at Tuskegee Army Airfield as a trainer. After the war, James stayed in the Army Air Forces and later the U.S. Air Force. He flew 101 combat missions during the Korean War. Several important command and staff assignments followed, and during the Vietnam War he served as the vice commander of the 8th Tactical Fighter Wing, flying 78 missions over Vietnam. In 1970, he was promoted to the rank of brigadier general. He eventually reached the rank of full general on August 29, 1975. At that rank, he commanded the North American Air Defense Command, one of the most important assignments in the military during the Cold War. He retired on February 2, 1978, after a career of 36 years and died three weeks later.

George C. Marshall
(December 31, 1880–October 16, 1959)

Career army officer. Educated at the Virginia Military Institute, Marshall showed enormous skill as an organizer and leader as well as an ability to deal effectively with political leaders. By September 1939, he was the chief of staff of the U.S. Army—the top soldier in the entire army—and in that capacity would oversee the expansion of the army by more than 40 times and the training and commitment to combat of those armies and air forces. On racial matters, he was conservative, believing that the military was not the proper place for what he saw as social experimentation. However, he was also committed to subordination of the military to civilian masters and an astute student of national strengths and characteristics. Whatever his own feelings on the matter, he understood that President Roosevelt wanted to see black combat aviation units and ensured that his subordinates in the Army Air Corps (and later Army Air Forces) understood that he would accept nothing but success on that matter. After the war, he retired from the army as a five-star general. He later served as secretary of state and secretary of defense.

William "Spike" Momyer
(September 23, 1916–)

Career air force officer. Momyer was commander of the 33rd Fighter Group, to which the 99th Fighter Squadron was attached from June until October 1943. Awarded the Distinguished Flying Cross and the Silver Star with two oak leaf clusters for service in North Africa, he wrote the damning report on the pilots of the 99th, which was later endorsed by General Edwin House, commander of the 12th Air Support Command. Aggressive in combat, he was criticized for the heavy losses the 33rd Fighter Group sustained under his command. He later commanded the 7th Air Force in the Vietnam War and in 1978 wrote his seminal book *Air Power in Three Wars*. Momyer retired from the air force in 1973 as a four-star general after commanding the Tactical Air Command.

Robert Moton
(August 17, 1867–May 31, 1940)

Second principal of Tuskegee Institute. Moton was born in Virginia and graduated from Hampton Institute in 1890. Shortly after graduating, he was appointed as commandant of cadets at Hampton and served in the administration. On the death of Booker T. Washington in 1915, the trustees of Tuskegee Institute appointed Moton to serves as the school's second principal. He held that position until 1935, during which period Tuskegee focused more on providing a college education to black youths.

Noel F. Parrish
(November 1, 1909–April 7, 1987)

Career army and air force officer. Born in Kentucky and raised in Alabama, Parrish graduated from Rice Institute in 1928 and originally enlisted in the army in 1930 and was assigned to the cavalry. After a year, he entered the cadet training program, after which he was commissioned in the Air Corps. He served in a variety of flying and training positions before he became the base commander at Tuskegee Army Airfield in February 1943. One of his early acts as commander was to have all "whites" and "colored" signs removed from the post. While some blacks, especially black newspapers such as the *Pittsburgh Courier*, claimed that he hid his disdain for blacks behind a smooth and polished style, most of the pilots in the program believed that he had their best interest in mind. He was committed to the success of the experiment, in part because he believed that maintaining segregation was inefficient. He retired from the air force on October 1, 1964, as a brigadier general.

Frederick Douglas Patterson
(October 10, 1901–April 26, 1988)

Third principal of Tuskegee Institute (1935–1953). Born in Washington, D.C., and orphaned while young, Patterson held a doctorate of veterinary medicine from Iowa State College and a PhD in bacteriology from Cornell University. Patterson served as the director of Tuskegee's School of Agriculture before the school's trustees selected Patterson to lead the school. While president, he formed the United Negro College Fund (1944). In 1987, he was awarded the Presidential Medal of Freedom.

John C. Robinson
(1903–March 1954)

Known as the "Brown Condor of Ethiopia." Born in Carrabella, Florida, and raised largely in Gulfport, Mississippi, Robinson graduated from Tuskegee Institute in 1924. He later became the first black student accepted into the Curtiss Wright Aeronautical Institute in Chicago. He then worked for the Curtiss Flying Service and later opened his own flying school. His May 1934, landing at the Tuskegee Institute marked the beginning of interest in aviation at the school. Robinson later served as a colonel in the fledgling Ethiopian air force during the war with Italy. After returning from the war, Robinson became a hero to black Americans both for his skills as a pilot and for fighting to defend the last African nation under indigenous rule. In 1944, Robinson returned to Ethiopia, where he continued his involvement in aviation as well as business. Seriously injured in a plane crash on March 13, 1954, he died two weeks later and was buried in Addis Ababa.

Eleanor Roosevelt
(October 11, 1884–November 7, 1962)

First Lady of the United States (1933–1945). Roosevelt, niece of President Theodore Roosevelt and a distant cousin of Franklin D. Roosevelt, shared her future husband's New York City upbringing. Her mother died when she was eight, and her father was institutionalized for alcoholism when she was 10. At the age of 23, she married Franklin. Throughout her life, she espoused progressive causes, including rights for women and blacks. When her husband became president in 1933, she used her position as First Lady to speak for the issues she supported. Her support for black civil rights led to rumors among her opponents of the existence of "Eleanor's Clubs," secret clubs of black women domestic workers who, inspired by the First Lady, vowed to disobey white employers. She made a point of not following segregation laws in Alabama when she attended a conference there in 1938. In 1939, she famously resigned her membership in the Daughters of the American Revolution after it refused to let the black singer Marian Anderson sing at Constitution Hall, which they owned. Mrs. Roosevelt then pressured her husband to have the secretary of the interior allow Anderson to sing at the Lincoln Memorial. She showed her support for the Tuskegee Airmen when, on a visit to Tuskegee in the spring of 1941, she went for an airplane ride with "Chief" Anderson at the controls. After her husband's death, she continued to champion progressive causes, including civil rights for blacks, until her own death.

Henry "Harry" H. Schwartz
(May 18, 1869–April 24, 1955)

Democratic senator from Wyoming (1937–1943). Schwartz, originally from Ohio, represented a state with a tiny black population. While some in Congress argued that the original bill to begin the Civilian Pilot Training Program (CPTP) contained no provisions to exclude backs, Schwartz believed that without language explicitly directing the establishment of the program at a Negro college, no such program would be established because of opposition from the War Department. He therefore inserted an amendment into Public Law 18, the appropriations bill that directed the establishment of a CPTP at one or more Negro colleges. When after the law was passed and the Air Corps still did not establish any program at a Negro college, he made a personal visit to General Arnold demanding that the Air Corps fulfill the requirements of the law.

Robert R. Selway Jr.
(December 31, 1902–September 12, 1967)

Career Air Corps officer. A 1924 graduate of West Point, he was a pilot of great experience but also an ardent segregationist who apparently had little enthusiasm for his mission to lead black airmen. He commanded the 332nd Fighter Group from June until October 1943. He became the commander of the 477th Bombardment Group at Selfridge Airfield in early 1945. He instituted policies to maintain strict segregation, in line with the policies of his superiors, which precipitated the so-called Freeman Field Mutiny.

George "Spanky" Spencer Roberts
(September 24, 1818–March 1984)

Career air force officer. Born and raised in Fairmount, West Virginia, Roberts attended West Virginia State College and earned his private pilot's license in the Civilian Pilot Training Program. Graduating in the first class of cadets from the Tuskegee program, he commanded the 99th Fighter Squadron until August 1942 when Davis assumed command. Roberts later served in every command and staff position in the 99th. He reassumed command of the 99th in September 1943 after Davis left to assume command of the 332nd Fighter Group. He assumed command of the 332nd on June 9, 1945. He flew 78 combat missions during the war. Roberts brought the 332nd back to the United States and oversaw its deactivation. He stayed in the air force, retiring as a colonel in 1968, and took up a career at Wells Fargo. He died in Sacramento, California.

Henry L. Stimson
(September 21, 1867–October 20, 1950)

Secretary of war during World War II. Stimson, a lifelong Republican from New York, attended Phillips Academy in Andover, Massachusetts, Yale College, and Harvard Law School. After a successful law career and less successful political career, Stimson served as the secretary of war from 1911 to 1913 under President Howard Taft. He served in France as an artillery officer during World War I, mustering out with the rank of colonel. He served as governor general of the Philippines from 1927 to 1929, during which time he opposed Philippine independence. He served as secretary of state from 1929 to 1933 under President Herbert Hoover. When World War II started in Europe, President Franklin D. Roosevelt appointed the Republican Stimson to be secretary of war, based on experience and his staunch anti-Germany and anti-Japan stance. He remained in office until 1945, after the war ended.

Robert B. Tresville
(May 9, 1921–June 24, 1944)

Fifth black graduate of West Point. Tresville became the first black West Point cadet accepted straight into the Army Air Forces in January 1943. A native of Galveston, Texas, Tresville's father had been a career soldier, serving as the bandmaster for the 24th Infantry. Tresville attended flight training at Tuskegee Army Airfield in the summer and fall of 1942 while still a cadet. By January 1944 when the 332nd Fighter group deployed, Captain Tresville commanded the 100th Fighter Squadron. He flew 24 missions before being killed in action over the Tyrrhenian Sea near Corsica. The day of his death, a cable announcing his promotion to the rank of major arrived at the 332nd.

Charles Young
(March 12, 1864–January 8, 1922)

Career Regular Army officer and third African American to graduate from West Point. Born into slavery in Kentucky, Young moved with his family to Riply, Ohio, after the Civil War, where he grew up. He went to an otherwise white high school, graduating at the top when he was 16, and worked for a while as a teacher in a black school. He took the examination for appointment to West Point and scored second. After the top scorer declined the appointment, Young was appointed to West Point. He graduated in 1889 and was branched cavalry, serving in the 9th and 10th Cavalries. In addition to troop duties in the West and in the Philippines, Young taught ROTC at Wilberforce College in Ohio, acted as superintendent of Sequoia and General Grant National Parks, and served as military attaché to Haiti and Liberia. In 1916, Young became the first

African American promoted to lieutenant colonel in the Regular Army. However, when the United States entered World War I, his color and rank became an issue. Because most of the company grade officers in the 9th and 10th Cavalry Regiments were white, for Young to serve in a position comparable to his rank would mean having a black man in command of white men in combat. Officially, he was put on medical furlough in June 1917 because of high blood pressure. He returned to work at Wilberforce, but in November 1918, he rode a horse from Ohio to Washington, D.C., to demonstrate his physical fitness. With the war over, he was returned to active service and again served as attaché to Liberia. He died of a kidney infection while on a mission to Nigeria. He was returned to the United States and buried with full military honors.

Coleman A. Young
(May 24, 1918–November 29, 1997)

First black mayor of Detroit. Born in Tuscaloosa, Alabama, but having moved with his family to Detroit in 1923, Young worked for the Ford Motor Company and soon became a labor organizer. He later worked for the post office and, along with his brother, began organizing a union of postal workers. In the army, he had been accepted into the pilot training program and assigned to the 477th, where he served as a bombardier and navigator. He was one of the officers who organized the so-called Freeman Field Mutiny. After the war, he returned to Detroit and became involved in politics. In 1960, he was elected to help draft the new state constitution for Michigan. In 1964, he was elected to the state senate. In 1974, he was elected to the first of five mayoral terms, with a campaign that focused heavily on the issue of the black grievances against the predominantly white police force.

Primary Documents

Document 1: Army War College 1925 Memorandum on "The Use of Negro Man Power in War," first page. This memorandum formed much of the official army stance toward the use of black soldiers, particularly drafted black soldiers, during war. The study was ostensibly based on the experience of black units in World War I and on scientific facts, but it was actually a compilation of racist assumptions, stereotypes, and pseudosciences presented as a straightforward study. The paper starts with a few assumptions and then presents some "facts" about blacks that form the basis of the "problem" of using black soldiers. The paper notes that blacks form a considerable part of the population of the United States, are citizens, and should be expected to bear their share of the burden in war. Nothing in that list of assumptions would be offensive to black leaders, black veterans, or black soldiers. In the next section, however, section III, several "facts" about black men are stated that disqualify them from combat or leadership positions—the black man is a coward, is easily swayed by crowds, has not the initiative of a white man, has a sense of inferiority regarding the white man, and is not intelligent. Such bigotry masquerading as simple statements of fact and official policy would do much to block efforts of black men such as Cadet Benjamin O. Davis Jr. to enter the Air Corps. Men who commanded divisions and larger formation during World War II would have served in the army in 1925 and would have spent much of their professional life when these ideas were widely accepted among whites.

THE ARMY WAR COLLEGE,
OFFICE OF THE COMMANDANT

Washington Barracks, D.C.
October 30, 1925.

MEMORANDUM FOR THE CHIEF OF STAFF:
Subject: The use of negro man power in war.

I. Papers accompanying.
Reference "A". Analysis of the physical, mental, moral and psychological qualities and characteristics of the negro as a sub-species of the human family.
Reference "B". Performance of the negro in past wars.
Reference "C". The negro officer.
Reference "D". Negro political activity in the World War.
Reference "E". Plan for the organization and employment in war of the negro man power drafted and found physically and mentally qualified for military service.

II. The problem presented.
Under the Constitution the negro has the rights of citizenship. He forms a considerable part of the population of the United States. It is evident that he must bear his share of the burden of war.
To what extent shall negro man power be used in a military effort contemplated by the War Department General Mobilization Plan?
How shall it be organized?
How shall it be officered?
How shall it be trained and employed in the Theatre of Operations and the Zone of the Interior?
What standards should be used in the appointment and promotion of negro officers?

III. Facts bearing upon the problem.
1. The negro is physically qualified for combat duty.
He is by nature subservient and believes himself to be inferior to the white man.
He is most susceptible to the influence of crowd psychology.
He can not control himself in the fear of danger to the extent the white man can.
He has not the initiative and resourcefulness of the white man.
He is mentally inferior to the white man.
Reference "A".

Army War College. "The Use of Negro Man Power in War," October 30, 1925. Air Force Historical Research Agency, Maxwell AFB, Alabama.

Document 2: War Department order of March 19, 1941, constituting the 99th Pursuit Squadron, and ordering its activation at Chanute Field, Illinois, on April 1, 1941. In order to get the new squadron functioning, the order called for the transfer of seven men each from the two existing black Regular Army infantry regiments, the 24th and 25th, to provide the initial enlisted support for the new Air Corps squadron. Those 14 enlisted men would be the first black men to serve in an aviation unit in the U.S. military. As the 24th Regiment and the 25th Regiment were part of the old "Buffalo Soldier" units, the transfer of these 14 men provided a tangible link between the Buffalo Soldiers and the Tuskegee Airmen.

WAR DEPARTMENT
The Adjutant General's Office
Washington

AG 320.2 (2-18-41)   March 19, 1941.
M (Ret) M-C

SUBJECT: Constitution and Activation of Units.

TO: The Commanding Generals,
           Fourth and Eighth Corps Areas,
           And Chanute Field, Illinois.

    1. The 99th Pursuit Squadron and Air Base Detachment are hereby constituted and will be activated at Chanute Field, Illinois, by the Commanding General on or about April 1, 1941, with eventual station at Tuskegee, Alabama. The Squadron will be organized in accordance with Table of Organization 1-15.

    2. The 24th Infantry will furnish seven (7) men as a part of the cadre. These enlisted men will be transferred in their present grades and ratings and will have the following qualifications:

> 1 to be First Sergeant
> 1 to be Mess Sergeant
> 1 to be Clerk, administrative
> 4 to be Cooks.

    3. The 25th Infantry will furnish seven (7) men for the remainder of the cadre. These enlisted men will be transferred in their present grades and ratings and will have the following qualifications:

> 1 to be Supply Sergeant
> 4 to be Cooks
> 2 to be Clerks, administrative.

    3. The Commanding Generals of the Fourth and Eighth Corps Areas will issue the necessary orders to transfer the enlisted men from Fort Benning, Georgia,

and Fort Huachuca, Arizona, respectively, to Chanute Field, Rantoul, Illinois, on or about April 1, 1941, as requested by the Commanding General, Chanute Field, Rantoul, Illinois.

a. Movement will be effected in the most economical manner.

b. Individual equipment, except clothing, as shown for peace in column 3, Tables of Basic Allowances, plus trunk lockers, will be taken. Clothing will be in accordance with column 2 (Mobilization), Tables of Basic Allowances, as modified by War Department Circular No. 8, 1941.

c. Travel by privately owned automobile is authorized as provided in paragraph 1 i, AR 35-4820.

d. Direct correspondence in all matters relating to these movements is authorized.

e. Report by radio to this office

Date of departure

Estimated time of arrival

4. Obligate the procurement authorities cited below to the extent necessary:

Travel of the Army

FD 1437 P 50-0623, P 82-0600, A 0410-01. (For travel of enlisted men; and for travel of dependents of enlisted men of the first three grades.)

Army Transportation—Rail

QM 1620 P 54-0110, P 54-0284, P 54-1378, P 54-0701 A 0525-01 "D". (For packing, crating, and shipping authorized household goods allowances.)

By order of the Secretary of War:

L.S. Ostrander
Adjutant General.

Copies furnished:
The Commanding Generals,
All Armies, GHQ Air Force and Corps Areas.
The Chief of Staff, GHQ, and Commanding Officers
of Exempted Stations.
The Chiefs of Arms, Services and Bureaus and the Divisions of the War Department General Staff.

U.S. War Department. "Constitution and Activation of Units," March 19, 1941. Air Force Historical Research Agency, Maxwell AFB, Alabama.

Document 3: War Department order of December 27, 1941, constituting the 100th Pursuit [*sic*] Squadron and ordering its activation at Tuskegee Army Airfield. The orders make clear that the 100th was "a colored unit." This practice of identifying black units as such was apparently considered necessary so that no one in the army bureaucracy would make an inadvertent decision that might assign a white man to such a unit or take a black man from such a unit and assign him to a white unit. Such inefficiencies were the price to be paid to maintain segregation. Since Tuskegee Army Airfield was still under construction, the orders specify that the 100th would be constituted when the facilities at Tuskegee were adequate for the unit rather than on a specified date.

AG 320.2 (12-8-41)
R—AAF   December 27, 1941.

Constitution and Activation of
The 100th Pursuit Squadron.

Commanding General,
Southeast Air Corps Training Center.

1. The 100th Pursuit Squadron, a colored unit, is constituted and will be activated when facilities permit at Tuskegee Air Base. The necessary Base and Service personnel will be increased for the expansion of the Tuskegee Air Base.

2. Cadres will be furnished by existing units at Tuskegee Air Base.

By order of the Secretary of War:
Otto Johnson

Adjutant General.

Copies furnished:

Commanding Generals,
    Field Forces and
    Second and
    Third Armies.
Chief of the Army Air Forces.
Chief of the Air Corps.

U.S. War Department. "Constitution and Activation of the 100th Pursuit Squadron," December 27, 1941. Air Force Historical Research Agency, Maxwell AFB, Alabama.

Document 4: War Department orders of July 4, 1942, constituting the Head-quarters of the 332nd Fighter Group, the 332nd Fighter Control Squadron, the 301st Fighter Squadron, and the 302nd Fighter Squadron. As with the 100th Pursuit Squadron, no specific date for activation was given, stating only that activation should occur "at the earliest practical date," with the unit commanders making that determination. With the rapid expansion of the Army Air Forces during the period, orders for multiple units, often un-connected, were published together. Notice how again the orders had to indicate that the 332nd was "a colored unit."

CONFIDENTIAL

The Adjutant General's Office
Washington

AG 320.2 (7-3-42)   July 4, 1942
MR-M-AF

SUBJECT: Constitution, Activation, Reassignment and Redesignation of certain Army Air Forces Units.

TO: Commanding Generals,
             Air Service Command
             Eighth Air Force
             Third Air Force.

  1.   The following units are constituted and will be activated at the earliest prac-ticable date by the commanders concerned, as indicated below:

Unit	Station of Activation	Activated by CG and assigned to:
Army Air Forces Storage Depot	Pierce Arrow Building, Great Arrow Avenue, Buffalo, N.Y.	Air Service Command
Sub Depot	Chico, Calif.	Air Service Command
Sub Depot	Blythe, Calif.	Air Service Command
Sub Depot	Memphis, Tenn.	Air Service Command
VIII Troop Carrier Command, Hq & Hq Sq	Stout Field Indianapolis, Ind.	Eighth Air Force
380th Base Hq and Air Base Sq (Reduced)	Camp Davis, N. C.	Third Air Force

*Hq. 332d Fighter Gp Tuskegee, Ala. Third Air Force
332d Fighter Control Sq
301st Fighter Sq
302d Fighter Sq

* A colored unit

2. Authorized enlisted strength and grades will be published in a separate communication.

3. Cadre personnel for these units will be taken from units under the control of the commander concerned.

4. Filler personnel for these units will be requisitioned in the usual manner.

CONFIDENTIAL

CONFIDENTIAL

U.S. War Department. "Constitution, Activation, Reassignment and Redesignation of Certain Army Air Forces Units," July 4, 1942. Air Force Historical Research Agency, Maxwell AFB, Alabama.

Document 5: "General Orders No 14" of October 18, 1942, activating the 332nd Fighter Group, assigning the 100th Fighter Squadron to the 332nd Fighter Group, and assigning the 332nd Fighter Group to the Third Air Force. The exact size of the "experiment" was unknown in the early days of the war, and the 100th Fighter Squadron was originally envisioned as a sister squadron to the 99th, while the 301st and the 302nd would also be paired. However, the 99th was trained and deployed far earlier than the other three black fighter squadrons, so the 100th was instead assigned to the 332nd Fighter Group along with the 301st and 302nd Fighter Squadrons.

Tuskegee, Alabama

18 October, 1942.

GENERAL ORDERS)
:
NO.   14)

SECTION I—ACTIVATION OF THE 332D FIGHTER GROUP
SECTION II—REASSIGNMENT OF THE 100TH FIGHTER SQUADRON

I—ACTIVATION OF THE 332D FIGHTER GROUP

     1.   PAC letter, WD, AGO, file: AG 320.2 (7-3-42) MR-M-AF, July 4 1942, Subject: "Constitution, Activation, Reassignment and Redesignation of Certain Army Air Force Units", and General Orders, #180, Hq., Third Air Force, Tampa, Fla., dated July 9, 1942, the following named unit having been constituted is activated as of October 18, 1942, and assigned to the Third Air Force:

Unit	Station of Activation
Hq. 332D Fighter Group	Tuskegee Army Flying School,
332D Fighter Control Sq.	Tuskegee, Alabama
301st Fighter Sq.	
302D Fighter Sq.	

II—REASSIGNMENT OF THE 100TH FIGHTER SQUADRON

     1.   PAC letter, WD, AGO, file: AG 320.2 (7-3-42) MR-M-AF, July 4, 1942, Subject: "Constitution, Activation, Reassignment and Redesignation of Certain Army Air Forces Units", and General Orders, #180, Hq., Third Air Force, Tampa, Fla., dated July 9, 1942, the following unit is relieved from its present assignment and reassigned as indicated:

Unit	New Assignment
100th Fighter Squadron	332D Fighter Group

By order of Colonel KIMBLE:

CLYDE H. BYNUM
1st Lt., A. C.,
Asst. Adjutant.

OFFICIAL:

CLYDE H. BYNUM,
1st Lt., A. C.,
Asst. Adjutant.

Kimble, Frederick von. "General Orders No. 14," October 18, 1942. Air Force Historical Research Agency, Maxwell AFB, Alabama.

Document 6: Memorandum from Major General Edwin J. House on the combat efficiency of the 99th Pursuit Squadron. This was the memo written largely by Colonel Momyer that set off such a firestorm when its contents became disseminated. While the memo praises Lieutenant Colonel Davis, most of the memo is critical of the combat abilities of the 99th as a whole. In particular, the memo states that while "ground discipline and the ability to accomplish and execute orders promptly are excellent," the unit lacked air discipline, aggressiveness, physical stamina, and apparently courage. The memo advises that the 99th would be better employed using older aircraft to patrol the west coast of Africa, where enemy contact was increasingly unlikely. Their reassignment to a quiet sector would free up their current aircraft for use by white units.

The writer really shows his prejudices in paragraph 4 and 6. In paragraph 4, he explains that expert opinion holds that blacks are not physically or mentally equipped to be pilots and that, besides, social difficulties made the use of a black squadron difficult, specifically mentioning that having black men and white men sleeping and eating in the same area was problematic. In other words, because of what he believed about the abilities of blacks and the need to maintain the military's version of Jim Crow, he did not want black fighter units regardless of the performance of the 99th. In paragraph 6, he further states that based on the experience of the 99th, any "colored" group being formed in the United States—the 332nd Fighter Group—be kept in the United States. Here, laid bare, was the racist argument—the conduct of one black unit applied to all.

HEADQUARTERS XII AIR SUPPORT COMMAND
APO #766

16 September 1943

SUBJECT: Combat Efficiency of the 99th Fighter Squadron.

TO: Major General J. K. Cannon, USA, Deputy Commander, Northwest
African Tactical Air Force, APO #509, U. S. Army.

1. On June 12th, 1943, I took command of the XII Air Support Command.
With one of the Groups assigned to the Command was the 99th Fighter Squadron,
which I visited quite frequently. Their Commanding Officer, Lt. Col. Davis, particularly impressed me. On the day of the 99th's first encounter with enemy aircraft, I
happened to be on the airdrome and was very complimentary and encouraging to
the personnel I met. At that time one of the colored correspondents asked me if I
thought there should be a colored group, and I answered to the effect that I saw
no reason why there should not be such a group in the near future. Since that day,
I have compared the operating efficiency of the 99th Fighter Squadron with that
of a white fighter squadron operating in the same group and with the same type of
equipment. I quote from a report by an officer who has been in the best position to
observe carefully the work of the 99th Squadron over its entire combat period:

"The ground discipline and ability to accomplish and execute orders
promptly are excellent. Air discipline has not been completely satisfactory. The
ability to work and fight as a team has not yet been acquired. Their formation flying has been very satisfactory until jumped by enemy aircraft, when the squadron seems to disintegrate. This has repeatedly been brought to the attention of the
Squadron, but attempts to correct this deficiency so far have been unfruitful. On
one particular occasion, a flight of twelve JU 88's, with an escort of six ME 109's,
was observed to be bombing Pantelleria. The 99th Squadron, instead of pressing
home the attack against the bombers, allowed themselves to become engaged with
the 109's. The unit has shown a lack of aggressive spirit that is necessary for a well-
organized fighter squadron. On numerous instances when assigned to dive bomb a
specified target in which the anti-aircraft fire was light and inaccurate, they chose
the secondary target which was undefended. On one occasion, they were assigned
a mission with one squadron of this Group to bomb a target in the toe of Italy; the
99th turned back before the reaching of the target because of the weather. The
other squadron went on to the target and pressed home the attack. As later substan-
tiated, the weather was considered operational.

"Up to the present moment, the 99th Squadron averages approximately
28 sorties per man. Their operations since being placed on combat duty have been
considerably easier than past operations due to the nature of the tactical situation. However, the Squadron Commander of the 99th requested during the battle
of Sicily to be removed from operations for a period of three days, and longer if
possible. The reason given was that his pilots were suffering from pilot's fatigue.

The Squadron's Surgeon submitted a medical report stating that the pilots of the 99th should be removed from combat duty because of the strenuous and rigorous conditions under which they have been operating. In comparison, the pilots of this Group had an average of approximately 70 sorties and had been in operations for nine continuous months.

"Based on the performance of the 99th Fighter Squadron to date, it is my opinion that they are not of the fighting caliber of any squadron in this Group. They have failed to display the aggressiveness and desire for combat that are necessary to a first-class fighting organization. It may be expected that we will get less work and less operational time out of the 99th Fighter Squadron than any squadron in this Group."

2. At the present time the 99th Squadron is not in the Naples area because there is insufficient room on the P-40 field on which to place them. It is our intention to bring them into the area as soon as space is available. We also brought forward two Spitfire Groups less squadrons because of lack of space.

3. Shortly before the Naples operation, a radiogram came to me stating that Lt. Col. Davis had been selected to return to the United States to command a colored group. Although with the knowledge that in turning the command of the 99th Squadron over to the next ranking officer would not approach the standard of Davis, I relieved Davis for his new assignment.

4. On many discussions held with officers of all professions, including medical, the consensus of opinion seems to be that the negro type has not the proper reflexes to make a first-class, fighter pilot. Also, on rapid moves that must be a part of this Command, housing and massing difficulties arise because the time has not yet arrived when white and colored soldiers will mess at the same table and sleep in the same barracks. No details in this connection have been brought out because it is desired that administrative features not be a part of this report.

5. I believe it would be much better to assign the 99th to the Northwest African Coastal Air Force, equip it with P-39's and make the present P-40's available to this Command as replacements for the active operations still to come in this theater.

6. It is recommended that if and when a colored group is formed in the United States, it be retained for either the eastern or western defense zone and a white fighter group be released for movement overseas.

EDWIN J. HOUSE
Major General, U.S.A. (by J.H.C.)
Commanding

COPY

House, Edwin J. "Combat Efficiency of the 99th Pursuit Squadron," September 16, 1943. Air Force Historical Research Agency, Maxwell AFB, Alabama.

Document 7: "Narrative Mission Account No. 23," July 12, 1944. The initial report and its supplement document a typical escort mission, when the 100th, 301st, and 302nd Fighter Squadrons escorted B-24s from the 49th Bomb Wing to their targets at Nimes. Although the initial report listed only one enemy fighter shot down, the supplement lists four confirmed and one possible. One pilot, Lieutenant Rhodes, was shot down, but he was able to bail out. Six of the planes from the 332nd landed at other fields other than their home field at Ramitelli, probably because of mechanical problems or fuel shortages, and the initial report noted that final tallies would not be known until all pilots were debriefed. While the report lists only one bomber lost, Missing Aircrew Reports from the 49th Bomb Wing show three bombers lost that day.

D-CV/med

HEADQUARTERS 332ND FIGHTER GROUP
A.P.O. 520, U.S. ARMY

12 July 1944.

NARRATIVE MISSION REPORT NO. 23

MISSION NO. 23, 100th, 301st, and 302nd Ftr Squadrons.

1. MISSION AND TARGET: To provide close cover, escort, penetration, target cover and withdrawal for B-24's to the 49th Bomb Wing.

2. AIRCRAFT AND CHRONOLOGY: 42 A/C took-off from Ramitelli A/D at 0751 hours. 8 returned early (6 spares, 2 mech). Line R/V with bombers at 1011 hours at 23,000 ft.

3. ROUTE: Base to line R/V with bombers at 47° 57'N–07° 10'E to target, rallied left and returned directly to base.

4. RENDEZVOUS, FORMATION AND ASSAULT: R/V at 47° 47'N–07° 10'E at 23,000 ft. as briefed. Bombers in fair formation due to heavy overcast. The 100th was middle, 301st lead and 302nd high as bombers reached the target.

5.   RESULTS OF BOMBING: Bombers reported excellent pattern over T/A, direct hits were observed in the M/Y's according to bomber pilot landing here. Left Bombers at Isle of Corsica–NW tip.

6.   STRAFING: Nil.

7.   ENEMY AIR—RESISTANCE AND ACTIVITY: 6 FW 190's peeling off slowly and in line dived down through the bomber formation at an extremely high rate of speed having peeled off at 10 o'clock above, after diving through formation did a split "S", made tight turns to the left the split "S" again with 1 believed th have been hit and crashed out of second split "S", confirmation being made of crash by other pilots of the flight.

Other pilots returning to base report other encounters, return of pilot concerned will be necessary before confirmation or securing details.

8.   FLAK: MAH tracking type from Toulon to target area.

9.   SIGNIFICANT OBSERVATIONS: 12 E/A believed to be FW 190's observed but not encountered due to great distance, 30 M/V's observed in Toulon Harbor, approximately 60 Ftr's in revetments on A/D around Toulon.

10.   WEATHER: 8/10 to 10/10 enroute T/A and return 3,000 to 25,000 ft with heavy thunderstorms—zero visibility in places—field completely closed on return to base.

11.   AIR—SEA RESCUE: Nil.

12.   RADIO SECURITY: Good.

13.   FRIENDLY A/C LOST OR IN DIFFICULTY: 1 of our pilots, Lt Rhodes bailed out in vicinity of Viterbo. Pilot is reported safe. Excessive black smoke was observed coming from plane. 1 B-24 shot down over T/A—6 chutes observed.

14.   ENEMY A/C SEEN DESTROYED BY OTHER GROUPS: Nil. 1 FW 190 was shot down by one of our pilots, Lt Sawyer.—confirmed by Lt Wiggins.

CONCLUSIONS

15. VICTORIES AND LOSSES:

Victories

Destroyed	Prob. Dist.	Damaged
1 FW 190 Lt Sawyer	0	0

Total
    1 FW 190

LOSSES

OUR LOSSES:	FLAK	FIGHTERS	OTHERS
Lost	0	0	1
Missing	0	0	0
Damaged (non-repairable)	0	0	0
Damaged (repairable)	0	0	0
Wounded	0	0	0

16. SORTIES: 33.

17. FORMATION LEADERS AND FLT LEADERS: 100TH, Lts Pullam, Crockett Curtis; 301st, Lts Elsberry, Ballard, Downs; 302nd, Lts Watson, Smith and McGee.

18. COMMENTS: Bad weather and visibility enroute and over target prevented our formation from keeping together. 17 A/C were with the bombers on penetration, target cover and withdrawal.

19. CORRECTIONS OF TELEPHONIC MISSION REPORTS: 6 pilots at friendly fields. NOTE: 2 FW 190's believed destroyed—arrival of pilot concerned is necessary for confirmation. Pilot at F/F—supplement will follow.

CORNELIUS VINCENT Jr.,
Capt, AC,
S-2.

D-CV/mcd

HEADQUARTERS 332ND FIGHTER GROUP
A.P.O. 520, U.S. ARMY

13 July 1944.

SUPPLEMENT TO NARRATIVE REPORT #23, DATED 12 JULY 1944

MISSION NO. 23, 100th, 301st and 302nd Ftr Sqs.

2. AIRCRAFT AND CHRONOLOGY: 11 early returns (6 spares, 2 mech, 3 weather).

7. ENEMY AIR—RESISTANCE AND ACTIVITY: Lt Elsberry reported that 16 FW 190's attacked the bomber formation at 9 o'clock to the bombers. His flight was weaving to the left of the bombers and dropped their tanks and turned into the enemy fighters. The fighters started turning away but Lt Elsberry caught 1 FW 190 in range and fired a short 30° deflection shot causing the plane to fall off on left wing, as heavy black smoke poured out of fuselage. Lt Elsberry claims 1 FW 190 probably destroyed.

Another FW 190 turned in front of Lt Elsberry who came into range in a 30° dive and started firing, observing hits on left wing. The FW 190 began to roll. Lt Elsberry continued firing short bursts as the FW 190 crashed to the ground from a split "S". Lt Elsberry claims 1 FW 190 destroyed.

About a minute later another FW 190 pulled in front of Lt Elsberry and executed a turn as if to get away. Lt Elsberry got a lead shot on the FW 190 firing a two second burst. Two members of his flight, Lts Dunne and Friend, saw the FW 190 crash to the ground and explode. Lt Elsberry claims 1 FW 190 destroyed.

Another FW 190, in a 45° dive, shot by Lt Elsberry on the right. He caught the FW 190 going down. With only his left wing guns firing, he then kicked right rudder to keep his sight on the FW 190 and observed hits on the left wing near the fuselage. The FW 190 started spiralling. The plane continued in a dive. The pilot attempted to pull out too late and crashed into the ground. Lt Elsberry claims 1 FW destroyed.

15. VICTORIES AND LOSSES:

VICTORIES

Destroyed	Prob. Dest.	Damaged
4	1	0

16. SORTIES: 31.

17. FORMATION LEADER: Lt Elsberry instead of Lt Pullam as previously reported.

CORNELIUS VINCENT Jr.,
Capt, AC,
S-2.

Vincent, Cornelius, Jr. "Narrative Mission Account No. 23," July 12, 1944. Air Force Historical Research Agency, Maxwell AFB, Alabama.

Document 8: "Narrative Mission Report No. 28," July 18, 1944. After each mission, pilots would be debriefed. During debriefing, each pilot would give an account of the mission, including details of formations, targets, enemy, and other pertinent subjects. While the pilot recounted the details, an enlisted man would write down the narrative, either with a typewriter or with shorthand, to be typed out later in a formal report. The report would be analyzed by intelligence officers (G2) and other sections hoping to find trends or lessons from each mission. Afterward, the reports were filed away and eventually archived and finally declassified. Modern researchers can learn many details from missions from the narratives that survive. Often a summary narrative of the mission would be created using several narratives from individual pilots. The report included here was from a mission to "furnish penetration, target cover and withdrawal" for a bombing mission over the city of Memmingen in southern Germany. In the mission, three planes from the 332nd went missing, and one of the bombers exploded, while the unit was credited with 11 aerial victories, including three enemy aircraft shot down by Lieutenant Lester.

18 July 1944.

NARRATIVE MISSION REPORT NO. 28

ENEMY AIR—RESISTANCE AND ACTIVITY: As escort approached the Udine and Treviso Areas approximately 0950–1000 hours, 30-35 ME 109's prepared to attack bombers to their right at about 25,000 ft. ME 109's came in units of two and five and the fives would split "S" away. Attacks were made at 3 o'clock above and 5 o'clock low. E/A were not aggressive in their attacks—used poor evasive tactics all seeming to attempt split "S's" at any altitude at which attacked by our fighters. Our claims in the Udine Area being 9 ME 109's destroyed and 1 damaged. The 21 P-51's engaged in the encounter returned to base while 36 continued to target. All ME 109's were either black or very dark with red marking on cowling near nose.

Approximately 30–40 enemy A/C were observed in target area SE. Those observed were ME 109's, FW 190's, FW 189's and ME 210's. T/E ships were not observed to have attacked bombers but stayed out of range at same altitude of bombers as if directing operations. As 4 FW 190's dived from approximately 26,000 ft on our bombers at 25,000 ft, 2 of our fighters tacked on to the rear 2 destroying both. Our claims in this area were 2 FW 190's destroyed. Neither attempted evasive action. It should be noted that while these 4 E/A dived upon bombers 6 other FW 190's provided top cover. This action took place at approximately 1030 hours. No specific markings noted on FW 190's.

HEADQUARTERS 332ND FIGHTER GROUP
A.P.O. 520, U.S. ARMY

18 July 1944.

NARRATIVE MISSION REPORT NO. 28

MISSION no. 28, 99th, 100th, 301st, and 302nd Fighter Squadrons.

1. MISSION AND TARGET: To furnish penetration, target cover and withdrawal for the 5th Bomb wing to Memmingen A/D.

2. AIRCRAFT AND CHRONOLOGY: 66 A/C took-off from Ramitelli A/D at 0750 hours. 8 returned early (6 mech and 2 spares). 36 A/C over target at 1035 hours. 54 down at base at 1325 hours, 1 A/C at Fermo A/D–

3. ROUTE: Base to line R/V with bombers at 0925 hours at 26,000 ft, 45° 32'N–12° 40'E to target and returned directly to base.

4. RENDEZVOUS, FORMATION AND ASSAULT: R/V at 45° 32'N–12° 40'E—bombers were late; scheduled R/V was 47° 06'N–11° 12'E. Bomber formation was good and easy to cover. The 301st was lead Sq; the 99th was low; the 302nd middle; the 100th high.

5. RESULTS OF BOMBING: Bombs straddled target and columns of black smoke were seen.

6. STRAFING: Nil.

7. ENEMY AIR—RESISTANCE AND ACTIVITY: (See attached sheet).

8.   FLAK: SIA over target—SAH—MIH at Brenner Pass.

9.   SIGNIFICANT OBSERVATIONS: 15 T/E A/C observed dispersed at Portoguaro 45° 45'N–12° 50'E.

10.   WEATHER: Overcast enroute—CAVU over target.

11.   AIR—SEA RESCUE: Nil.

12.   RADIO SECURITY: Good.

13.   FRIENDLY A/C LOST OR IN DIFFICULTY: 1 B-24 at 48° 35'N–10° 45'E exploded.

14.   ENEMY A/C SEEN DESTROYED BY OTHER GROUP: Nil.

CONCLUSIONS

15.   VICTORIES AND LOSSES:

Victories:

Destroyed:	Prob. Dest:	Damaged:
1 FW 190 Lt Bailey	0	1 ME 109 Capt Turner
1 FW 190 Lt Toppins		
3 ME 109's Lt Lester		
2 ME 109's Lt Holsclaw		
1 ME 109 Lt Palmer		
1 ME 109 Lt Archer		
1 ME 109 Lt Romine		
1 ME 109 Lt Warner		
TOTALS;		
9 me 109'S	0	1 ME 109
2 FW 190's		

LOSSES:

OUR LOSSES:	FLAK:	FIGHTERS:	OTHERS:
Lost	0	0	0
Missing	0	0	3
Damaged (non-repairable)	0	0	0
Damaged (repairable)	0	0	0
Wounded	0	0	0

Lt Hutton last heard from at approximately 1030 at 19,000 ft NE of Venice 25 to 30 miles, headed toward base.

Lts Irving and Browne were last seen in Kempton Area 47° 43'N–10° 20'E at 1045 hours. Last seen in vicinity of E/A.

16. SORTIES: 57.

17. FORMATION LEADERS AND FLT LEADERS: Capt Rayford. 99th, Lts Driver, Mills, Lawson, Toppins; 100th, Capt Turner, Lts Dickson, Briggs, Holsclaw; 301st, Capt Rayford, Capt Elsberry, Lts Govan, Gomer; 302nd, Lts McGee, Kirkpatrick, Walker and Bussey.

18. COMMENTS: This marks the first mission of the 99th Ftr Sq as a complete unit in long range escort with the 15th AF.

19. CORRECTIONS OF TELEPHONIC MISSION REPORTS: SIGNIFICANT OBSERVATIONS classed as Nil should read 15 T/E A/C observed dispersed at Portoguaro—45° 45'H–12° 50'E. E/A encountered should read 2 FW 190's destroyed in Memmingen Area and 9 ME 109's destroyed and 1 ME damaged in Udine and Trevio Areas.

CORNELIUS VINCENT Jr.,
Capt, AC,
S-2.

Vincent, Cornelius, Jr. "Narrative Mission Report No. 28," July 18, 1944. Air Force Historical Research Agency, Maxwell AFB, Alabama.

Document 9: "General Orders Number 2972, Award of the Distinguished Flying Cross" to Colonel Benjamin O. Davis Jr. for his leadership on the mission to escort bombers on an attack on industrial targets near Munich, Germany. On that mission, the bombers under escort were attacked by more than 100 enemy fighters, yet because of the skill of Colonel Davis in maneuvering and positioning his fighters, only two bombers were shot down by the enemy, while the 332nd could claim to have shot down five enemy fighters. With this award, Colonel Davis became the first African American to be awarded this high honor for aerial combat.

C-UPD-bmr

HEADQUARTERS
FIFTEENTH AIR FORCE
APO   520

31 August 1944.

GENERAL ORDERS)
        :
NUMBER   2972)

Award of the Distinguished Flying Cross I

SECTION I—AWARD OF THE DISTINGUISHED FLYING CROSS

Under the provisions of AR 600-45, as amended, and pursuant to authority contained in Circular No. 89, Headquarters NATOUSA, 10 July 1944, the Distinguished Flying Cross is awarded the following named officer, Air Corps, United States Army, residence and citation as indicated:

BENJAMIN O. DAVIS, JR., 0-20146, Colonel, Headquarters, 332nd Fighter Group. For extraordinary achievement in aerial flight as pilot of a P-47 type aircraft. Colonel Davis led his Group as escort to heavy bombers on a mission against industrial targets in Germany on 9 June 1944. Enroute, the bomber formation was attacked by approximately one-hundred (100) enemy fighters. Faced with the problem of protecting the large bomber formation with the comparatively few fighters under his control, Colonel Davis so skillfully disposed his squadrons that in spite of the large number of enemy fighters, the bomber formation suffered only a few losses. During the engagement, Colonel Davis led one (1) flight against more than fifteen (15) enemy fighters which were making repeated attacks on one (1) group of bombers. His aggressive spirit and determined leadership caused his men to rout the enemy fighters and emerge with five (5) victories. By his outstanding courage, leadership and combat ability, Colonel Davis has reflected great credit upon himself and the Armed Forces of the United States of America. Residence at appointment: Washington, D.C

By command of Major General TWINING:

R. K. TAYLOR
Colonel, GSC,
Chief of Staff.

OFFICIAL
        J.M. IVIMS,
        Colonel, AGD
        Adjutant General.

DISTRIBUTION: "D"
        Plus: 1-Individual concerned

Twining, Nathan Farragut. "General Orders No. 2972, Award of the Distinguished Flying Cross," August 31, 1944. Air Force Historical Research Agency, Maxwell AFB, Alabama.

Document 10: "Narrative Mission Report No. 246" for the mission of March 24, 1945. The mission, escorting the B-17s of the 5th Air Wing on an attack on the Daimler-Benz tank assembly plant near Berlin, was one of the longest missions flown by the 5th Air Force during the war, and the 332nd Fighter Group would later be awarded the Distinguished Unit Citation for its service that day. By the date of the mission, the 332nd Fighter Group consisted of three squadrons, all of which participated. As with most mission reports, enemy fighters were seen but sometimes did not attack. The mission also includes sightings of and attacks by Me-262 jet fighters, which drew the attention of Army Air Forces intelligence officers. The report also recorded a tragedy that was all too common in the air war—one of the B-17s was hit by flak near Prague, Czechoslovakia, and spiraled to the ground. None of the pilots of the 332nd saw any parachutes come from the stricken bomber, which would indicate that all crew members probably died when their plane hit the ground.

Of note is that while escorting the bombers, the fighter pilots were expected to strafe targets of opportunity on the ground, and two pilots of the 332nd reported strafing and damaging locomotives and railcars during the mission. The comment at the end, that the pilots of the 332nd did not see the P-38 fighters belonging to the 1st Fighter Group, which was supposed to escort the bombers on part of the mission, was a cause of some controversy.

D-RBW/jch

HEADQUARTERS 332ND FIGHTER GROUP
Office of the Intelligence Officer
A.P.O. 520, U. S. Army

24 March 1945.

NARRATIVE MISSION REPORT NO. 246

MISSION NO. 246—99TH, 100TH, 301ST Fighter Squadrons.

1. MISSION: To provide close escort on penetration to prudent limit of endurance for B-17's of 5th Bomb Wing attacking DAIMLER/BENZ TANK ASSEMBLY PLANT, BERLIN, GERMANY.

2. AIRCRAFT STATISTICS: 59 P-51's of at 0930 hours. Effective sorties: 54. Non-effective sorties: 5; 4 mechanical, 1 cockpit.

38 A/C R/V at 1145 hours. 43 A/C in T/A at 1215 hours.
52 A/C down at base at 1800 hours. 2 A/C at FF.
1 lost: At 1215 hours at 5210N–1205E at 26,000 feet
1 P-51 had its right wing shot off in an encounter with 3 ME-262's.
Pilot is believed to have parachuted.
4 missing: 2 A/C were last heard from over R/T at 1400 hours as they
attempted to contact Rimini A/D. 1 A/C was last seen at 1215 hours at
26,000 feet above 5210N–1205E in area of encounter with E/A. 1 A/C
was last seen at 1315 hours at 22,000 feet above 4900N–1345E. A/C
was in no apparent difficulty.

3. NARRATIVE DESCRIPTION OF MISSION: 59 P-51'S took off from Ramitelli
A/D at 0930 hours. 5 A/C returned early and were classed as NES. Proceeding on
briefed course 38 A/C R/V with assigned bombers at 1145 hours at 25,000 feet above
5020N–1313E. Though 16 other P-51's were in the same area they did not R/V with
designated lead group of B-17's (as directed by group leader) but did furnish general
route cover on penetration and later engaged attacking enemy fighters. After R/V
close escort on penetration was furnished to assigned bombers as briefed. At 1205
hours two P-51's withdrew from 5130N–1205E at 26,000 feet. At 1210 hours 9 P-51's
withdrew from 5210N–1205E at 26,000 feet. 43 P-51's continued on course to the
area of 5208N–1304E where at 1210 hours 12 E/A were encountered in a running engagement that lasted until 1225 hours and extended into the immediate vicinity and
over Berlin. After the encounter the remaining P-51's made a Fighter Sweep of the
T/A. On withdrawal 2 P-51's strafed rail traffic at 1310 hours at 4825N–1330E, 2 additional P-51's strafed rail traffic at 4825N–1240E at 1315 hours. At 1315 hours 1 other
P-51 strafed rail traffic at 4803N–1331E. 52 P-51's were down at base by 1800 hours.
1 P-51 is lost and 4 are missing and 2 are at FF. Formation Leader: Col. Davis.

4. E/A (air)
    a. Seen (not encountered): 30 ME-262's, 3 FW-190's, 1 ME-163 and 1 P-51 type
A/C (painted black and bearing German markings) were seen between 1210 and
1215 hours in the area of 5150N–1300E and 5210N–1205E at 27 to 28,000 feet. Those
E/A were not attacking B-17's, but it is believed they were preparing to intercept
escorted bombers.
    b. Encountered: 4 ME-262's were encountered at 1208 hours at 5208N–1304E
at 26,000 feet. These 4 E/A directed their attack against the lower eschelon of the
land group of B-17's from 7 o'clock high. 2 ME 262's were damaged. E/A were not
aggressive to fighters.
        1 ME 262 made a pass on fighters at 1212 hours in area of 5210N–1304E
from 20,000 feet. The ME-262 made one pass from 1 o'clock high then broke off
contact. No damage was done by the ME-262.
        3 ME-262's were encountered at 1215 hours in the vicinity of 5218N–1306E
at 26,000 feet. The 3 ME 262's were making an attack from 5 o'clock high on the lead
group of B-17's when our A/C attacked and damaged 1 ME 262.

9 ME 262's and 1 ME 163 were engaged from 1210 to 1225 hours in the vicinity of 5150N–1300E at 27,000 feet as the E/A dived through a formation of B-17's. 17 P-51's engaged these 10 E/A destroying 3 ME 262's and probably destroying 2 ME 262's and 1 ME 163. The E/A were unaggressive and were not inclined to engage our fighters.

7 ME 262's were engaged at 1215 hours in the area of 5210N–1205E at 26,000 feet when E/A made passes from 9 o'clock low and 6 o'clock high in formations of 4 and 3 respectively. 1 ME 262 scored a direct hit against 1 P-51, knocking off its right wing.

Total Claims: 3 ME 262's destroyed, 2 ME 262's and 1 ME 163 probably destroyed, and 3 ME 262's damaged.

5.   FLAK: Nil.

6.   OBSERVATIONS: Nil.

7.   RADIO SECURITY: Satisfactory.

8.   FRIENDLY A/C: At 1343 hours 1 B-17 was seen hit by flak and began spinning earthward above Prague. No chutes were seen.

9.   STRAFING: 2 P-51's strafed rail traffic at 4825N–1330E at 1310 hours. Claims; 1 locomotive damaged.
   2 P-51's strafed rail traffic at 4825N–1240E at 1315 hours. Claims: 3 RR cars damaged.
   1 P-51 strafed rail traffic at 4803N–1331E at 1315 hours. Claims: 1 locomotive damaged.
   Total strafing claims: 2 locomotives and 3 RR cars damaged.

10.   COMMENTS: 1st Fighter Group P-38's were not seen when this Group began escort.

11.   CORRECTIONS TO TELEPHONE MISSION REPORT: Nil.

Ray B. Ware,
Captain, Air Corps,
S-2.

Ware, Ray B. "Narrative Mission Report No. 246," March 24, 1945. Air Force Historical Research Agency, Maxwell AFB, Alabama.

Document 11: Narrative accounts by Thurston L. Gaines Jr., Richard S. Harder, Edward M. Thomas, and Vincent I. Mitchell of the 99th Fighter Squadron and Robert W. Williams, Samuel W. Watts Jr., Joseph E. Chineworth, Charles V. Brantley, Reid E. Thompson, Roscoe C. Brown, and Earl R. Lane of the 100th Fighter Squadron of their encounter with German jet fighters in the skies over Berlin on March 24, 1945. These extended narratives came from the same mission as above. Although the war in Europe had only about six weeks left, Allied intelligence was unsure how long Germany could hold out, and they were concerned about German jet fighters, fearing that Germany might still be able to inflict heavy losses on American aircraft. The mission on March 24 had been one of the longest missions flown by the 15th Air Force during the war, when its B-17 bombers struck a German tank factory near Berlin. All three squadrons of the 332nd were assigned escort duties, some 59 Mustangs in all. Army Air Force Intelligence (S-2) officers used such narratives in their analysis of how many jet fighters the Germans were able to field and how effective they were in combat and, most important, to try to glean tactics or techniques that would allow Allied pilots to shoot down the much faster jets.

D-RBW/mcd

HEADQUARTERS 332ND FIGHTER GROUP
Office of the Intelligence Officer
A.P.O. 520, U.S. Army

26 March 1945.

ENCOUNTERS WITH JET AIRCRAFT IN BERLIN AREA, 24 MARCH 1945

Narrative of encounter by F/O Thurston L. Gaines, Jr., 99th Fighter Squadron, 332nd Fighter Group.

On 24 March 1945, I was flying number four (4) position in yellow flight furnishing penetration cover for B-17's of the 5th Bomb Wing. At approximately 1210 hours, we were escorting B-17's at an altitude of 27,000 feet about thirty (30) miles southwest of the target, when three (3) ME-262's were seen diving on the bomber formation from about thirty thousand (30,000) feet. The ME-262's were in string and made their attack from five o'clock high at the rear section of the bombers. The first jet missed his bomber apparently and continued his flight under the bomber formation without altering his course. The second jet made his attack in a glide and after firing a burst from his guns applied power to his engine. This was evidenced by the fact that a puff of dark smoke was emitted from the jet nacelles. This jet continued his attack under the bomber formation and started a turn to the right. Immediately after observing the puff of smoke from the jets, a B-17 was seen to do an abrupt high wing over to the right and started to spin in the same direction. The second ME-262 to make a pass at the bomber fired from approximately 1,500 feet. By the time I had released my wing tanks, the jet aircraft had made his pass and as I gave pursuit, I soon discovered that his rate of speed was too fast for [me] to close in on him. Consequently, I started a climbing turn to the right at approximately 20,000 feet when I observed an ME-262 in a steep right turn about one o-clock slightly high. I pulled the nose of my aircraft up and started firing from about 2,000 feet, with thirty-five degree deflection head-on and closed to approximately 800 feet, with seventy degree deflection. No strikes were observed nor did the enemy aircraft attempt to take evasive action. It appeared that the jet pilot did not see me because he made no attempt to bear his guns on my aircraft but instead continued in a steep right turn. The rate of closure was not exceptionally fast for an almost head-on approach, and I would estimate that I fired a good three second burst at a climbing deflection shot. All of the ME-262's that I observed in the area appeared to be black with blue-gray under surface. No markings, belly tanks, or rockets were observed and I did not observe contrails during the encounters.

Narrative of encounter by Lt Richard S. Harder, 99th Fighter Squadron, 332nd Fighter Group.

I was leading a flight of four (4) P-51's escorting B-17's of the 5th Bomb Wing when at approximately 1208 hours, 26,000 feet, 4 ME-262's made an attack from five o'clock high in string at the lower right echelon of the lead bombers. The number four (4) jet broke high and left and climbed straight up; the number one (1) jet continued down while the two (2) jets in the middle rolled out to the right and went straight down. My flight gave chase and I pursued the two (2) jets that turned to the right and commenced firing from about 3,000 feet, ten to twenty degree deflection shots, about two second bursts. I ceased firing from approximately 900 feet when I observed that it was impossible to close in any further. I observed strikes on the fuselage of one jet aircraft and black smoke was seen coming from the jet orifice. I followed the jets down and pulled out at around 10,000 feet. Climbing back to altitude, I observed three (3) jets at 1215 hours coming in at the bombers from five o'clock high but they did not reach the bombers as I turned my flight into them. Number one (1) jet dived straight down and number three (3) jet pulled straight up into a steep climb. The jet aircraft in the middle turned to the right and my flight started turning inside of him. I immediately opened fire from 2,000 feet, twenty to thirty degree deflection shots of very short bursts. I continued firing until I closed to within 900 feet before breaking off the attack. I observed hits on the fuselage and a puff of black smoke was seen as the jet apparently applied more power and pulled away. The first four (4) ME-262's appeared to be very aggressive and pressed their attack upon the bombers. The last three (3) ME-262's encountered seemed reluctant to engage fighters and appeared less experienced than the former. I could not observe any marking or belly tanks. There were no contrails. The colors were dark with a blue-gray under surface.

Narrative of encounter by Lts Robert W. Williams, and Samuel W. Watts, Jr., 100th Fighter Squadron, 332nd Fighter Group.

At about 1215 hours, while escorting B-17's of the 5th Bomb Wing, Lt Brown, the flight leader, called in enemy aircraft attacking our bombers. We were higher than the enemy aircraft and had the advantage, so we thought. When I saw the first enemy aircraft, they were in somewhat of a line abreast formation, making very shallow turns. They must have been cruising at least 450 MPH because I had an indicated 380 MPH after my dive with everything full forward. The jets continued almost straight and in a slight dive, disappearing in the distance. At 1220 hours, my wingman called to me that we were being attacked by two (2) ME-262's from five o'clock high. They came in, in a close formation and fired at my wingman. I was about 500 feet above them, so I rolled over into a steep wing-over and developed a high-speed stall from which I recovered but immediately developed another. When I pulled out, I dropped down almost in trail of the jet aircraft. I noticed a simultaneous trail of propulsion from both aircraft. They continued straight through in a shallow dive for almost a minute after the attack and while still in very close formation, they started a shallow left turn. I picked up a 2 ½ Radil lead on the jet on the right and fired a long burst. I fired another burst and held it for about two seconds. I noticed hits on the aircraft and saw him fall out of formation and I believe he went down. I had to break off the attack because my wingman called to me for help. In these encounters I observed that the jets stay under the bombers and attack beneath where they cannot be seen by fighters. They fly a close formation using jet propulsion intermittently. They were very unaggressive to fighters. Jets take advantage of their speed and make shallow turns in order to not lose speed.

Narrative of encounter by Lt Joseph E. Chineworth, 100th Fighter Squadron, 332nd Fighter Group.

At approximately 1215 hours while engaged in escorting B-17's of the 5th Bomb Wing, my flight was attacked by three (3) ME-262's. I was flying number two position and was at 29,000 feet at the time of the attack. The jets came in from ten o'clock low and passed under us, making a fairly tight 180 degree turn to the left. At this time we were to the left of the bombers and above them. While the jets were in their turn, we dropped tanks and started a dive to the left of the enemy aircraft, pursuing them for 5,000 feet downward. At this point I lost my flight leader and picked up the number four man in our flight. Together, we went after another ME-262 that had just passed in front of us. I made a ninety degree left turn and was on the tail of the jet about 1,500 feet away. I fired three long bursts and then my guns stopped. I saw hits and pieces flew off his plane. Black smoke came from the enemy aircraft as he started into what appeared to be an uncontrolled dive. I used a five degree to a zero degree deflection shot at him. My ship was equipped with the new K-14 gun sight. As I was pursuing the jet, I had my throttle full forward but I did not notice my air speed or my manifold pressure at the time, but as I pulled away I was indicating from 355 to 375 MPH at 17,000 feet. My attack lasted for about five minutes. I saw approximately nine (9) ME-262's. Several of the jets I saw were not using power as

I saw no smoke or contrails. The jets climb without using their power. Their approach to the bombers was without the use of power. They appeared unaggressive to fighters. They flew almost in a "U" formation with one behind the other.

Narrative of encounter by Lt Charles V. Brentley, 100th Fighter Squadron, 332nd Fighter Group.

Between 1200 and 1220 hours, while flying as escort for B-17's of the 5th Bomb Wing, my element leader and I encountered an ME-262. We were at an altitude of 25,000 feet flying practically abreast when two (2) ME-262's came in from behind and slightly below us. Both aircraft appeared to be coasting as I saw no indication of power. One (1) jet was between us and the other one was to my flight leader's right. I dropped my nose, being well within range, and made several bursts on the ship that was in front of me from dead astern. My flight leader fired on the other. The jets broke in a slow turn in opposite directions, pulling us apart. I followed my target in a dive for a short while observing hits on the fuselage. I then broke off to join my flight leader. The dive was very shallow and at no time did I go below 20,000 feet. As I broke away, the ME-262 steepened its rate of turn and dive. It was seen by my flight leader and other pilots to go down in flames. I encountered another ME-262 while joining my flight leader. This ME-262 passed me at approximately ninety degrees. I fired but no hits were observed. I was unable to pick up the correct lead and could not turn fast enough because of one wing tank which had stuck. The jets were able to pull away from us without using power. Altitude is essential in successfully combating the fast jet aircraft.

Narrative of encounter by Lt Reid E. Thompson, 100th Fighter Squadron, 332nd Fighter Group.

Between 1200 and 1220 hours, while weaving over bomber of the 5th Bomb Wing, three (3) ME-262's made a pass at the bombers from seven o'clock low.

I was at an altitude of 26,000 feet when I saw the ME-262's come up, make a pass, level off and go zooming up and over the bombers at one o'clock. They also did a wing-over and made another pass from two o'clock high. I called in the enemy aircraft and told my flight leader I was going down to intercept them. I peeled down with my tanks on and reached a speed of 300 MPH. On the way down a flight of five of our aircraft passed me and I broke away to the left and dropped my tanks. In the turn I saw an ME-163 in a turn to the left at two o'clock to me. I tightened my turn and fired two bursts with a seventy degree deflection, but I was out of range, at about 4,000 feet. The jet went into a dive almost vertical and I dived behind him, still out of range and looking for him to pull up and allow me a shot at him. We began to dive from 26,000 feet and on the way down, he did three barrel rolls to the left and I rolled with him. On the completion of the rolls, I pulled out of the dive at 10,000 feet and leveled off at about 6,000 feet. I estimated the jet to be about 4,000 feet in front of me and when I last saw him, he was still going down. I circled the area where I last saw him and located a puff of smoke and wreckage where I judged him to have gone in. I then joined a friendly aircraft and left the area. The jet appeared unaggressive and employed a dive as evasive action.

Narrative of encounter by Lt Roscoe C. Brown, 100th Fighter Squadron, 332nd Fighter Group.

I was on the west side of the third and fourth sections of B-17's of the 5th Bomb Wing at about 27,000 feet when at 1215 hours, we noticed three (3) ME-262's coming in at the bombers at eleven o'clock, breaking to one o'clock. The attack was below the bombers. The jets were attacking individually rather than in formation. I called the flight to drop tanks and peeled right on the three (3) ME-262's. I fired at one (1) from 2,400 feet, having him in the extreme range of my K-14 gun sight. He went into a dive and I went with him down to 22,000 feet, where I broke off pursuit because of the exceptional diving speed of the jet. I climbed back to 27,000 feet. It was then that I sighted a formation of four (4) ME-262's under the bombers at about 24,000 feet. They were below me going north. I was going south. I peeled down on them toward their rear but almost immediately, I saw a lone ME-262 at 24,000 feet, climbing at ninety degrees to me and 2,500 feet from me. I pulled up at him in a fifteen degree climb and fired three long bursts at him from 2,000 feet at eight o'clock to him. Almost immediately, the pilot bailed out from 24,500 feet. I saw flames burst from the jet orifices of the enemy aircraft. The attack on the bombers was ineffective because of the prompt action of my flight in breaking up the attack. The jets appeared unaggressive to fighters and used diving speed as evasive action. They seem to employ the tactics of attacking bombers from below where they are not easily visible to fighters.

Narrative of encounter by Capt Edward M. Thomas and Lt. Vincent I. Mitchell, 99th Fighter Squadron, 332nd Fighter Group.

Our formation was about thirty miles southwest of the target when I saw two (2) ME-262's make a pass on a box of B-17's off to our left at approximately 1208 hours. The pass was made from five o'clock high. We dropped tanks and followed them from the bombers' altitude which was 26,000 feet to about 20,000 feet, without gaining on them. At approximately 20,000 feet, the two (2) jets started a wide right turn and my flight started cutting off the turn, trying to close the range and pick up a deflection. The two (2) ME-262's were in loose string, so we attempted to catch the rear jet. Lt Mitchell, who had joined my flight, closed with me to a range of about 450 yards and started firing from a forty-five degree deflection and we both observed on the jet. He apparently had not realized we were so close on him, for as soon as the hits were observed, he pulled his nose up, did a quarter roll to the right, and split "S'd" away from us. In the meantime, the first ME-262 had tightened his turn until he was almost head-on to us, thereby preventing us from following the second jet. The ME-262 then broke to his left and pulled up and away from us. These two (2) jet aircraft pilots appeared to be experienced which was evidenced by their tactics in this encounter. They used power after we were observed in the area.

Narrative of encounter by Lt Earl R. Lane, 100th Fighter Squadron, 332nd Fighter Group.

I was flying number three position in a flight of four aircraft covering B-17's of the 5th Bomb Wing. I was at 29,000 feet at the time. At about 1210 hours I noticed four aircraft, apparently enemy, in string passing from three o'clock to nine o'clock under the bombers. They were completely out of range. I did not notice any damage to the bombers. After seeing these aircraft I began looking around. We "S'd" across the bombers and made a turn back to the right when I saw an ME-262. The ME-262 was in thirty degree dive, coming across the bomber formation. He appeared as if he was peeling for an attack on the bombers. I came in for a thirty degree deflection shot from 2,000 feet. He did not quite fill my gun sight. I fired three short bursts and saw the plane emitting smoke. A piece of the plane, either the canopy or one of the jet orifices, flew off. I then pulled up and circled over the spot where he went down. I saw another piece hit close to the first piece. I was at 17,000 feet when I broke off the encounter. The jet was a steel blue-grey camouflage. After this encounter I teamed up with another friendly aircraft and headed for home. Before leaving the area, a black P-51 with German markings approached me at 22,000 feet at five o'clock. The friendly pilot I was with yelled "break right!" I did so and the enemy aircraft broke off and flew north. The jets I saw were not using power. They were unaggressive to fighters and dived and climbed but seldom turned. In attacking bombers the jets came out of the sun and flew across the middle of the bombers from five to ten o'clock, or came up low and behind the last bombers. There is a need for fast speed in areas where jets are expected. Also it is essential to weave close to the bombers when affording cover because the low attack on bombers by jets cannot be observed easily from a distance.

RAY B. WARE,
Capt, Air Corps,
S-2.

Gaines, Thurston L., Jr., Richard S. Harder, Edward M. Thomas, Vincent I. Mitchell, Robert W. Williams, Samuel W. Watts Jr., Joseph E. Chineworth, Charles V. Brantley, Reid E. Thompson, Roscoe C. Brown, and Earl R. Lane. "Encounters with Jet Aircraft in Berlin Area," March 26, 1945. Air Force Historical Research Agency, Maxwell AFB, Alabama.

Document 12: Orders for the awarding of the Silver Star Medal to Colonel Benjamin O. Davis Jr. for "gallantry in action" during a mission on April 15, 1945. The orders for the award, as with most, came in a group of awards to many soldiers. For Colonel Davis's award, the citation emphasizes that the target was a difficult one but that Colonel Davis's skill, bravery, and tenacity ensured mission accomplishment.

RESTRICTED

SECTION III—AWARDS OF THE SILVER STAR

Under the provisions of AR 600-45, as amended, and pursuant to authority contained in Circular No. 73, MTOUSA, 12 May 1945, the Silver Star is awarded the following named personnel, Air Corps, United States Army, residence and citation as indicated:

BENJAMIN O. DAVIS, JR., 0-20146, Colonel, Headquarters 332nd Ftr Gp. For gallantry in action as pilot of a P-51 type aircraft. On 15 April 1945, Colonel Davis led a group formation to strafe enemy rail targets in Austria. Keenly realizing the necessity for successfully accomplishing this important mission, Colonel Davis assigned himself to lead the mission. He exhibited expert navigational skill in leading his group through low clouds and haze to reach the assigned target area. Fully aware that the enemy could not be surprised because the area had previously been strafed during the day, Colonel Davis split his group into three squadrons in order to thoroughly cover the entire area. Without thought of personal safety, he led one squadron of twelve aircraft down to strafe despite the intense ground fire that blanketed the area and the difficult terrain features that made strafing hazardous. Loading his squadron gallanlty on repeated passes, Colonel Davis courageously pressed his attack until he had destroyed or damaged six (6) locomotives. The thorough planning, outstanding leadership and professional skill displayed by Colonel Davis enabled the group to destroy or damage thirty-five (35) locomotives, eight (8) oil cars forty four (44) other units of rolling stock, four (4) barges, four (4) motor transports on a flat car and one (1) aircraft in the air to thoroughly disrupt the enemy's transportation facilities. Despite the hazard presented and when he might have withdrawn, Colonel Davis remained in the target area more than an hour and only reformed his squadron when no further targets were available. By his conspicuous gallantry, and devotion to duty as evidenced throughout sixty (60) successful missions against the enemy, Colonel Davis has reflected great credit upon himself and the Armed Forces of the United States of America. Residence at appointment: Washington, D.C.

U.S. Army Air Forces. "Awards of the Silver Star," May 31, 1945. Air Force Historical Research Agency, Maxwell AFB, Alabama.

██████████

Document 13: "Special Account." This excerpt, from an official report, documents one of the final formations of the 332nd Fighter Group under the command of Colonel Benjamin O. Davis Jr. before he returned to the United States to take command of the 477th Composite Group. The report notes that Davis received the first Silver Star Medal received by any member of the 332nd Fighter Group. It also lists other awards presented to other members of the 332nd that day and quotes Colonel Davis's farewell letter to the men and officers of the 332nd Fighter Group. The letter, although brief, reflects the pride Colonel Davis had in his men and recognizes that the joy that victory in Europe gave them all was tempered by the understanding that the war in the Pacific was not over and that the war against Japan might still have a long way to go. Davis, like military leaders around the world and throughout time, found parting from men with whom he had been through so much difficult, but he was through and through a soldier and understood his duty above all else.

I. SPECIAL ACCOUNTS

June 1945.

On 8 June 1945 final combat awards were presented to pilots and enlisted men of this Group by Colonel Y. H. Taylor, Commanding Officer of the 306th Fighter Wing at an impressive ceremony. The Silver Star, the first to be received by any member of the 332nd Fighter Group, was awarded to Colonel Benjamin O. Davis, Jr. Distinguished Flying Crosses were awarded to Gordon M. Rapier, Jimmy Lanham, Gentry E. Barnes, Bertram W. Wilson, Robert W. Williams and Carl E. Cary. Air Medals were awarded to William H. Hollomon, III, Charles A. Lane, Jr., Samuel Matthews, Felix M. McCrory and Frank A. Jackson, Jr. The Bronze star was awarded to Samuel W. Henderson, First Sergeant of the 99th Fighter Squadron.

Troops passed in review to close the ceremony and bid farewell to Colonel Davis as Commanding Officer of the Group.

A few hours later Colonel Davis with fifteen officers and twenty-five enlisted men stepped into B-17's to depart for the United States.

Colonel Davis was to assume command of the 477th Composite Group located at Godman Field, Kentucky. In a farewell letter to members of this command Colonel Davis wrote: "In parting I would like to say that it has been a signal honor to be a part of such a fine organization as the 332nd Fighter Group. It is with regret that I leave you with whom I have been so closely associated during the past many months. We have been through much together, and the many common experiences we share make it most difficult for me to tear away so abruptly. However, the war is but half won, and we cannot let up until Japan is defeated. In the words of Brigadier General D.C. Strother who recently commanded our Fighter Command, the 332nd has been a credit to itself and the Army Air Forces. All of us who have been connected with the 332nd know this to be a fact. I am proud to have been associated with you, and I am certain that even if we do not serve together in war time, we will meet again in peace. I wish all of you Godspeed and may all of us carry on in the future as nobly as we have in the past."

On 9 June 1945 Major George S. Roberts assumed command of the 332nd Fighter Group. Major Roberts had previously commanded the 99th Fighter Squadron and had served as Deputy Commander of the 332nd Fighter Group for many months.

On 12 June 1945, the 332nd Fighter Group was relieved from assignment to the XV Fighter Command (Prov) and assigned to the 305th Bombardment Wing (H).

U.S. Army Air Forces. "Special Account," June 1945. Air Force Historical Research Agency, Maxwell AFB, Alabama.

Document 14: General Order 84, of October 25, 1945, awarding battle honors to the 332nd Fighter Group for its performance on the mission of March 24, 1945, when it escorted bombers attacking the Daimler-Benz tank factory near Berlin. Although the war was over by the time the recognition came, the delay was normal. After an act by an individual or unit occurred, someone, usually a higher-ranking officer, would submit that person or unit for recognition. The process of evaluating the application could take months or even years before a decision was made and orders were written. Although the war ended in September 1945 and the massive U.S. military was about the start its rapid reduction in the size, the processing of enormous amounts of paperwork continued, and the 332nd Fighter Group got its proper official recognition for its heroic service in the attack on the tank factory.

GENERAL ORDERS ⎫   WAR DEPARTMENT
No. 84   ⎭   Washington 25, D. C., 5 October 1945

BATTLE HONORS.—As authorized by Executive Order 9396 (sec. I, WD Bul. 22, 1943), superseding Executive Order 9075 (sec. III, WD Bul. 11, 1942), citations of the following units in the general orders indicated are confirmed under the provisions of section IV, WD Circular 333, 1943, in the name of the President of the United States as public evidence of deserved honor and distinction. The citations read as follows:

1. The *9th Weather Reconnaissance Squadron (Prov)* is cited for outstanding performance of duty in action against the enemy from 8 to 29 December 1944). Despite extremely hazardous weather conditions and determined enemy fighter and ground resistance, the *9th Weather Reconnaissance Squadron (Prov)* executed 81 perilous missions over enemy-held territory. During the period 8 to 18 December 1944, the courageous airmen of this squadron flew 19 dangerous low-level reconnaissance missions over the Roer River dam area. Flying at times with a ceiling of only 100 feet, through heavy antiaircraft defenses and an enemy balloon barrage, the squadron secured vital weather information which was of great assistance in operations against the stubbornly resisting enemy. From 18 to 29 December 1944 during the critical Ardennes Campaign, the daring and aggressive sorties flown by the aviators of the *9th Weather Reconnaissance Squadron (Prov)* kept the Allies constantly informed of weather developments. Maintenance personnel worked day

and night to keep every aircraft in condition durin the sustained operations of this period. The outstanding determination and technical skill of the officers and men of the *9th Weather Reconnaissance Squadron (Prov)* from 8 to 29 December 1944 were of inestimable aid to the American and British air forces in striking a telling blow against the desperate German army. (General Orders 62, Headquarters Ninth Air Force, 2 May 1945, as approved by the Commanding General, United States Forces, European Theatre (Main).)

2. *The Military Police Platoon, 9th Infantry Division*, is cited for extraordinary gallantry and outstanding performance of duty from 9 to 15 March 1945, during which time it maintained traffic control on the Ludendorf Bridge at Remagen and in the Rhine bridgehead area, braving constant heavy artillery fire and air attacks to keep supply, evacuation, and troop movements running smoothly over this vital link. The sector in which the platoon operated was a target for 24 hours of each day for heavy artillery concentrations, air attacks, and on two occasions V-2 weapons. Under this murderous fire, the MP's stood at their posts, unable to take cover, as casualties to themselves and to passing troops and vehicles mounted each day. When one of their own number fell, another MP stepped forward to take his place. The bridgehead over the Rhine was completely dependent upon the Ludendorf span; necessary troops and supplies had to strengthen the bridgehead in a steady stream, or all would be lost. It was the coolly competent direction by the *Military Police Platoon* which insured their crossing the Rhine despite the heavy, constant shelling. Vehicles were hit and reinforcements wounded; in every case the MP's stood ready to clear the bridge, and did so quickly. When drivers of vehicles in convoy stopped to seek cover during shelling, the MP's went out to them, forced then back into vehicles, or took over themselves to keep the vital artery clear. The high casualties on the bridge and its approaches made it necessary for the *Military Police Platoon* to take over their care, which they did quickly and competently, setting up an aid station and an evacuation system. One of the first wire lines across the bridge 2 August 1945, as approved by the Commander in Chief United States Army Forces, Pacific.)

15. The *332d Fighter Group* is cited for outstanding performance of duty in armed conflict with the enemy. On 23 May 1945, the group was assigned the mission of escorting heavy bombardment type aircraft attacking the vital Daimler-Benz tank assembly plant at Berlin, Germany. Realizing the strategic importance of the mission and fully cognizant of the amount of enemy resistance to be expected and the long range to be covered, the ground crews worked tirelessly and with enthusiasm to have their aircraft at the peak of mechanical condition to insure the success of the operation. On 24 March 1945, fifty-nine P-51 type aircraft were airborne and set course for the rendezvous with the bomber formation. Through superior navigation and maintenance of strict flight discipline the group formation reached the bomber formation at the designated time and place. Nearing the target approximately 25 enemy aircraft were encountered which included ME262's which launched relentless attacks in a desperate effort to break up and destroy the bomber formations. Displaying outstanding courage, aggressiveness, and combat technique, the group immediately engaged the enemy formation in aerial combat. In the ensuing engagement that continued over the target area, the gallant pilots of the *332d Fighter Group* battled against the enemy fighter to prevent the breaking up of the bomber formation and thus jeopardizing the successful completion of this vitally important mission. Through their superior skill and determination, the group destroyed

three enemy aircraft, probably destroyed three, and damaged three. Among their claims were eight of the highly rated enemy jet-propelled aircraft with no losses sustained by the *332d Fighter Group.* Leaving the target area and en route to base after completion of their primary task, aircraft of the group conducted strafing attacks against enemy ground installation and transportation with outstanding success. By the conspicuous gallantry, professional skill and determination of the pilots, together with the outstanding technical skill and devotion to duty of the ground personnel, the *332d Fighter Group* has reflected great credit on itself and the armed forced of the United States. (General Orders 3674, Headquarters Fifteenth Air Force, 9 August 1945, as approved by the Commanding General, United States Forces, Mediterranean Theater.)

U.S. War Department. "General Orders No. 84," October 25, 1945. Air Force Historical Research Agency, Maxwell AFB, Alabama.

———

Document 15: Executive Order 9981. Throughout World War II, the National Association for the Advancement of Colored People and others demanded an end to segregation in the armed forces, repeatedly pointing out the inconsistencies of black Americans fighting for freedom and democracy in a segregated military. Opponents of integration insisted that the military should not be used as a social laboratory and that the military would integrate when society did. In 1946, the Gillem Board reviewed policy toward black soldiers and found that the army had failed to make the best use of black soldiers during World War II. The board recommended that segregation be retained but that in the peacetime establishment, blacks should constitute about 10 percent of the army and be given equal opportunity for advancement and that some base facilities should be integrated. Black leaders were not mollified by the recommendations because of the retention of military segregation. In November 1947, A. Phillip Randolph, whose threatened "March on Washington" in 1941 had led to President Franklin Roosevelt issuing Executive Order 8802, creating the Fair Employment Practices Commission, helped found the Committee Against Jim Crow in Military Service and Training. Opponents of segregation were encouraged when President Harry Truman issued his Civil Rights Message to Congress in February 1948, which, among other things, called for ending discrimination in the military. President Truman had been especially disturbed by a recent photograph of a black man who had been lynched while wearing his army uniform—his sergeant's stripes clearly showing on the bloodied, beaten body. Southern congressmen and military leaders opposed desegregating the military, and the president's call was largely ignored.

In March 1948, the United States established a peacetime draft. Randolph led protests in major cities throughout the summer of 1948, urging young black men to refuse to register for the draft, arguing that "prison is better than Army Jim Crow." As in 1917 and 1941, some black leaders feared that the refusal of blacks to serve would be used as an excuse to continue to deny civil rights to all blacks. Truman, however, wanted to end military segregation from a mixture of wanting to avoid black resistance to the peacetime draft and a genuine concern that military segregation was not in the best interests of the nation. President Truman was annoyed that his earlier call had been ignored by Congress and decided to use his authority to issue an executive order. The use of the executive order, which presidents can use for issues that specifically concern the federal government, would bypass Congress, but the military would still be required to comply. On July 26, Truman issued Executive Order 9981, which stated that "there shall be equality of treatment and opportunity for all persons in the armed services without regard to race, color, religion or national origin" and that "This policy shall be put into effect as rapidly as possible." While some black leaders criticized the executive order as weak in not ordering the immediate desegregation of the military, it did signal a drastic change by the U.S. government toward supporting integration instead of segregation.

EXECUTIVE ORDER 9981

Establishing the President's Committee on Equality of Treatment and Opportunity In the Armed Forces.

WHEREAS it is essential that there be maintained in the armed services of the United States the highest standards of democracy, with equality of treatment and opportunity for all those who serve in our country's defense:

NOW THEREFORE, by virtue of the authority vested in me as President of the United States, by the Constitution and the statutes of the United States, and as Commander in Chief of the armed services, it is hereby ordered as follows:

1. It is hereby declared to be the policy of the President that there shall be equality of treatment and opportunity for all persons in the armed services without regard to race, color, religion or national origin. This policy shall be put into effect as rapidly as possible, having due regard to the time required to effectuate any necessary changes without impairing efficiency or morale.

2. There shall be created in the National Military Establishment an advisory committee to be known as the President's Committee on Equality of Treatment and Opportunity in the Armed Services, which shall be composed of seven members to be designated by the President.

3. The Committee is authorized on behalf of the President to examine into the rules, procedures and practices of the Armed Services in order to determine in what respect such rules, procedures and practices may be altered or improved with a view to carrying out the policy of this order. The Committee shall confer and advise the Secretary of Defense, the Secretary of the Army, the Secretary of the Navy, and the Secretary of the Air Force, and shall make such recommendations to the President and to said Secretaries as in the judgment of the Committee will effectuate the policy hereof.

4. All executive departments and agencies of the Federal Government are authorized and directed to cooperate with the Committee in its work, and to furnish the Committee such information or the services of such persons as the Committee may require in the performance of its duties.

5. When requested by the Committee to do so, persons in the armed services or in any of the executive departments and agencies of the Federal Government shall testify before the Committee and shall make available for use of the Committee such documents and other information as the Committee may require.

6. The Committee shall continue to exist until such time as the President shall terminate its existence by Executive order.

Harry Truman

The White House
July 26, 1948

Truman, Harry S. "Executive Order 9981," July 26, 1948. Air Force Historical Research Agency, Maxwell AFB, Alabama.

━━━━━━━

Document 16: Official U.S. Air Force Lineage and Honors Histories. Every unit in the military carries an official lineage. The lineages of the current 99th, 332nd, and 477th show their commanders, locations, missions, and other pertinent data during World War II and to the present.

Lineage and Honors History
of the
99 Flying Training Squadron (AETC)

Lineage. Constituted 99 Pursuit Squadron on 19 Mar 1941. Activated on 22 Mar 1941. Redesignated: 99 Fighter Squadron on 15 May 1942; 99 Fighter Squadron, Single Engine, on 28 Feb 1944. Inactivated on 1 Jul 1949. Redesignated 99 Flying Training Squadron on 29 Apr 1988. Activated on 1 Jul 1988. Inactivated on 1 Apr 1993. Activated on 14 May 1993.

Assignments. Army Air Corps, 22 Mar 1941; Air Corps Technical Training Command, 26 Mar 1941; Southeast Air Corps (later, Southeast Army Air Forces) Training Center, 5 Nov 1941 (attached to III Fighter Command, 19 Aug 1942–c. 2 Apr 1943); Twelfth Air Force, 24 Apr 1943; XII Air Support (later, XII Tactical Air) Command, 28 May 1943 (attached to 33 Fighter Group, 29 May 1943; 324 Fighter Group, c. 29 Jun 1943; 33 Fighter Group, 19 Jul 1943; 79 Fighter Group, 16 Oct 1943; 324 Fighter Group, 1 Apr–6 Jun 1944); 332 Fighter Group, 1 May 1944 (attached to 86 Fighter Group, 11–30 Jun 1944); 477 Composite Group, 22 Jun 1945; 332 Fighter Group, 1 Jul 1947–1 Jul 1949. 82 Flying Training Wing, 1 Jun 1988; 82 Operations Group, 15 Dec 1991–1 Apr 1993. 12 Operations Group, 14 May 1993–.

Stations. Chanute Field, IL, 22 Mar 1941; Maxwell Field, AL, 5 Nov 1941; Tuskegee, AL, 10 Nov 1941–2 Apr 1943; Casablanca, French Morocco, 24 Apr 1943; Qued N'ja, French Morocco, 29 Apr 1943; Fardjouna, Tunisia, 7 Jun 1943; Licata, Sicily, 28 Jul 1943; Termini, Sicily, 4 Sep 1943; Barcellona, Sicily, 17 Sep 1943; Foggia, Italy, 17 Oct 1943; Madna, Italy, 22 Nov 1943; Capodichino, Italy, 16 Jan 1944; Cercola, Italy, 2 Apr 1944; Pignataro, Italy, 10 May 1944; Ciampino, Italy, 11 Jun 1944; Orbetello, Italy, 17 Jun 1944; Ramitelli, Italy, 6 Jul 1944; Cattolica, Italy, c. 5 May–Jun 1945; Godman Field, KY, 22 Jun 1945; Lockbourne AAB (later, AFB), OH, 13 Mar 1946–1 Jul 1949. Williams AFB, AZ, 1 Jun 1988–1 Apr 1993. Randolph AFB, TX, 14 May 1993–.

Commanders. Capt Harold R. Maddux, 22 Mar 1941; 2 Lt Clyde H. Bynum, 10 Nov 1941; Capt Alonzo S. Ward, 6 Dec 1941; 1 Lt George S. Roberts, 1 Jun 1942; Lt Col Benjamin O. Davis Jr., 22 Aug 1942; Maj George S. Roberts, 2 Sep 1943; Capt Erwin B. Lawrence Jr., 13 Apr 1944; Maj George S. Roberts, 1 Sep 1944; Capt Alfonso W. Davis, 20 Oct 1944; Maj William A. Campbell, 29 Oct 1944; Unknown, Jun–22 Jun 1945; Capt Wendell M. Lucas, 22 Jun 1945; Maj William A. Campbell, 3 Jul 1945; Capt Melvin T. Jackson, Jul 1947; Capt Marion R. Rodgers, Apr 1948–1 Jul 1949. Lt Col Johnny Jarnagin, 1 Jul 1988; Lt Col Stephen T. Fenton, 5 Jun 1990; Lt Col James M. Bower, 17 Jul 1992–1 Apr 1993. Lt Col Michael K. Davis, 14 May 1993; Lt Col Scott E. Wuestoff, 14 Jul 1995; Lt Col Joseph F. Barron, 19 Jul 1996; Lt Col Steven C. Waters, 26 Jun 1998; Lt Col James B. Kotowski, 24 Apr 2000; Lt Col Donald R. Simpson, 30 Apr 2001; Lt Col Randall W. Gibb, 10 Dec 2002; Lt Col James A. Garrett, 14 Jun 2004–.

Aircraft. P-40, 1943–1944; P-51, 1944–1945; P-47, 1945–1949. T-38, 1988–1993; 1993–; T-1, 1993–.

Operations. Organized as the first African-American flying unit in the Air Corps. Earned three Distinguished Unit Citations in World War II. Combat in Mediterranean and European theaters of operation (MTO and ETO), 2 Jun 1943–30 Apr 1945. Undergraduate pilot training, 1988–1993; 1993–.

Service Streamers. World War II American Theater.

Campaign Streamers. World War II: Sicily; Naples-Foggia; Anzio; Rome-Arno; Southern France; North Apennines; Po Valley; Air Offensive, Europe; Normandy; Northern France; Rhineland; Central Europe; Air Combat, EAME Theater.

Armed Forces Expeditionary Streamers. None.

Decorations. Distinguished Unit Citations: Sicily, [Jun–Jul] 1943; Cassino, 12–14 May 1944; Germany, 24 Mar 1945. Air Force Outstanding Unit Awards: 1 Apr 1991–31 Mar 1993; 14 May–30 Jun 1993; 1 Jul 1993–30 Jun 1994; 1 Jul 1995–30 Jun 1996; 1 Jul 1996–30 Jun 1998; 1 Jul 1998–30 Jun 2000; 1 Jul 2002–30 Jun 2004.

Lineage, Assignments, Components, Stations, and Honors through 26 Apr 2007.

Commanders, Aircraft, and Operations through 31 Dec 2005.

Supersedes statement prepared on 16 May 1995.

Emblem. Approved on 24 Jun 1944.

Prepared by Patsy Robertson.

Reviewed by Daniel Haulman.

Lineage and Honors History
of the
332nd Expeditionary Operations Group (ACC)

Lineage. Established as 332nd Fighter Group on 4 Jul 1942. Activated on 13 Oct 1942. Inactivated on 19 Oct 1945. Activated on 1 Jul 1947. Inactivated on 1 Jul 1949. Redesignated 332nd Air Expeditionary Group, and converted to provisional status, on 19 Nov 1998. Activated on 1 Dec 1998. Redesignated 332d Expeditionary Operations Group on 12 Aug 2002.

Assignments. Third Air Force, 13 Oct 1942; First Air Force, 23 Jul 1943; Twelfth Air Force, c. 27 Jan 1944; XII Air Force Training and Replacement Command (Provisional), 3 Feb 1944; XII Fighter Command, 10 Feb 1944; 62nd Fighter Wing, 10 Feb 1944; Fifteenth Air Force, 22 May 1944; 306th Fighter Wing, 22 May 1944; 305th Bombardment Wing, 12 Jun–Sep 1945; unkn, Sep–19 Oct 1945. Ninth Air Force, 1 Jul 1947; 332nd Fighter Wing, 15 Aug 1947–1 Jul 1949. 9th Air and Space Expeditionary Task Force-Southern Watch, 1 Dec 1998–.

Components. Squadrons. 9th Expeditionary Fighter: 16–28 Dec 1998. 18th Expeditionary Fighter: 1 Dec 1998–2 Mar 1999. 34th Expeditionary Fighter: 1 Dec 1998–2 Mar 1999. 55th Expeditionary Fighter: 19 Jan–4 May 1999. 68th Expeditionary Fighter: 3 Mar–23 Apr 1999. 69th Expeditionary Fighter: 23 Apr–1 Oct 1999. 70th Expeditionary Fighter: 4 May–1 Oct 1999. 99th Fighter: 1 May 1944–22 Jun 1945 (detached 1 May–6 Jun and 11–30 Jun 1944); 1 Jul 1947–1 Jul 1949. 100th Fighter: 13 Oct 1942–19 Oct 1945; 1 Jul 1947–1 Jul 1949. 301st Fighter: 13 Oct 1942–19 Oct 1945; 1 Jul 1947–1 Jul 1949. 302nd Fighter: 13 Oct 1942–6 Mar 1945. 332nd Expeditionary Rescue: 1 Dec 1998–. 355th Expeditionary Fighter: 1–21 Dec 1998. 391st Expeditionary Fighter: 19 Jan–9 Mar 1999. 522nd Expeditionary Fighter: 15 Dec 1998–8 Feb 1999.

Stations. Tuskegee, AL, 13 Oct 1942; Selfridge Field, MI, 29 Mar 1943; Oscoda, MI, 12 Apr 1943; Selfridge Field, MI, 9 Jul–22 Dec 1943; Montecorvino, Italy, 8 Feb 1944; Capodichino, Italy, 15 Apr 1944; Ramitelli Airfield, Italy, 28 May 1944; Cattolica, Italy, c. 4 May 1945; Lucera, Italy, c. 18 Jul–Sep 1945; Camp Kilmer, NJ, 17–19 Oct 1945. Lockbourne AAB (later, AFB), OH, 1 Jul 1947–1 Jul 1949. Al Jaber, Kuwait, 1 Dec 1998–.

Commanders. Lt Col Sam W. Westbrook, Jr., by 19 Oct 1942; Col Robert R. Selway, Jr., 16 May 1943; Col Benjamin O. Davis, Jr., 8 Oct 1943; Maj George S. Roberts, 3 Nov 1944; Col Benjamin O. Davis, Jr., 24 Dec 1944; Maj George S. Roberts, 9 Jun 1945– unkn. Unkn, 1 Jul–27 Aug 1947; Maj William A. Campbell, 28 Aug 1947–1 Jul 1949.

Aircraft. P-40, 1943–1944; P-39, 1943–1944; P-47, 1944; P-51, 1944–1945. P(later F)-47, 1947–1949.

Operations. Only all-African-American fighter group in World War II, also known informally as "The Tuskegee Airman." Trained for combat at Tuskegee, Alabama and bases in Michigan with P-39 and P-40 aircraft. Moved to Italy, January–early February 1944. Began combat with Twelfth Air Force on 5 February. Used P-39s to escort convoys, protect harbors, and fly armed reconnaissance missions. Converted to P-47s during April–May 1944 and to P-51s in June. Operated with Fifteenth Air Force from May 1944 to April 1945, being engaged primarily in protecting bombers that struck such objectives as oil refineries, factories, airfields, and marshalling yards in Italy, France, Germany, Poland, Czechoslovakia, Austria, Hungary, Yugoslavia, Rumania, Bulgaria, and Greece. Also made strafing attacks on airdromes, railroads, highways, bridges, river traffic, troop concentrations, radar facilities, power stations, and other targets. Received a DUC for a mission on 24 March 1945 when the group escorted B-17s during a raid on a tank factory at Berlin, fought the interceptors that attacked the formation, and strafed transportation facilities while flying back to the base in Italy. Returned to the U.S. in October and inactivated on 19 Oct 1945. Activated again in July 1947 as a part of Tactical Air Command (TAC). Trained with P(later F)-47s, ferried aircraft, and took part in TAC exercises. Inactivated two years later on 1 July 1949.

Service Streamers. World War II American Theater.

Campaign Streamers. World War II: Rome-Arno; Normandy; Northern France; Southern France; North Apennines; Rhineland; Central Europe; Po Valley; Air Combat, EAME Theater.

Armed Forces Expeditionary Streamers. None.

Decorations. Distinguished Unit Citation: Germany, 24 Mar 1945.

Lineage through 12 Aug 2002.

Assignments, Components, Stations, and Honors through 6 Dec 1999.

Commanders, Aircraft, and Operations through 1 Jul 1949.

Supersedes published information contained in Maurer Maurer (ed.), Air Force Combat Units of World War II (Washington: USGPO, 1983).

Emblem. Approved on 15 Jan 1943.

Prepared by Judy G. Endicott.

Lineage and Honors History
of the
477 Fighter Group (AFRC)

Lineage. Established as 477 Bombardment Group (Medium) on 13 May 1943. Activated on 1 Jun 1943. Inactivated on 25 Aug 1943. Activated on 15 Jan 1944. Redesignated 477 Composite Group on 22 Jun 1945. Inactivated on 1 Jul 1947. Redesignated: 477 Special Operations Group on 31 Jul 1985; 477 Expeditionary Special Operations Group, and converted to provisional status, on 24 Jan 2005. Redesignated 477 Special Operations Group, and withdrawn from provisional status, on 11 Aug 2006. Redesignated 477 Fighter Group on 21 Sep 2007. Activated on 1 Oct 2007.

Assignments. Third Air Force, 1 Jun–25 Aug 1943. First Air Force, 15 Jan 1944; Ninth Air Force, 1 Jan–1 Jul 1947. Air Force Special Operations Command to activate or inactivate at any time after 24 Jan 2005; withdrawn from provisional status, 11 Aug 2006; Tenth Air Force, 1 Oct 2007–.

Operational Components. Squadrons. 99 Fighter: 22 Jun1945–1 Jul 1947. 302 Fighter: 1 Oct 2007–. 616 Bombardment: 1 Jun–25 Aug 1943; 15 Jan 1944–22 Jun 1945. 617 Bombardment: 1 Jun–25 Aug 1943; 15 Apr 1944–1 Jul 1947. 618 Bombardment: 1 Jun–25 Aug 1943; 15 May 1944–8 Oct 1945. 619 Bombardment: 1 Jun–25 Aug 1943; 27 May 1944–22 Jun 1945.

Stations. MacDill Field, FL, 1 Jun–25 Aug 1943. Selfridge Field, MI, 15 Jan 1944; Godman Field, KY, 6 May 1944; Freeman Field, IN, 5 Mar 1945; Godman Field, KY, 26 Apr 1945; Lockbourne AAB, OH, 13 Mar 1946–1 Jul 1947. Elmendorf AFB, AK, 1 Oct 2007–.

Commanders. Lt Col Andrew O. Lerche, 1943. Col Robert R. Selway Jr., 21 Jan 1944; Col Benjamin O. Davis Jr., 21 Jun 1945–1 Jul 1947. Col Eric S. Overturf, 1 Oct 2007–.

Aircraft. B-26, 1943. B-25, 1944–1947; P-47, 1945–1947. F-22, 2007–.

Operations. One of only two African-American flying groups in the Army Air Forces during World War II, and the only African-American bombardment group. The group had no African-American personnel assigned until its second period of activation, beginning in 1944. Pilots of the group during its second active period had received primary, basic, and advanced flight training at Tuskegee, Alabama, but the group itself was never stationed there. Although the 477th Bombardment Group did not deploy overseas and enter combat during World War II, like the 332d Fighter Group, it also contributed to the lifting of racial barriers within the U.S. armed forces. When the 99th Fighter Squadron transferred from the 332d Fighter Group to the 477th Bombardment Group in 1945, the group was redesignated a composite group, and Colonel Benjamin O. Davis, who had commanded both the 99th Fighter Squadron and the 332d Fighter Group, became commander of the 477th Composite Group. He went on to become the first African-American general in the U.S. Air Force. The group inactivated in 1947. After serving briefly as a provisional group, the 477th was activated in October 2007 in Alaska, flying F-22 aircraft.

Service Streamers. American Theater, World War II.

Campaign Streamers. None.

Armed Forces Expeditionary Streamers. None.

Decorations. Air Force Outstanding Unit Award: 1 Oct 2007–14 Sep 2009.

Lineage, Assignments, Components, Stations, Aircraft, and Honors through 1 Jan 2011.

Commanders and Operations through 2007.

Supersedes statement prepared on 8 Apr 2005.

Emblem. Approved on 5 Oct 2007.

Prepared by Patsy Robertson.

Reviewed by Daniel Haulman.

Robertson, Patsy. "Lineage and Honors History of the 99 Flying Training Squadron (AETC)," 2007. Air Force Historical Research Agency, Maxwell AFB, Alabama.

Document 17: Official comparison of the performance of the 99th Fighter Squadron with similar squadrons between July 3, 1943, and January 31, 1944. Particularly significant are paragraphs 1 and 6. Paragraph 1 establishes that the performance of the 99th was similar to other units flying the P-40 at that time, while paragraph 6 draws attention to the discrepancy between the actual statics of the 99th and the claims of inferior performance by the 99th made in the House Memorandum of September 16, 1943.

OPERATIONS OF THE 99TH FIGHTER SQUADRON
COMPARED WITH OTHER P-40 SQUADRONS
IN MTO
3 July 1943–31 January 1944

1. An examination of the record of the 99th Fighter Squadron reveals no significant general difference between this squadron and the balance of the P-40 squadrons in the MTO.

2. From July through September the 99th operated from Licata, Sicily, its operations were largely beach patrol with occasional escort and bombing missions, similar to those of other P-40 squadrons. With but five exceptions, P-40's encountered no enemy aircraft, other than on missions to Sardinia in which the 99th did not participate, during the period 17 July to 16 October. On these five occasions the 99th flew no missions or was engaged elsewhere. Table I shows the activities of the 99th on the occasions when other P-40 squadrons encountered enemy aircraft.

3. In October, the 99th was moved to Foggia and until 16 January operated on the east coat of Italy in support of ground troops, its missions being mainly against gun positions, supply and ammunition stores and shipping. No enemy aircraft were

encountered during this period. On 18 January, a mission was flown over the Gulf of Gaeta and for the balance of the month, missions were flown over the Anzio beach head and vicinity. Table II summarizes the activities and claims and losses of the 99th compared with the average of all other P-40 squadrons in the XII Air Force from July 1943 through January 1944.

4.   Over the 7-month period July 1943 though January 1944, the 99th had about 12% fewer objective bombing and about 10 percent more armed patrol and reconnaissance missions than the average of all other P-40 squadrons in the XII Air Force. In other categories the percentages were very close as shown in Table III.

5.   From October forward the 99th was attached to the 79th Fighter Group. A comparison of the operations in December and January of the 99th with that of the three squadrons (85, 86, 87) assigned to the 79th Group shows their activities to be similar in nature but that the 99th had only 79% as many sorties as the other squadrons. The 99th destroyed 12 E/A while losing 2; the other squadrons destroyed 3 E/A while losing 0.3 on the average. Table IV compares the squadrons of the 79th Group with the attached 99th December and January.

6.   It is recommended that Major General Edwin J. House's memorandum to Major General J.K. Cannon dated 16 September 1943, Subject "Combat Efficiency of the 99th Fighter Squadron", General Cannon's endorsement to the Commanding General, Northwest African Air Force, and Lt. General Spaatz's indorsement to the Commanding General, Army Air Force be studied in connection with the attached statistical report since it sheds light on the comparison from a qualitative and theater point of view.

Statistical Control Division
Office of Management Control
30 March 1944

Retain or destroy this copy in accordance with AR 380-5. Do not return.

U.S. Army Air Forces. "Operations of the 99th Fighter Squadron Compared with Other P-40 Squadrons in MTO," March 30, 1944. Air Force Historical Research Agency, Maxwell AFB, Alabama.

Glossary

A-20 Havoc: A two-engine light bomber built by the Douglas Aircraft Company. It carried a crew of two or three. The Havoc was armed with seven 7.7-millimeter machine guns and could carry up to 4,000 pounds of bombs.

Air Division: A unit in the Army Air Forces containing between three and five wings. An air division was normally commanded by a major general.

Allies: Name given to an alliance of nations that fought against Germany and its allies during World War II. In the West, the Allies were dominated by the United States and the United Kingdom. The alliance included the dominions of the British Empire, such as such as Canada, Australia, New Zealand, and South Africa, along with British colonies. In addition, the governments in exile and the armed forces that managed to escape from many occupied countries such as the Netherlands were also part of the Allies, as was China. The other major nation in the Allies was the Soviet Union, even though it was neutral in the war against Japan until August 8, 1945, shortly before the end of the war.

Articles of War: A law code of the United States that applied to people in the armed forces on active duty. The code covered situations unique to military service that civilian laws did not cover. The Articles of War were replaced by the Uniform Code of Military Justice in 1951.

Axis: Name given to a loose alliance of nations with which the United States and its allies were at war during World War II. The Axis began in September 1940 when Germany, Italy, and Japan signed the Tripartite Pact. Other nations joined the Axis alliance during the war, including Hungary, which joined on November 20, 1940, followed by Romania on November 23, 1940. Bulgaria joined on March 1, 1941. Other nations, such as Finland, fought on the side of the Axis without formally joining the alliance, while puppet states formed in Axis-occupied countries and colonies officially joined.

B-17 Flying Fortress: Heavy bomber, built by the Boeing Company. It carried a crew of 10 and was powered by four piston engines. The Flying Fortress was armed with 10 .50-caliber machine guns and could carry up to 8,000 pounds of bombs. With machine gunners in the top, bottom, front, back, and sides, along with its high speed and altitude, the Flying Fortress was thought to not need fighter escorts. This assumption proved incorrect when the bombing campaign began.

B-24 Liberator: Heavy bomber, built by the Consolidated Aircraft Company. It carried a crew of 7 to 10, depending on the model, and was powered by four piston engines. The Liberator was armed with 10 .50-caliber machine guns and could carry up to 8,000 pounds of bombs. The dual tail configuration gave the B-24 a distinctive appearance. It filled much of the same role as the B-17.

B-25 Mitchell: Medium bomber built by North American Aviation. It carried a crew of six and was powered by two piston engines. The Mitchell was armed with 12 to 18 .50-caliber machine guns and could carry up to 6,000 pounds of bombs.

Bombardier: A crew member on a bomber. The bombardier was a highly trained commissioned officer. He sat in the Plexiglas nose of a bomber and, using a complicated mechanical computerized bombsight, normally the Norden bombsight, would calculate factors such as airspeed, aircraft speed, wind direction and speed, and altitude to place the bombs on their intended targets. The bombardier had effective control over the aircraft during the bomb run in order to line it up with the target as closely as possible.

Buffalo Soldiers: Name given to the black members of four regiments in the Regular Army created in 1866. The regiments were the 9th and 10th Cavalry Regiments and the 24th and 25th Infantry Regiments.

Cadet: A soldier in training to become a commissioned officer. Soldiers at the Military Academy at West Point were cadets, as were members of ROTC units. Cadets in training to become pilots who had completed their general commissioning program but had not completed pilot training were normally held in the status as aviation cadets until they completed pilot training.

Commissioned Officer: Military ranks from second lieutenant through general. Officers are granted a commission from the president with the advice and consent of the Senate. A commission gives an officer the right to command soldiers and the responsibility to take charge. Except in certain circumstances, an officer has the right to resign his or her commission.

Company Grade Officer: A second lieutenant, first lieutenant, or captain.

Court-Martial: A trial under military laws.

Drop Tank: An externally mounted auxiliary fuel tank carried by an airplane—usually a fighter airplane—to extend its range. Because the added weight and drag of the tanks makes the airplane less maneuverable, drop tanks are equipped with a mechanism that allows the pilot to jettison them prior to engaging in aerial combat. Normally, a plane draws the fuel from the drop tank first, then switches to the internal fuel tank after exhausting all the fuel in the drop tank or after jettisoning it for combat.

Enlisted Man: A soldier who is not an officer or a warrant officer. Enlisted soldiers are in the ranks of private through sergeant major.

Field Grade Officer: A major, lieutenant colonel, or colonel.

Flak: Air defense artillery, from the German *Fliegerabwehrkanone,* meaning "aircraft defense cannon." Air crews used the term to refer to the explosions and deadly shrapnel from the explosions. Air defense gun crews would set their rounds to explode at a certain altitude based on observations of approaching aircraft or intelligence reports and fire into the air. Pilots in formation or on a bombing run were required to ignore the flak and remain on their assigned flight path, hoping that their plane would not be hit by the explosions.

Free French Forces: A military force created by those members of the French military who deserted after France surrendered and found their way to Allied lines in order to continue the fight against Nazi Germany.

General Charles de Gaulle emerged as the leader of the movement. The Free French fought on the side of the Allies, usually with American equipment. As French colonies or territories were liberated from Vichy or Axis forces, the Free French assumed control. Technically, the Free French were committing treason, and their capture in battle often resulted in death.

Fuselage: The main body of an airplane.

Grounds Crews: The enlisted men who maintained, armed, and fueled the aircraft.

Group: A unit in the U.S. Army Air Forces equal to a regiment in ground forces. A group was normally commanded by a colonel. Most groups contained three squadrons, although they could have more.

Jim Crow: A system of legal and social norms created after Reconstruction in the American South following the Civil War. Jim Crow was named for a stock character in minstrel shows. The Jim Crow system denied basic civil rights to most blacks and kept blacks in a position subordinate to whites.

Navigator: A member of a crew on a bomber. The navigator was normally a commissioned officer. He sat in a station behind the pilot and co-pilot and was responsible for determining the location of the aircraft and the direction to the target or other locations. The navigator would use a combination of methods to determine location, such as maps and aerial photographs, star charts, sextants, compass, and a watch. The best navigators usually served in the squadron or group commander's airplane or in special pathfinder aircraft that would fly ahead of the main body and mark targets with incendiaries.

Noncommissioned Officer: An enlisted soldier in the ranks of corporal through sergeant major. Noncommissioned officers usually had authority over lower-ranking enlisted men assigned to them.

Officers Candidate Schools: A system of schools run by the military to select and train promising enlisted men to serve as officers for the greatly expanded wartime army. Failure rates were intentionally high. A course normally lasted three months. Most were branch specific, meaning that they trained an officer candidate to serve as a lieutenant in a specific branch, such as artillery or infantry.

Officers Reserve Corps: A part of the Organized Reserves of the Army, this functioned mainly as a list of reserve officers until men on it were brought onto active duty.

P-40 Warhawk: Long-range single-seat fighter and ground attack aircraft built by the Curtiss-Wright Corporation and powered by a single piston engine. The Warhawk was armed with six .50-caliber machine guns and could carry up to 1,000 pounds of bombs.

P-47 Thunderbolt: Long-range single-seat fighter aircraft built by Republic Aviation and powered by a single reciprocating engine. The Thunderbolt was armed with eight .50-caliber machine guns and could carry up to 2,500 pounds of bombs.

P-51 Mustang: Long-range single-seat fighter aircraft built by North American Aviation and powered by a single piston engine. The Mustang was armed with six .50-caliber machine guns and could carry up to 2,000 pounds of bombs.

Ranks: Enlisted ranks in the army at the start of World War II went (from lowest to highest) from private, private first class, corporal, sergeant, staff sergeant, technical sergeant, first sergeant, and master sergeant. Changes in early 1942 added technician ranks. For officers, the ranks were second lieutenant, first lieutenant, captain, major, lieutenant colonel, colonel, brigadier general, major general, lieutenant general, and general.

Regular Army: The permanent army that exists during peacetime and wartime. During the world wars, the Regular Army was part of what was called the Army of the United States, which also included the National Guard on active service, the Reserves, and selectees. Most of the senior leadership of the wartime army came from the Regular Army.

Reserve Officers Training Corps (ROTC):   A program run by the army at civilian colleges through which men who completed the course were offered a reserve commission. Men who thus earned a reserve commission could then serve as officers in the Organized Reserves, in the National Guard, or, depending on the needs of the army, on active duty.

Selective Service: Informally called the draft, Selective Service was a system run at the city, town, or county level by boards composed of prominent civilians who were supposed to consider the health, intelligence, number of dependents, and role in the economy of a young man and then assign him to a category. From this pool, Selective Service boards would then decide which young men had to perform compulsory military service to fill the quota assigned to a community based on its population. Men so chosen to serve were termed "selectees" or, more informally, "draftees."

Sortie: A unit of measure for the number of missions an air unit performed. A sortie was credited each time an aircraft took off on a mission.

Squadron: A unit in air and cavalry units comparable to a battalion in infantry units. A squadron is normally commanded by a lieutenant colonel and, in air units, contains two to four flights.

Strafe: A method of attacking ground and sea targets by an aircraft. In strafing, an aircraft would fly in a straight line over a target—such as troops on a road, rolling stock, parked aircraft, or other suitable targets—and fire a long burst of machine gun fire, usually from two guns mounted side-by-side.

Technicians: A series of three enlisted ranks comparable to noncommissioned officers but normally having high technical skills rather than leadership responsibilities.

Third Reich: Term used to describe Germany under the rule of the Nazis (1933–1945). The term *Reich* is German for "empire." According to some German theorists, the First Reich had been the Holy Roman Empire, a loose confederation of central European states that existed from 962 CE until 1806. The Second Reich was the German Empire of 1871 to 1918. Adolf Hitler disliked the term Third Reich and preferred to call his Germany the "Thousand Year Reich." He was off by 988 years.

USO: United Service Organization. The USO was a charity organization established to bring culture, entertainment, and refreshments to American servicemen and servicewomen around the world. The USO ran canteens close to the front. American entertainers from the film, recording, and stage industries were recruited to travel to sites in the United States and abroad to perform for the troops.

Vichy France: The government of France during much of World War II from June 1940 after France surrendered to Nazi Germany. The Germans occupied northern France and the Atlantic coast. The remainder of the country was ruled from a new French government that met in the resort town of Vichy. The Vichy government had limited authority over the governance of the occupied area, as German policies had supremacy. Vichy in theory was also the capital of all overseas French colonial possessions. In reality, Vichy had little control over the colonies. Vichy was pro-Germany and assisted Germany in oppressing the people of France. The Germans took direct control over all France in November 1942 after the successful Allied invasion of French North Africa, but the Vichy government continued to function as a collaborationist government until the liberation of France in late 1944.

War Department: A cabinet-level agency of the federal government. The War Department was headed by a civilian secretary of war. The War Department oversaw the army, including the Army Air Corps, but not the navy or Marine Corps, which were under a separate Navy Department. In 1947, the War Department was divided into the Department of the Army and the Department of the Air Force, and both were moved, along with the Department of the Navy, to the subcabinet level. A new Department of Defense became the cabinet-level representative for all the armed forces.

Warrant Officer: A series of officer ranks below a second lieutenant but above all enlisted soldiers. Warrant officers were normally chosen from enlisted soldiers who showed great skill and intelligence. Whereas commissioned officers were supposed to be primarily leaders, warrant officers were technical experts on a particular subject.

West Point: An informal name for the U.S. Military Academy at West Point, New York. Cadets at West Point are appointed by a member of Congress. They undergo a four-year undergraduate degree program while also training in military tactics and leadership. Graduates formed the nucleus of the long-term Regular Army officer corps.

Wing: A unit in the Army Air Forces comparable to a brigade in land forces. A wing normally had three groups and was commanded by a brigadier general.

Annotated Bibliography

Bone, Walter J. *Silver Wings: A History of the United States Air Force*. New York: Simon & Schuster, 1993.

Covers the development of the air force from its origins in the Army Signal Corps in 1907 through the development of an independent air force in 1947 to Operation Desert Storm—the war against Iraq in 1990–1991. Bone deals extensively with the development of air doctrine and equipment as well as organizational developments. While the Tuskegee Airmen and integration form only a small part of this study, *Silver Wings* provides a background of the development of the Army Air Forces in which the Tuskegee Airmen served as well as their later impact.

Boyne, Walter J. *Beyond the Wild Blue: A History of the U.S. Air Force, 1947–1997*. New York: St. Martin's Press, 1997.

A solid overview of the first 50 years of the air force as a separate branch of the American military establishment. Emphasizes the people, equipment, and missions that shaped the development of the U.S. Air Force.

Broadnax, Samuel L. *Blue Skies, Black Wings: African American Pioneers of Aviation*. Westport, CT: Praeger, 2007.

A personal account from one of the Tuskegee Airmen who traces the struggles of blacks in the United States, especially in the South, and the rise of black interest in aviation. Broadnax shows how the interest of African Americans in flying was often blocked by white Americans, who refused to accept that blacks were capable of mastering the complex set of skills needed to fly an airplane. Broadnax includes many personal memories of the training programs at Tuskegee.

Bruscino, Thomas. *A Nation Forged in War: How World War II Taught Americans to Get Along*. Knoxville: University of Tennessee Press, 2010.

A nuanced study about the lasting impact of the shared military experience on redefining who was considered an "American." The war broke down much of the antagonism between old stock whites and other ethnic groups and between various Protestant denominations, Catholics, Orthodox Christians, Mormons, and Jews. As Bruscino rightly points out, blacks were excluded from this process as a result of racial segregation in the military, and the generally harmonious relations between ethnic and religious groups in the United States after the war did not extend to relations between blacks and whites.

Bucholtz, Chris. *332nd Fighter Group—Tuskegee Airmen*. New York: Osprey Publishing, 2007.

Part of Osprey's Aviation Elite Units series, *332nd Fighter Group* provides background, contexts, and mostly combat history of the 332nd. As with most Osprey volumes, this one contains numerous contemporary photographs and color paintings to highlight pivotal moments in the history of the 332nd and to put faces and images on the stories. The volume is largely celebratory and focuses on the victories and exploits of the 332nd more than the larger implications of their service.

Cornish, Dudley Taylor. *The Sable Arm: Black Troops in the Union Army, 1861–1865*. Lawrence: University Press of Kansas, 1987.

Groundbreaking and influential work on black soldiers in the Union army during the Civil War. Cornish provides valuable insight to understanding blacks who served in the army, why the they served, what they did, and how they were treated.

Craven, Wesley Frank, and James Lea Cate. *The Army Air Forces in World War II*. 7 vols. Chicago: University of Chicago Press, 1948–1958.

A seven-volume official history of U.S. Army Air Corps and U.S. Army Air Forces during the war. Despite the enormous amount of research about the air war that has been conducted since this series was first published, it has held up well. Volume 1, *Plans and Early Operations, January 1939 to August 1942*, Volume 2, *Europe: Torch to Pointblank, August 1942 to December 1943*, and especially Volume 3, *Europe: Argument to V.E. Day, January 1944 to May 1945* are especially relevant to the understanding the larger issues of the entirety of the American air war in Europe and the role of the 99th Fighter Squadron and later the 332nd Fighter Group in context from an operational standpoint.

Dalfiume, Richard M. *Desegregation of the US Armed Forces: Fighting on Two Fronts, 1939–1953.* **Columbia: University of Missouri Press, 1969.**

As this work shows, racial integration of the military did not happen instantaneously with President Harry S. Truman's issuance of Executive Order 9981 in 1948 but took years to implement. The executive order was an important milestone, but it resulted from the experience of World War II, both through the demonstrated inefficiency of segregation and from the proof offered by the Tuskegee Airmen and others that blacks could and would fight for the United States and were capable of performing dangerous tasks, mastering complex skills, and serving as leaders. Dalfiume demonstrates that desegregation came because blacks forced the issue to the forefront.

Davis, Benjamin O., Jr. *Benjamin O. Davis, Jr., American: An Autobiography.* **Washington, DC: Smithsonian Institution Scholarly Press, 2000.**

Davis's account of his life from his earliest memories until after his retirement from the air force as a lieutenant general. His shameful treatment at as a cadet West Point is chronicled, but throughout that gauntlet and beyond, Davis was carried by an innate sense of self-worth instilled in him by his father, a career soldier. Davis makes clear the pivotal role that his being tasked by the Roosevelt administration to lead an experimental black squadron was on him. Davis recounts his early years as a young black man from a middle-class family whose father was a dedicated soldier and how he too became the consummate professional soldier, albeit one with a lifelong love of flying. He recounts the obstacles placed in his way by racist attitudes and practices but also documents his determination to surmount them and bring them down. What emerges is a determined military man who sought to make the nation live up to the high ideals he believed it stood for. Davis's ability to work within the army system while always maintaining his own dignity and that of his men made him instrumental to the success of the "Tuskegee Experiment."

Dobak, William A., and Thomas D. Phillips. *The Black Regulars, 1866–1898.* **Norman: University of Oklahoma Press, 1998.**

A history of the so-called Buffalo Soldiers—the four black regiments in the Regular Army between the end of the Civil War and the Spanish-American War. These four regiments were the first black units in the Regular Army and would remain the only such units until after World War II. Dobak and Phillips argue that the black Regulars, constituting around 10 percent of the peacetime of the army between the until the Spanish-American War, were neither despised and maltreated by the army nor elite Indian fighters. Instead, the 9th and 10th Cavalry Regiments and the 24th and 25th Infantry Regiments were treated in a similar fashion as white regiments in the small peacetime army and performed on a similar level. Minor differences did exist, though. Black Regulars were less likely to desert, more likely to keep a wife without army permission (which was only for officers and noncommissioned officers), and less likely to be literate. But for all soldiers, the peacetime army had little prestige in society at large, and the army was too small to maintain two separate systems. The black Regulars constituted a diminishing percentage of the Regular Army because of its expansion after the Spanish-American War.

Donaldson, Gary A. *The History of African-Americans in the Military*. Malabar, FL: Krieger, 1991.

A survey of black participation in the American military from the colonial period into the all-volunteer force instituted after the end of the draft in 1973. Donaldson argues that blacks participated in American wars in part from the hope that loyal service would lead to recognition of basic civil and human rights after the war ended, but instead blacks found broken promises and renewed oppression. Only with World War II did the old pattern begin the break down, and eventually the military desegregated. However, new patterns emerged during the Vietnam War when the civil rights movement took away the tendency to keep blacks out of frontline units and replaced it with an increased tendency to use blacks in the infantry. Military integration proved to be more superficial than realized, and the stresses of the draft and the Vietnam War broke the apparent racial harmony in the armed forces. In the years since the Vietnam War, under the all-volunteer force, the military has become one of the most successfully integrated institutions in the United States.

Dryden, Charles W. *A-Train: Memoirs of a Tuskegee Airman*. Tuscaloosa: University of Alabama Press, 1997.

Dryden was one of the Tuskegee Airmen who chose after the war to remain in the military, and he served in the air force into the Vietnam War era, when he retired as a lieutenant colonel. The book takes its title from the name he painted on the nose of his airplanes: *A-Train*. Dryden provides an insider's look at the process of integration, from the earlier days of the "Tuskegee Experiment" to his later years as a career Regular Air Force pilot in the integrated military. Much of his narrative concerns the familiar stories of good humor found in military units and aerial combat, but other sections underscore the blatant unfairness of Jim Crow, such as when black officers watched German prisoners of war use the Post Exchange, from which black American soldiers were barred. Despite such indignities, Dryden found much that he enjoyed of life in the air force, and he kept faith that the days of the segregated military were coming to an end.

Edgerton, Robert B. *Hidden Heroism: Black Soldiers in America's Wars.* **Boulder, CO: Westview, 2001.**

Overview of the history of the participation of blacks in American wars. Edgerton shows that while blacks fought on both sides in the Revolutionary War, in the years since they have fought in every American war except the Mexican War. Despite this involvement of blacks as fighting men, a myth of black men as "natural cowards" was used to keep blacks from serving during peacetime. Black participation in wars, including during the colonial period and Revolution, followed a pattern of black participation increasing as wars got longer and less popular. The participation of blacks as fighters was initially celebrated by white America, but a short time after the end of each war, the public memory of black participation was increasingly denigrated and later denied. Blacks were systematically erased from the public memory of wars. The perception that black men would not fight for the country despite their record of doing just that and the prohibitions against them serving in peacetime was used to justify slavery and later keeping blacks subordinate to whites and denying them the right to vote. The civil rights movement, which restored the right to vote to black men, had the ironic effect of increasing the use of black men on the front lines during the Vietnam War.

Fletcher, Marvin E. *America's First Black General: Benjamin O. Davis, Sr., 1880–1970.* **Lawrence: University Press of Kansas, 1989.**

Documents the 50-year career of the senior Davis, from his first taste of the military as a high school cadet until his retirement after World War II. Davis came from a middle-class black family from Washington, D.C., and he carried that middle-class outlook his entire life. Denied the chance to attend West Point because of his skin color, he enlisted as a private, which horrified his family. Like white middle-class families, the Davis family saw enlisted service as beneath them. Davis eventually was commissioned by examination after serving in all enlisted ranks from private to sergeant major. His career as an officer followed an unusual path, as each promotion made more difficult the policy of preventing black officers from commanding white enlisted men and avoiding, if at all possible, placing one in a position superior to a white officer. As a result, Davis spent much of his time advising or commanding black National Guard units, teaching ROTC at black colleges (including Tuskegee Institute), and serving as a military liaison to Liberia. Davis was aware that his appointment to general officer in World War II was mostly to ward off criticism of army policies to black soldiers, but Davis used his position to constantly lobby for equitable treatment of blacks soldiers. While he did not cross General Dwight D. Eisenhower by calling for the end of racial segregation, his recommendations, if enacted, would have done just that. *America's First Black General* includes an excellent introduction by Benjamin O. Davis Jr.

Francis, Charles E. *The Tuskegee Airmen: The Men Who Changed a Nation*. 4th ed. Boston: Branden Publishing, 1997.

Originally published in 1955, *The Tuskegee Airmen* was one of the first popular histories of the Tuskegee Airmen after the war. Francis, a member of the Tuskegee Airmen, provides a heroic view of them, stressing the obstacles placed in their way as they strived to become combat aviators. Francis includes short biographies of key enlisted men as well as officers who served in the various units, lists of who served in which units, graduating classes from Tuskegee, and other details of their existence.

Gropmen, Alan. *The Air Force Integrates, 1945–1964*. Washington, DC: Government Printing Office, 1978.

Official history of the integration of the air force, concurrent with the establishment of the air force as a separate branch of the military. Despite an official line that the air force simply did not create segregated units on independence, Gropmen shows that the air force initially began creating segregated units and only hesitantly gave up that plan following the issuing of Executive Order 9981 by President Harry S. Truman, ordering the desegregation of the military. In retrospect, the air force plan for segregated units was incredibly wasteful, and integration prevented the creation of a horribly inefficient system. Still, integration was largely one way, with black airmen allowed into white units rather than a true merging.

Hardesty, Von, and Dominick Pisano. *Black Wings: The American Black in Aviation*. Washington, DC: Smithsonian Institution Press, 1984.

A survey of African Americans who made flying their life's work, from early aviation pioneers to astronauts. Bessie Coleman, William J. Powell, and Cornelius R. Coffey broke barriers and encouraged others to fly when Jim Crow sought to deny that blacks were even capable of piloting an aircraft. Hardesty and Pisano take special note of the role that the Civilian Pilot Training Corps and the "Tuskegee Experiment" had in opening aviation as an avocation or as a career to generations of blacks. By the 1960s and 1970s, building on those who came before them, blacks could be found in positions of great responsibility in commercial and military aviation. This work puts the Tuskegee Airmen in long-term perspective of building on blacks who came before them and opening doors for blacks who came after them.

Hastie, William H. *On Clipped Wings: The Story of Jim Crow in the Army Air Corps.* **New York: National Association for the Advancement of Colored People, 1943.**

Pamphlet produced during World War II, Hastie used statistics to demonstrate that the Army Air Forces followed racist policies that not only humiliated most blacks by placing them in units that performed unskilled menial tasks but that also were wasteful of manpower and talent and worked against the war effort. Hastie wrote this pamphlet after he resigned as civilian assistant to the secretary of war in disgust over the continued existence and, as he saw it, entrenchment of military segregation and Jim Crow.

Homan, Lynn M., and Thomas Reilly. *Black Knights: The Story of the Tuskegee Airmen.* **Gretna, LA: Pelican Publishing, 2001.**

Standard account of the Tuskegee Airmen, both pilots and ground crews from before their formation until after the war. The authors mined the After Action Reports from the 99th Fighter Squadron and the 332nd Fighter Group to provide detailed accounts of many of the battles fought over the skies of Europe. The authors also drew on numerous interviews to describe the selection and training of the Tuskegee Airmen and their struggles against racism during the war. The sections on the 477th Bombardment Group helps fill a void in the historiography.

Homan, Lynn M., and Thomas Reilly. *Tuskegee Airmen.* **Charleston, SC: Arcadia Publishing, 1998.**

Part of Arcadia's Images of America series, this volume contains a short but solid introduction to the Tuskegee Airmen, but its real strength is in the hundreds of photographs of black aviation pioneers, black leaders, and the men who actually served as Tuskegee Airmen. The photographs, many never published before, allow readers to see the Tuskegee Airmen training, fighting, and enjoying themselves. The chapters cover different periods and places in the

Tuskegee Airmen's story. Not surprisingly, many of the photos look similar to thousands of other photos from the war years, except for the prevalence of black men and some women. The last chapters show the legacy of the Tuskegee Airmen in the integrated air force in the Korean and Vietnam wars.

Jakeman, Robert J. *The Divided Skies: Establishing Segregated Flight Training at Tuskegee Alabama, 1934–1942.* **Tuscaloosa: University of Alabama Press, 1992.**

The occasion when the first five young black men received their Air Corps pilot wings at Tuskegee Army Airfield in March 1942 came after an intense and difficult struggle to open military aviation to blacks. Jakeman chronicles prewar black interest in aviation, the rising civil rights movement, and the need for military pilots who came together on that late winter day. He shows that while blacks wanted barriers removed and opportunities opened without segregation, many whites did not want to see black pilots at all. The result was the "Tuskegee Experiment," which totally pleased few but was an important step toward eliminating racial barriers.

Lee, Ulysses. *The Employment of Negro Troops.* **Washington, DC: Government Printing Office, 1966.**

Part of the Green series, the official history of the U.S. Army in World War II. Provides an overview of the participation of blacks in the army, including the Army Air Forces. The work was intended to be a history of policies toward black troops rather than a narrative of the use of black troops during the war. Lee argues that the civilian background, especially the lack of education, as well as entrenched racist attitudes, made the employment of large numbers of black troops in frontline units difficult. Blacks never achieved the numbers of frontline combat troops black leaders desired, but the changing nature of war meant that the army created far more support troops, both black and white, that it had intended to in prewar planning.

McGovern, James R. *Black Eagle: General Daniel "Chappie" James, Jr.* **Tuscaloosa: University of Alabama Press, 1985.**

"Chappie" James, from Florida, earned his college degree from Tuskegee Institute and went on to complete pilot training at the Tuskegee program in July 1943 and deployed to join the 332nd. His talent and drive soon marked him as a stand out among a group of excellent pilots. When he retired from the air force more than three decades later, he was the first black four-star general in

American history. This biography focuses on his military career, as he rose in rank and stature in the air force, in a period of transition of the relationship between the races.

MacGregor, Morris J., Jr. *Integration of the Armed Forces, 1940–1965.* **Washington, DC: Center for Military History, 1989.**

Solid overview of the integration of all branches of the U.S. military. MacGregor demonstrates the pivotal role that the Tuskegee Airmen played in changing attitudes toward the idea of black military service, especially for President Harry S. Truman. The Air Corps, like the Marine Corps, was all white and was seen as an elite service. For black men to serve as commissioned officers and fighter pilots in the previously all-white Air Corps dealt a serious blow to the color line, but inequities remained throughout the war. Despite the success of the Tuskegee Airmen, the commissioning of the first black navy officers, and the establishment of black combat marine units, most blacks in the war still performed the low-skilled, demeaning, or backbreaking jobs as in World War I. MacGregor shows the various branches responded in myriad ways to orders to create more black units and more black officers and, eventually, to integrate. The shortcomings in public education for black Americans was a major problem in bringing African Americans into formerly all-white units on an equitable basis. The story is largely progressive, for its ends before the stresses of the Vietnam War and the inequities of the draft exposed racial tensions beneath the facade of successful integration.

McGuire, Phillip. *He, Too, Spoke for Democracy: Judge Hastie, World War II, and the Black Soldier.* **Westport, CT: Greenwood, 1988.**

Detailed study of one of the more overlooked figures in the struggle for racial integration. Hastie (and others) assumed that his appointment as civilian aide to the secretary of war was mostly about quelling black opposition to military policies regarding African American soldiers, but Hastie used his position to push hard for black officers, back combat units, black pilots, and integration of the military. While he found the entrenched racism of the military and government exasperating, in retrospect he accomplished much in his two years in the position and laid the groundwork for the desegregation of the military after World War II.

Moye, J. Todd. *Freedom Flyers: The Tuskegee Airmen of World War II.* **Oxford: Oxford University Press, 2010.**

Eminently readable account of the creation of the pilot training program for black cadets at Tuskegee through the postwar integration of the U.S. Air Force.

Moye argues that the Tuskegee "experiment" never would have come about had not the National Association for the Advancement of Colored People put political pressure on the Roosevelt administration to force the Army Air Corps to open pilot positions to black men. Moye emphasizes the experiences of young black men from often ethnically mixed communities in the urban North who found themselves deep in the Jim Crow South.

Osur, Alan M. *Blacks in the Army Air Force during World War II: The Problem of Race Relations*. Washington, DC: Office of Air Force History, 1976.

Study by an air force officer on the overall role blacks played in the Army Air Forces during the war. The Tuskegee Airmen were a small, albeit prominent percentage of all blacks who served in the Air Forces. Most black airmen were relegated to more demeaning and unskilled duties during the war. Osur documents the frustrations blacks inside and outside the military felt over clearly unfair and discriminatory policies and actions. Occasionally, the friction boiled over into protests and even riots at several installations, forcing Army Air Forces leaders to acknowledge that "separate but equal" was a charade and that allowing one or two black combat groups was not a satisfactory response to black demands for equitable treatment in the military.

Palmer, Walter J. A. *Flying with Eagles*. Indianapolis: Nova Graphics, Inc., 1993.

Palmer, who flew more than 150 combat missions over Europe during World War II, served with the 99th Fighter Squadron during most of the war. Palmer was a man in his early 20s who loved flying and thought little of the potential to be killed until a close friend of his fell to German bullets. In this personal account, Palmer recounts his many missions, recalling that the men in the 99th knew that they carried the hopes of millions of blacks in the United States while they fought Nazis and fascists in Europe but never dreamed that they would reach near legendary status in the years after the war.

Perret, Geoffrey. *Victory: The Army Air Forces in World War II*. New York: Random House, 1993.

A study of the leaders of the Army Air Forces. Perret shows how battles of personalities often decided what was built, how aircraft were designed, and how campaigns were waged. Perret underscores that the wartime Air Forces was growing fast and feeling its way into a waging an air war of a scale and ferocity men had barely dreamed of before. Perret also includes the views of the men who had to carry out the policies of the generals in the cold and deadly skies over Europe.

Pisano, Dominick. *To Fill the Skies with Pilots: The Civilian Pilot Training Program, 1939–1949.* Urbana: University of Illinois Press, 1993.

Readable history of the Civilian Pilot Training Program (CPTP) from its origins in 1939 into the years immediately after the end of World War II. *To Fill the Skies* shows that the program was created from a mixture of desires of both commercial and military aviation proponents. The struggle to include blacks and women in the program was sharp but quickly settled. While not focused on the CPTP at black colleges, Pisano provides context for the program and puts the establishment of programs at black colleges such as Howard and Tuskegee Institute into the larger issue of the desire of the government to create more pilots. Pisano argues that the program was largely successful and fulfilled the desires of the military and commercial aviation.

Sandler, Stanley. *Segregated Skies: All Black Combat Squadrons of World War II.* Washington, DC: Smithsonian Institution Press, 1998.

A combination popular and scholarly history of the 332nd Fighter Group and the 477th Bomber Group. Sandler emphasizes the additional burden placed on these men by segregation and racism. They trained and fought knowing that every shortcoming would be commented on and that powerful elements within the military and American society at large wanted them to fail. Sandler takes particular aim at charges made at the end of the war that the 332nd performed at a level far below that of similarly equipped white fighter groups, using statistics to demonstrate that the 332nd Fighter Group performed on par with the high standards required for all fighter groups in the Army Air Forces.

Scott, Lawrence P., and William M. Womack Sr. *Double V: The Civil Rights Struggle of the Tuskegee Airmen.* East Lansing: Michigan State University Press, 1994.

Places story of the Tuskegee Airmen within the context of the early civil rights movement. Scott and Womack argue that the men of the 99th Fighter Squadron and later the 332nd Fighter Group were highly sensitive to their role in proving that blacks could and would fight for the United States but were also keen to ensure that their service would not follow the normal pattern of degradation or erasure from public memory after the war. The officers and men of the 332nd and 477th were well aware that they were making an important step not only in challenging military segregation but also on the whole issue of routinely denying basic civil rights to African Americans. *Double V* also focuses on the unrest in the 477th and the so-called Freeman Field Mutiny, arguing that it set the pattern for nonviolent protests of the postwar civil rights movement, such as the bus boycotts in Shreveport, Louisiana, and Birmingham, Alabama.

Silvera, John D. *The Negro in World War II*. New York: Arno Press, 1969.

Part of the American Negro, His History and Literature series, this volume is a compilation of articles on many facets of African American life during the war in both the military and the civilian world. What is clear is the enormous impact that the war had on black life, setting in motion many currents that would bring about greater changes in later decades.

Smith, Charlene McGee. *Tuskegee Airman: The Biography of Charles E. McGee*. Boston: Branden Publishing, 1999.

Biography of Charles McGee from central Illinois, who graduated from the Tuskegee program in 1943. Written by his daughter, *Tuskegee Airman* offers an interesting portrait of an African American from a small town in the Midwest near Chanute Field who entered the program after it had been running for more than a year but while the war was still in a bloody period and the end uncertain.

Stillman, Richard J., II *Integration of the Negro in the US Armed Forces*. New York: Praeger, 1968.

Stillman, an expert in public administration, looks at the racial integration of the military as a case study of integration by a large, bureaucratic government agency. While not focused on the Tuskegee Airmen or the U.S. Army Air Forces in particular, the legacy of the Tuskegee Airmen provided an important step to ending separate units for blacks in the military.

Stout, Jay A. *The Men Who Killed the Luftwaffe: The U.S. Army Air Forces against Germany in World War II*. Mechanicsburg, PA: Stackpole Books, 2010.

Stirring account of the transformation of the U.S. Army Air Corps, which numbered some 45,000 men in 1939, as it expanded many times over and eventually defeated the Luftwaffe. Stout shows the development of strategies, tactics, aircraft, and doctrine as the U.S. Army Air Forces came to challenge and then destroy the once mighty Luftwaffe.

Strickland, Patricia. *The Putt-Putt Air Force: The Story of the Civilian Pilot Training Program and the War Training Service, 1939–1944.* Washington, DC: Department of Transportation/Federal Aviation Administration, Aviation Education Staff, 1971.

Largely celebratory work on the programs to train civilians to fly airplanes. Strickland focuses on the role that small, light aircraft, such as the Piper Cub, played as trainer aircraft.

Thole, Lou. *Forgotten Fields of America: World War II Bases and Training Then and Now.* Vol. 3. Missoula, MT: Pictorial Histories Publishing, 2003.

Nostalgic look at former army airfields throughout the nation that had been constructed in haste between 1940 and 1942. Despite the need to get the new airfields operational quickly, the exacting standards of construction demanded by the Army Air Forces created impressive bases and auxiliary fields, yet most of them were closed soon after the war, the buildings sold and dismantled, and the lands reverted to private use. Thole includes images and brief histories from Tuskegee Army Airfield and surrounding landing strips in the years after the army closed the base. Part of the irony shown in this book is that while Moton Field, at Tuskegee Institute, has a memorial to the Tuskegee Airmen and is closely associated with them, the former Tuskegee Army Airfield is largely forgotten.

Tucker, Phillip Thomas. *Father of the Tuskegee Airmen, John C Robinson.* Dulles, VA: Potomac Books, 2010.

Biography of the man hailed as the "Black Lindbergh" and later as the "Brown Condor of Ethiopia." Robinson, a graduate of Tuskegee Institute, saw aviation as a way for African Americans to advance socially and economically, and he personally broke barriers placed in the way of blacks who wanted to fly. Robinson's exploits in Ethiopia, actually fighting against fascism and for the last black nation under an indigenous ruler, made him a hero to African Americans and a powerful voice inspiring blacks to take to the air. His personal popularity and links to Tuskegee Institute helped bring the Civilian Pilot Training Program and later the Army Air Forces to Tuskegee, cementing the link between the school and black aviation.

Washington, George L. *The History of Military and Civilian Pilot Training of Negroes at Tuskegee, Alabama, 1939–1945.* **Washington, DC: George L. Washington, 1972.**

Self-published account of the establishment and operation of the Civilian Pilot Training Program at Tuskegee Institute and the later development of the army's program to provide precommissioning and flight training in Tuskegee. Covers the period when the institute established Moton Field and later the shift of most military training from the campus to the newly constructed Tuskegee Army Airfield.

Wynn, Neil A. *The African American Experience during World War II.* **Lanham, MD: Rowan & Littlefield, 2010.**

Part of a series on the history of African Americans, Wynn argues that the war years were a time when African Americans found new freedoms and made substantial economic gains but also a time of increased oppression and racial tension. Wynn sees President Harry S. Truman's 1948 issuance of Executive Order 9981 calling for the desegregation of the armed forces a direct result of the African American contribution to the American victory in World War II. The civil rights movement would build on the gains made during the war years, but much ground remained to be covered.

Index

About the Author

BARRY M. STENTIFORD received his doctorate in history from the University of Alabama. He is an associate professor of military history at the U.S. Army's School of Advanced Military Studies. He is the coeditor of the *Jim Crow Encyclopedia* and taught at Grambling State University for more than a decade. He served in the U.S. Air Force in the 1980s.

Edwards Brothers Malloy
Thorofare, NJ USA
April 16, 2013